RELIGION, CONFLICT AND MILITARY INTERVENTION

For Keith, Gill and Miriam

Religion, Conflict and Military Intervention

Edited by

ROSEMARY DURWARD
Royal Military Academy Sandhurst, UK

and

LEE MARSDEN
University of East Anglia, UK

ASHGATE

Published by
Ashgate Publishing Limited
Wey Court East
Union Road
Farnham
Surrey, GU9 7PT
England

Ashgate Publishing Company
Suite 420
101 Cherry Street
Burlington
VT 05401-4405
USA

www.ashgate.com

British Library Cataloguing in Publication Data
Religion, conflict and military intervention.
1. War--Religious aspects--Christianity. 2. War--Religious aspects--Islam. 3. Conflict management--Religious aspects--Christianity. 4. Conflict management--Religious aspects--Islam. 5. Iraq War, 2003-
I. Durward, Rosemary. II. Marsden, Lee.
261.8'73-dc22

Library of Congress Cataloging-in-Publication Data
Religion, conflict, and military intervention / [edited] by Rosemary Durward and Lee Marsden.
p. cm.
Includes bibliographical references and index.
ISBN 978-0-7546-7871-7 (hardback) -- ISBN 978-0-7546-9721-3 (ebook)
1. Religion and politics. 2. Intervention (International law) I. Durward, Rosemary. II. Marsden, Lee.
BL65.P7R432655 2009
201'.7273--dc22

2009031218

ISBN 978-0-7546-7871-7 (hbk)
ISBN 978-0-7546-9721-3 (ebk)

FSC
Mixed Sources
Product group from well-managed forests and other controlled sources
www.fsc.org Cert no. SGS-COC-2482
© 1996 Forest Stewardship Council

Printed and bound in Great Britain by
TJ International Ltd, Padstow, Cornwall

Contents

List of Figures

Notes on Contributors

Shazadi Beg holds a Master's degree in international law from Southampton University, UK. She has practiced as a barrister for more than 15 years in human rights and criminal law.

Rosemary Durward is Senior Lecturer in the Defence and International Affairs Department at the Royal Military Academy Sandhurst.

Rebecca Glazier is a doctoral candidate in Political Science at University of California Santa Barbara.

Nicholas Kerton-Johnson is an honorary lecturer in politics at the University of Bristol.

Sandy Mergenschroer-Livingston is a doctoral candidate at Aberdeen University, UK and attended New Orleans Baptist Theological Seminary.

Ivan Manokha is Vice-Dean and Lecturer in International Relations at the Institut d'études politique de Paris (Sciences Po).

Lee Marsden is Lecturer in Politics and International Relations at the University of East Anglia.

Kunal Mukherjee is a doctoral candidate at the University of Nottingham.

Serena K. Sharma teaches in the Department of International Relations at the London School of Economics and Political Science.

Acknowledgements

Producing an edited volume requires tremendous amounts of cooperation between editors, publishers and authors to produce the finished work. In this process the editors are particularly indebted not only to the contributors but to the many people who gave freely of their time and efforts in organising conferences, panels, reviews and providing extensive feedback to help shape the volume you have before you. Special thanks are due to Paul Cornish, Head, International Security Programme and Carrington Professor of International Security, Chatham House and Sara Silvestri, City University, for their encouragement. Special thanks are due to staff at the Royal Military Academy Sandhurst, especially the RMAS Commandant, Major General D.J. Rutherford-Jones, the Director of Studies, Sean McKnight and the team that helped organise the 'Engaging with Religion for Building Peace: The Experience of Afghanistan and Iraq' conference that inspired the present volume. Amongst them are Matthew Bennett, Stuart Philip, Martin Smith, Stephen Deakin, Andrew Orgyll, Margaret Young and Chris MacLennan as well as numerous people who helped on the day, too many to mention, but important, nevertheless.

The editors would like to thank Vernon White, Tim Gibson, Tim Dean, George Wilkes, Shenaz Bunglawala, Connie Sherman, Nigel Whitnall and the anonymous reviewers for valuable comments, advice and assistance, although inevitably responsibility for any errors remains the responsibility of authors and editors alike. This publication would not have been possible without the wonderful cooperation and efficiency of Kirstin Howgate and all the team at Ashgate for which we are truly grateful. Last, but by no means least, we wish to acknowledge the debt of gratitude to Keith, Gill and Miriam who graciously and stoically endured the regular incursions of editing this book into family time. Thank you.

Chapter 1
Introduction

Rosemary Durward and Lee Marsden

For many years religion has been the neglected component of international relations, and yet in an age of globalisation and terror, religious identity has become an increasingly important influence upon the lives of those in the west and in the developing world. The secularisation thesis has been overtaken by a desire to understand how religious actors contribute to both conflict and the resolution of conflict. The initial shock of terrorism 'going global' on 11 September 2001 was followed by the steady realisation that its declared motivator, religion, was actually a familiar feature of conflict. It was a significant dynamic in the Balkans that had occupied Western military resources in the immediate post-Cold War period, as well as in many Cold War regional conflicts in the Middle East, Africa and Asia. Further, there was a surprising religious dimension evident in the response to terrorism. In the United States, President George Bush's policy and rhetoric used religious language that resonated with a religious American public, despite the United States constitution separating church and state.

The language of reconciliation used by President Barack Obama is also influenced by his Christian faith. There is no doubt, however, that Obama rejects any inference that policy can be formulated on the strength of what a church believes. Rather, he seeks policies that meet the criteria of 'reasonableness', to the ordinary citizen. There are many who anticipate a radical change in the role religion plays in conflict with the election of Barack Obama as President. Writing in *Foreign Affairs* on 'Renewing American Leadership', Obama wrote:

> In the Islamic world and beyond, combating the terrorists' prophets of fear will require more than lectures on democracy. We need to deepen our knowledge of the circumstances and beliefs that underpin extremism. A crucial debate is occurring within Islam. Some believe in a future of peace, tolerance, development, and democratization. Others embrace a rigid and violent intolerance of personal liberty and the world at large. To empower forces of moderation, America must make every effort to export opportunity – access to education and health care, trade and investment – and provide the kind of steady support for political reformers and civil society that enabled our victory in the Cold War. Our beliefs rest on hope; the extremists' rest on fear. That is why we can – and will – win this struggle. (Obama 2007)

Obama's thesis suggests that religious fundamentalism is caused by social deprivation and lack of political representation, placing the blame firmly on indigenous factors. Obama's strategy requires long-term patience and investment, and if successful, it promises to make recourse to military intervention less likely. In Iraq, American troops are withdrawing, leaving policing the conflict to the Iraqi government and its security forces. In Afghanistan, the battle against the Taliban by NATO and the US continues. In both cases, Obama's emphasis on a long-term peaceful solution through opportunity is a consequence of the partial failure of military intervention to stabilise Afghanistan and Iraq.

Religion can be a contributing factor in conflict or an inhibitor, and occasionally both at the same time. It has the potential to complicate military intervention or facilitate its success. There are people with no religious faith who use religion for political ends. There are others who see their faith and political action as coterminous and yet more who view religion (a human construct) and faith (God given) as distinct, preferring private faith to be uncorrupted by politics. This book is about conflict, religion and military intervention which, despite their many problems, continue to feature in the lives of individuals and communities world-wide. The idea for the book developed from a conference held in November 2007, entitled 'Engaging with Religion for Building Peace: The Experience of Afghanistan and Iraq'. The conference was at the Royal Military Academy Sandhurst, responsible for training British and Overseas Officer Cadets to be commissioned as officers into their respective armies, including the armies of Afghanistan and Iraq.

Twenty-four Officer Cadets commissioned into the British Army since December 2001 have died in Afghanistan and Iraq as of 30 June 2009. The total death toll of servicemen and women is over 1,200 in Afghanistan (Afghanistan 2009), and in excess of 4,600 in Iraq (Iraq 2009). Estimates vary of the total count of Iraqi and Afghan civilian deaths following military intervention. The Iraq Body Count estimate in April 2009 was somewhere between 92,000 and 100,000 (Radio Free Iraq 2009). Taking an aggregate of estimates from a variety of monitoring agencies, including Human Rights Watch, the UN Assistance Mission in Afghanistan (UNAMA) and the Afghanistan Rights Monitor (ARM), civilian deaths in Afghanistan directly attributable to the conflict are estimated to be between 7,500 and 10,500 as well as indirectly, between a further 3,000 to 20,000.

The context for this book is the religious dimension of violence in Afghanistan and Iraq. As this introductory chapter is being written, news is breaking that the decomposed bodies of two men, Jason Creswell from Aberdeen and Jason Swindlehurst from Lancashire have been handed in to the Iraqi authorities. They were security guards for GardaWorld, a Canadian security company. They had been guarding another captive, Peter Moore, a computer consultant, along with two guards Alan and Alec. They were training Iraqi civil servants at a Finance Ministry building when their compound was stormed by 40 gunmen on 29 May 2007. This is both tragic and poignant: the planned keynote speaker at the Sandhurst conference, Canon Andrew White, Anglican vicar of Baghdad, withdrew at the final hour because of signs that there might be the possibility of productive negotiations with the kidnappers enabling their release. Efforts were made by the British Foreign Office to handle this case in a low key manner, and no doubt there will be questions asked about their strategy. It will add to the litany of questions about the legality of military intervention in Iraq, the reliability of intelligence and the competence of the intelligence community, the wisdom of military intervention, and whether enough or too little force was used. But the starting point to any response, as Obama indicates, must be to try to understand the religious motivations behind this kind of violence.

The assumption behind this book is that the religious dimension of conflict in Afghanistan and Iraq has been underestimated. Religion defines the perpetrators of terrorist violence, and it influences the politico-strategic response, as well as tactics and outcomes from military intervention. The book seeks to respond to and develop Obama's thesis that more knowledge is needed about the circumstances of terrorism and the terrorists' religious beliefs and indeed the religious beliefs of states involved in conflict and military intervention. It does so by interpreting knowledge, not only in its epistemological sense, but ontologically, proposing that solutions will be found in a deeper level of engagement between faiths and new ways of thinking about conflict and its resolution in the policy arena. The book explores four main areas: religion and conflict; religious influences on military intervention; the need to disentangle religion from politics; and, religion and its relationship to conflict resolution. This approach highlights the importance of engaging with religious thinkers on their own terms, as theologians, for whom religion gives a different perspective on reality.

Religion and Conflict

The next two chapters highlight the plurality of belief in both Christianity and Islam in relation to war, influenced as much by context as by religious experience, belief and tradition. This pluralism challenges the claims of particular religions or religious sects to be the absolute arbiter of truth, with peaceful outcomes a product of the capacity of truth claims to be able to enter into dialogue with each other. Chapter 2 by Kunal Mukherjee, 'Islamism and Neo-Fundamentalism', explores the belief systems of Islamists. He provides an overview of Islamism by looking at it in a historical and then in a more contemporary context. The first half of the chapter examines some of the terms used in the existing body of scholarly literature, *fundamentalism*, *integrisme* and *jihadism*, and the problems associated with the use of such terms. It considers the historical background of Islamism and pays attention to the three phases of *revivalism*, *reformism* and *radicalism.* The second section then considers Islamism in a more contemporary context and in the shape of *neo-fundamentalism*, a term coined by French scholar Olivier Roy in his *Globalised Islam.* In the final section, there is an important discussion of how contemporary Islamism differs from the earlier period. Critically, the chapter highlights how Islamic fundamentalism is a cyclical phenomenon which occurs as a response to an acute period of social crisis, with the scope and intensity of the fundamentalist reaction ranging from spiritual reawakening to revolutionary violence. Mukherjee finds that this phenomenon is dependent on the pervasiveness of the crisis environment.

It is a point of coincidence and interest that Bin Laden's orchestrated terrorist attack on the United States World Trade Centre and Pentagon took place in 2001, at the start of the second millennium, a year of symbolic value for Christians marking the birth of Jesus – a prophet for Muslims; for Christians, the Son of God. It would be easy to assume that secularism in Europe and the United States, as well as the libertarian life-style of its citizens, means that the Christian tradition that took root in Europe in the early fourth century no longer influences decision-making on issues of conflict and military intervention. In Chapter 3, on 'God, the State and War', Rosemary Durward explores Christian attitudes to conflict and war, demonstrating a much more complex relationship between Christian faith and defence decision-making. The chapter reveals pluralism within Christianity, with differing interpretations of scripture, revelation and tradition leading to a variety of conclusions about the ethics of war. She argues that between different Christian traditions there is an opportunity for dialogue and to re-think the dualist paradigm that has dominated Christian thinking about the world and international relations discourse. With particular reference to Karl Barth's theology, Durward identifies the possibility of reshaping the whole Western philosophical and conceptual framework within which military power is exercised and reconciliation is sought. Taken together, these opening chapters show that in Islamic and Christian communities, there is an onus on members to mediate responsibly between their tradition, teaching and practice.

Religious Influences on Military Intervention

Setting aside Bin Laden and the Taliban whose actions prompted the intervention in Afghanistan, a feature of the campaigns in Afghanistan and Iraq was the lack of attention to the significance of religious leaders in the aftermath of military intervention. This had serious consequences for the stabilisation task. One casualty was the head of the Al-Khoei Foundation, Abdul Majid al-Khoei. Al Khoei was assassinated in April 2003 in Najaf near the Imam Ali Shrine. His family had enormous influence over the Shia community, with his father, Abu al-Qasim al-Khoei, spiritual leader of the Shia, having opposed Ayatollah Khomeini's establishment of the Islamic Republic of Iran. The safety of the son, who had returned from exile, should have been a priority given his moderating influence on the Shia community and his unifying role.

This error may have been because little thought was put into planning for occupation generally. Additionally, planners might have underestimated the positive effects religious leaders could have on faith communities because they believed Al Qaeda's claim to speak for all Muslims. The fact that church and state are separated in much of the West will have probably played a part in influencing the mindset. This book, on the contrary, finds the origins of early complacency to lie more deeply: in the seductiveness of secularism as a belief system in Europe; and, conversely, in the influence, in the US, of a relatively small but powerful right-wing evangelical lobby that saw invasion as an opportunity to export their values.

Secularism is an ideal that is cherished in Western political culture, particularly amongst Europe's intellectuals, influenced by Gibbon's historical judgement that the decline of the Roman world lay in 'the triumph of barbarism and religion' (Grayling 2008: 17). For Gibbon, religion must be treated as a phenomenon of human experience. On this basis, first there was ignorant religion, and then there was secular Enlightenment, the product of which was intellectual and political freedom and human rights. Islam does not accept a distinction between politics and religion. On this basis, Islam has been perceived by many Western political commentators to need similar enlightenment. The corollary to this reasoning is that, in historical terms, the West is at a much further stage in its intellectual, scientific and political progression but we suggest this argument is flawed.

The modern construction of the history of progress from religious ignorance to secular enlightenment and its causal link to terrorism by the unenlightened, neglects the possibility that Islamism is a response to the worldwide process that is ongoing and in constant flux, of freeing meaning and ideas from an ideological straitjacket. On that basis, it is not enlightenment within Islam that needs to be kick-started, nor freedom that needs to be exported, but freedom and dignity within the Islamic world that needs to be secured. Whether it is the Taliban, Al Qaeda or disparate Islamist militia speaking, the message is usually directed against modernising forces within Islam, as well as the United States and other Western forces that are alleged to be occupying Muslim lands. Local causes feature too, so that Islamist motivations are linked to specific and local political events to cause violence.

Rebecca Glazier in Chapter 4, 'Religiously Motivated Political Violence in Iraq', identifies religious nationalists, radical jihadists and sectarian combatants as sources of religious violence supported by outsiders coming into Iraq to support their causes. Glazier pays special attention to the role of providential belief in motivating jihad and martyrdom by suicide bombing. Amongst a range of responses, she highlights the possibility of shaping the context for intervention, so that jihadist belief ceases to have resonance. The issue of resonance relates to the conduct of intervention forces. But the current phase of Islamic radicalism is also rooted in the historic legacy of cultural insensitivity and violence towards Muslims leading to a sense of overwhelming humiliation by the West. It would be easy to tap into a narrative that shows Islam to be subordinated to a Judeo-Christian world, a feeling intensified by United States support for Israel. There is, for example, a Palestinian diaspora brought about by a lost war in 1948 and Israel's occupation of East Jerusalem, the West Bank and Gaza in 1967. Terrorism against Israelis by Hamas and the building of a wall by Israel ostensibly for its own security, nevertheless, reinforces a sense that security is divisible and selective. The Biblical narrative of the 'promised land' for the Jewish people and the location of sacred Muslim places in Jerusalem adds another layer of complication to attempts at a political solution to Israeli-Palestinian and wider Israeli-Arab relations.

So too, does the existence of Israeli religious extremism amongst a minority, which has obstructed attempts at peace. This extremism is in contradiction to most of the ancient Rabbinic literature on war, which urges the dissociation of Jews from any aspect of war-making. Rabbinic tradition identified laws relating to war through classifying each war by whether it was commanded or obligatory, permitted or contrary to divine law. According to Mishnah writing in the second century, the battles for self-defence recorded in the first five books of the Bible were 'obligatory', while the wars fought by King David to expand his territory were merely 'permitted' (Wilkes 2003: 11). George Wilkes interprets these delineations as, 'progressive limits to religious sanctions for subsequent military engagement rather than to expose a broad Biblical mandate for further wars'. The bulk of Rabbinic literature also treats the distinctions as a basis for considering justifiable military conduct. Rabbinic tradition recognises something like the Semitic herem or ban, an ordained slaughter of men, women and children without mercy. But from the Mishnah onwards, it dealt with the ban or herem as exceptions, no longer relevant, because the peoples concerned had intermarried to the point where they were no longer distinguishable. Even the ban on the Canaanites, according to Rabbinic interpretation, was preceded by peace negotiations, a practice identified with all of the wars of the biblical patriarchs (Deuteronomy 20:10; Wilkes 2003: 11). This is a long way away from the position of Israeli extremists who have sought to compare Arabs with the Amalekites (Exodus 17:8–16; Deuteronomy 25:17–19) and the Canaanites (Deuteronomy 20: 16–18) to whom no mercy is shown.

Another rallying point for Muslims against Western encroachment was the welcome given by Saudi Arabia, home of Mecca, to American troops when a coalition force expelled Iraq from Kuwait at the beginning of 1991. Al Qaeda's argument has been that the West has attempted to weaken Muslims by a policy of 'divide and conquer'. Historical events, such as the Crusades, have also had the power to unify Muslims although there are a great many myths surrounding this period of Muslim-Christian history and deconstructing them is part of a strategy to overcome parochialism and reinforce the sense of a common history. The common assumption that Muslims were passive victims of Christian aggression needs to be set in the context of the gradual retreat of Christian Europe against Muslim advance between 600 and 1400 Common Era (CE). In battling for Jerusalem during the Crusades, there was viciousness on both sides.

Muslim military conquest of Europe, followed by a degree of cultural osmosis, is deemed to have occurred from c.630 CE onwards, as Arabs moved from Mesopotamia past Jerusalem to Asia Minor and North Africa in just over 100 years. By 711 CE Arabs had crossed the Straits of Gibraltar into Spain, and by 732 CE they were in Poitiers. Pushed back to the Pyrenees, they remained on the Iberian

Peninsula until 1492. In the wake of military success, Muslim Arabs introduced academic developments, advancing the study of philosophy, mathematics, physics and astrology. They brought military prowess fighting on horseback, and adopting new navigation techniques. A great many of the skills brought by Muslim Arabs made the Italian city states extraordinarily prosperous. One mark of the cross-cultural exchange between Christian Europeans and Muslim Arabs in the early second millennium was the invention to something similar to the modern travellers cheque. This was instituted by the Knights Templar, a twelfth century religious and military order established and campaigning in the Holy Land, and thought to have been adopted from Muslim practice. The Templars would exchange the goods of Christian pilgrims for an encoded document determining its holders right to those goods to avoid the vagaries of banditry along the Pilgrim's Way. In return, Muslim military intervention in Europe was often welcomed by the indigenous population as preferable to rule by church authorities who, owning 25 per cent of the land, were growing rich at the expense of the majority. Relative freedom of religion, as defined by early Muslim warlords (c.630–750), meant that assimilation into Islam was voluntary rather than forced. Today, it is probable that there will be a degree of unintended cross-cultural exchange as a result of the military interventions in Iraq and Afghanistan.

It is evident that Crusaders and Muslims in Medieval Europe assumed that they had divine providence on their side to deliver victory. Assumptions about divine will continue to influence attitudes to war. Today's military chaplains provide support and succour to troops in the field while church leaders host parades and church services to honour the bravery of returning troops. At the same time a long established tradition of pacifism emphasises divine antipathy to warfare. Both traditions appeal to biblical interpretation and religious tradition in support of their differing interpretations of divine will. Lee Marsden in Chapter 5, 'God, War and Iraq', examines the approach of Christian churches to warfare, analysing Biblical accounts of warfare, exploring the pacifism of the early church and the emergence of just war theory. A brief history of the relationship between church and warfare provides a background to consider the Iraq war as a case study. He describes how President Bush's public statements fell just short of mentioning a crusade, but were deliberately designed to appeal to conservative evangelicals, at home and in the US military fighting abroad. This gave scope for an intensification of the conservative evangelical intent to engage in a spiritual battle against Islam. On this basis, the whole of the indigenous population was either the enemy or potential converts.

The rise of religious fundamentalism with global reach contributed to the growth of a neo-conservative elite in the United States, with an agenda to guarantee America's supremacy. As the world's greatest power economically and militarily, this necessarily means adopting and sustaining a *realpolitik* strategy to ensure its position over and against other states (Mason 2009: 136–42). We can speculate that as guarantor of security for itself and its allies, a change in United States presidency is unlikely to shift that agenda. President Carter, an outspoken

Christian and Democrat, tried to and was criticised for being soft on Communism; out of office his more moderate expression of faith put a distance between himself and his co-religionists in the Southern Baptist Convention, leading to his decision to leave in 2000. In Chapter 6, 'Trust Me! Jesus Would Go to War Too', Sandy Livingston explores the political alliance of Southern Baptist voters in the United States with the Republican party. The American political system is governed by competition between many factions which constantly vie for influence. Southern Baptists as one evangelical church amongst many, became a formidable force in American politics during the Bush years, helping to usher in many changes in the American political landscape, in pursuit of their particular religious and moral perspective.

The chapter takes a detailed look at the changing identity of the Southern Baptist voters and their loyalty to the Republican Party. The author proposes that their identity has been swept away from Christian values and has landed upon a rigid political construct. Livingston analyses how the vote has influenced American foreign policy and discusses the consequence of the Southern Baptist voter's influence for the relationship between religion and American politics in general. In light of the way in which theology is influenced by context, Livingston asks the question as to whether American foreign policy eventually led Southern Baptists to re- interpret their religious beliefs.

The close influence of religion on American politics during the Bush presidency has been remarkable, given the First Amendment to the United States constitution on the separation of church and state. In the United Kingdom, in the run up to the invasion of Iraq, faith and politics also seemed to merge. A British public that cherishes the *de facto* separation of church and state closely watched Prime Minister, Tony Blair's support for the US policy of military intervention in Iraq with grave uneasiness. Blair's conviction appeared to prioritise moral justifications based on private religious beliefs, over and above openly debated just war principles, which opposition from the Pope did not sway. The notion of the separation of church and state implies an institutional separation. It cannot enforce a separation of values from an individual's political motivation and action; in that sense the requirement to separate faith from politics may be unrealistic. Nevertheless, it appeared to be a Christian agenda that was driving forward a programme of military intervention in the wake of 11 September 2001. The apparent polarisation between Islam and a 'Christian' West surpassed Samuel Huntington's predictions of a clash of civilisations along cultural fault lines, between a secular West and Islam (Huntington 1993). Fundamentalists on both sides of the religious divide were confronting each other.

Disentangling Religion from Politics

Whilst it is important to appreciate the role that religion has had and continues to have in the formulation of policy, it is also critical to be able to disentangle the two. This is because religion can purport to confer authority and mandate actions and policies in the political arena, investing them with divine authority for political effect. This is arguably what George Bush was trying to do when he claimed that his policies were guided by a 'higher father' and fleetingly used the terminology of a crusade. Attempts at legitimisation on a religious basis need to be identified so that their validity can be challenged, and threats to security and the appropriate response can be debated objectively within a framework of international law.

A dominant value the United States strongly identifies with is that of 'freedom'. The term has resonance to Christians based on scripture and is also seen as part of the secular Enlightenment project, celebrated in the American War of Independence (1775–1783) and French Revolution (1789–1799). However, there are indications that 'freedom' has the characteristics of an ideology in American foreign policy. In Chapter 7, 'Coercive Solidarism: The Secular and Religious in US Exceptionalism', Nicholas Kerton-Johnson explores the connection between coercive solidarism and US freedom, particularly after 11 September 2001 and critiques US interventionist foreign policy. He exposes a tension between US support for liberal internationalism based on the equality of states, and its hegemonic desire to impose its own particular world view on international society. Consistent with Wightian revolutionism, US foreign policy aims at bringing about a utopian vision. However, the vision is divided between the US's support for liberal internationalism based on the equality of states, and its hegemonic desire to impose its own particular world view of freedom on international society.

Ivan Manokha attempts a different task – to disentangle just war and its role in justifying intervention on religious grounds, breaching Westphalian principles of sovereignty and territorial integrity, from humanitarian intervention motivated by ideology. In Chapter 8, 'The History of Modern Military Humanitarianism Revisited: The Ideology of Violence and the Violence of Ideology', Manokha describes feudalism as an ideology that depends for its justification on a notion of God that prescribes a hierarchy of social and economic relations. The divine dimension turns feudalism into an immutable system. He critiques the contemporary setting, asserting that once labour became a commodity, the necessity for coercion was removed, and along with it notions of divine right. Natural law became divorced from religious control as a consequence of capitalism and became significant in justifying humanitarian intervention. Humanitarian intervention, in turn, has a moral content but has the unintended consequence of contributing to the global hegemony of capitalism and unequal privilege. This is an example of an ideology in the negative sense, in which ideology as defined by Marx, is seen as a 'distorted form of knowledge' (Maclean 1988: 309).

Religion and ideology can be hard to untwine, when religion becomes systematised and total in its reach. Christian theologian, Don Cupitt (1989: 57) argued that religion is not 'true' but a tradition, like a culture or language, within which we frame our life project; to attempt to totalise it is mistaken. He asserted that theology is about spiritual power and subjection to spiritual power, but that historically, there was a presumption in favour of centralised authority, objective truth, ecclesiastical order and discipline, 'coming from Above, timeless, certain, ready-made, given and immutable'. For Cupitt, both religion and ideology need to be critiqued for the same tendency towards centralised and concentrated power, privileging 'Unity, selfsameness and presence.' He alleged that this privileging of unity in religion over the plurality of the real multi-faith world, mirrors the same will to power that afflicts the secular world. The secular Enlightenment is said to have freed politics from religion. There is a human tendency to find meaning in history, and to find identity in ideas as well as to kill for them. Responsibility lies with humanity, rather than religion. As Giandomenico Picco, Personal Representative to the Secretary-General for the United Nations Year of Dialogue Among Civilizations said in 1999, 'History does not kill. Religion does not rape women, the purity of blood does not destroy buildings and institutions do not fail. Only individuals do these things' (United Nations 2001).

Disentangling religion and politics is not easy, in part because Christianity and Islam have been influenced by the same ancient Greek philosophy that has influenced politics. For example, Plato's political concern was with justice and the escape from ignorance and he constructed a perfect state, *Magnesia*, which relied on moral absolutes and the enforcement of obedience. Plato's *Republic* was ruled by reason, and reason is ruled by knowledge of absolute good which is in the eternal. Plato's vision influenced early Islamic debate about what was required for just rule for Muslims (Walzer 1985) and provided a model for Islamic theocracies and secular authoritarian regimes.

Plato, alongside Aristotle, offers two alternative visions of the world, shaping Muslim and Christian thinking about the relationship between eternity and the material world. For Aristotle (384–322 BC), existence was in physical objects, including the idea that the mind and universals do not exist beyond the material things that are behind them. For Plato (c.427–347 BC), in contrast, eternal things are real and unchanging forms or ideas. Hence, 'good' is transcendent and unattainable, and the world is a perfect reflection of that reality, or form. Plato saw the world as the finite form of that eternal absolute good, a precursor to universals. Origen (c.185–254 CE), a Christian and Egyptian scholar and theologian teaching in Alexandria, was a neo-Platonist who wrote one of the first philosophical expositions of early Christian doctrine espousing universalism. He asserted that the human soul is pre-existent and eternal, distinct from Aristotle's view that the soul and body exist together (Ward 2009: 139).

Manokha's description of ideology sounds strangely like Plato's reality in the realm of universal ideas, with the material world a poor reflection. Manokha describes how ' ideological ideas are 'encouraged to a great extent' (Lukacs 1971) by a social reality which is 'inverted', that is, which appears different from what it really is and favours the development of ideas that express it inadequately, and may be shared by all social classes'.

Conflict Resolution

Exceptionalism and solidarism prevalent in states and religious groups engender rivalry, coercive behaviour and insecurity. History has shown that this is generally resolved by one or a group of states assuming a dominant position. Universalism challenges these 'isms' and reverses the movement towards a 'Clash of Civilizations' forecast by Samuel Huntington in the political realm. The universalist movement encourages intra- and inter-faith dialogue and draws on tradition in both Christianity and Islam.

A contemporary proponent of universalism is H.E. Mohammad Khatami, former President of the Islamic Republic of Iran who introduced the idea of a 'Dialogue Among Civilizations' in response to Samuel P. Huntington's 'Clash of Civilizations' thesis (Khatami 2000). In his dialogue Khatami asserted that 'Each and every human individual, living in each and every corner of time and place, is potentially included in the purview of Islam. The Islamic emphasis on essential human equality and its disdain for such elements as birth and blood, conquered the hearts of those yearning for justice and freedom'. He alludes to the synthesis of Persian wisdom, Greek rationalism and Islamic intuitive knowledge which rejects dualism that tries to separate human thought from divine revelation.

Khatami spoke of the Islamic civilisation's unity, and its plurality from the 'diversity of response' evoked in different nations. He spoke of the desirability of the emergence of a 'global culture', not ignoring local cultures but creating 'a unique and harmonious form' from the collection. This presents, according to Khatami, 'an alternative paradigm for international relations today' to the one 'based on the discourse of power and the glorification of might'. He urges that we replace that paradigm with a new one based on dialogue, appealing to 'the will for empathy and compassion', without which he sees no hope for order in the world. Khatami cites the value in interaction between cultures and deliberate interaction between members of civilisations such as scholars, artists, philosophers. He uses theological language, rather than secular language, which is better understood with knowledge of its religious tradition and philosophical underpinnings. Khatami was urging dialogue as the route to successful conflict resolution, supported by a meta-historical discussion of eternal human questions such as the ultimate meaning of life and death or goodness and evil:

> Without a discussion of fundamentals, and by simply confining attention to superficial issues, dialogue would not get us far from where we currently stand. When superficial issues masquerade as real, urgent and essential, and where no agreement, or at least mutual understanding, obtains among parties to dialogue concerning what is truly fundamental, in all likelihood misunderstanding and confusion will proliferate instead of any sense of empathy and compassion.

For forces undertaking military intervention and post conflict peace building, the definition and interpretation of 'good', will itself be influenced by conceptions of God or Allah.

The *Economist*'s Special Report on religion (*Economist* 2007: 20) wrote of the necessity not to dismiss inter-faith dialogue as 'liberal waffle' or 'naïve appeasement'. It reported on the progress of Sudanese Christians and Muslim leaders in Sudan in reducing the religious dimension of the conflict in 2000, and of the value of inter-faith dialogue in averting Muslim-Christian violence in Nigeria. Similarly, sectarianism in Northern Ireland, although expressed in class and economic rivalry, including crime, nevertheless had religious beginnings, and the 'beginning of the end' came when Roman Catholic and Protestant priests condemned the bombings in unison. Another possibly liberal method of reversing the cycle of violence has been through dialogue with the militants themselves.

The twenty-first century has already seen the 2,250 km border between Pakistan and Afghanistan become a decisive battleground in the fight against global terrorism. Shazadi Beg, in Chapter 9, 'Pakistan's Tribal Areas: A Battle for Jihad', puts forward a case for well structured interventions based on a real understanding of why individuals have become radicalised. Beg's chapter provides a unique insight into the border areas of Pakistan and Afghanistan, presenting a picture of corruption, tribal disenfranchisement and flourishing militancy. Drawing on experience in Yemen and other states implementing a rehabilitation strategy for radicalised Muslims, she advocates entering into the 'battle of ideas' by challenging beliefs through intellectual and theological discussion.

In Chapter 10, '"Just Peace" or Peace Postponed: *Jus Post Bellum* and the Aftermath of Iraq', Serena Sharma considers the conflict in Iraq, observing that in the modern period, just war thinkers have drawn a sharp distinction between the different phases of war. *Jus ad bellum* is clearly separated from the *jus in bello* and both have become separated from the concept of peace. Consequently, just war scholars working within this model have tended to treat the *jus post bellum* as a 'third just war category', completely autonomous from both *jus ad bellum* and *jus in bello*. On the contrary, the author argues, planning for peace should feature prior to the initiation of hostilities, and in this sense be part and parcel of the *jus ad bellum* calculation. The chapter argues for a conscious return to the Christian just war model where no discernible distinction is drawn between the different phases of war. In accordance with an Augustinian approach, considerations of peace should not be postponed until war's end, but rather, be present from the initiation of a conflict. It is on behalf of this rendering of peace which a meaningful *jus post bellum* must strive.

The neo-conservative assumption that there can be 'good' coming out of military intervention is neither new, nor necessarily absolutely wrong. It could, for example, be a 'good' thing if religious freedom were exported to countries that deny it (*Economist* 2007: 20), so long as it is not motivated by a desire to convert but rather, to have genuine pluralism in religious belief. The question in military intervention should always be, 'Whose good is served?' A further question that might usefully be asked, of ostensibly secular states such as the United States as well as religious ones is what kind of conception of God is influencing the concept of 'good' in consideration of just outcomes. In this approach to dialogue, in which free reign is given to the imagination, there might be some potentially unexpected consequences. If, for example, God were conceived of as female,[1] what would be the impact on the will to power generated under the dominant patriarchal motif imposed by Greek philosophy and religious tradition? Religion begs ontological questions about first principles. In the realm of meaning and its relationship to knowledge and reason, the religious and secular worlds have a great deal in common. Understanding this is the first step towards winning Obama's 'struggle'. President Obama said, in his Inaugural Address:

> To the Muslim world, we see a new way forward, based on mutual interest and mutual respect. To those leaders around the globe who seek to sow conflict, or blame their society's ills on the West, know that your people will judge you on what you can build, not what you destroy. (Obama 2009)

It is hoped that this book contributes to mutual understanding and respect, through greater understanding of religiously motivated terrorism and military intervention in the world, and most notably of the human struggle to live with conflict and deal with it constructively.

Bibliography

Afghanistan 2009. Operation Enduring Freedom. Available at: http://icasualties.org/oef/ (accessed 30 June 2009).

Cupitt, D. 1989. *Radicals and the Future of the Church*. London: SCM Press.

Grayling, A.C. 2008. *Britannica. Britannica's Guide to the Ideas that Made the Modern World*, introduction by A.C. Grayling. London: Constable and Robinson Ltd.

Economist 2007. In God's Name: A Special Report on Religion and Public Life. *The Economist*, 3 November, 1–20.

Huntington, S.P. 1993. The Clash of Civilizations? *Foreign Affairs*. Summer 72 (3), 22–44.

Iraq 2009. Iraq Coalition Casualty Count 2009. Available at: http://icasualties.org/Iraq/index.aspx (accessed 30 June 2009).

Khatami, M.K. 2000. Dialogue among Civilizations, Round Table, United Nations, New York. Online 5 September. Available at: http://www.unesco.org/dialogue/en/khatami.htm (accessed 5 July 2009).

Mason, P. 2009. *Meltdown: The End of the Age of Greed*. London and NY: Verso.

1 Modern feminists were not the first to feminise God. Julian of Norwich (c.1342–1415), for example, referred to God as mother.

Obama, B. 2007. Renewing American Leadership. *Foreign Affairs*, July–August.
Obama, B. 2009. President Barack Obama's Inaugural Address, Whitehouse. Online 21 January. Available at: http://www.whitehouse.gov/ (accessed 30 June 2009).
Picco, G. 1999. United Nations Year of Dialogue Among Civilizations. Online 2001. Available at: http://www.un.org/Dialogue/background.html (accessed 30 June 2009).
Radio Free Iraq 2009. Interview with IBC, first broadcast 24 April 2009. Available at: http://www.iraqbodycount.org/analysis/beyond/rfi/ (accessed 2 July 2009).
Ward, K. 2009. *The Big Questions in Science and Religion*. Pennsylvania: Templeton Foundation Press.
Walzer, M. 1985. al-Farabi (c.870–950) *al-Madina al-fadila, The Virtuous City*, trans. R. Walzer, *Al-Farabi on the Perfect State*. Oxford: Clarendon Press.
Wilkes, G. 2003. Judaism and Justice in War. In P. Robinson (ed.) *Just War in Comparative Perspective*. Aldershot: Ashgate.

PART 1
Religion and Conflict

Chapter 2
Islamism and Neo-fundamentalism

Kunal Mukherjee

'Islamic fundamentalism' of a particular virulent kind has been on the rise in recent times and is most likely to continue. Fundamentalism is a malaise of the twentieth century and it has afflicted almost every religious tradition, no matter how ancient (Noorani 2002: 1). Although this phenomenon is associated with most religious traditions, in recent times, it has been associated a lot more with Islam since Islam has been everywhere on the political scene. Islamic fundamentalism is perceived as a cyclical phenomenon, which occurs as a response to an acute period of social crises and the scope and intensity of the fundamentalist reaction ranging from spiritual reawakening to revolutionary violence depends on the pervasiveness of the crisis environment (Dekmejian 1985: 6). The aim of this chapter is to give readers an overview of Islamism by firstly looking at Islamism in a more historical context and then in a more contemporary one.

Islamism is the term used for the extreme politicised version of Islam that sees Islam in a state of constant conflict with the West, non-Muslims and insufficiently pious Muslims. Even within Islamism there are different categories, but it is important to understand that the Islamist category is a microscopic minority and not representative of the Muslim people.

The first half of this chapter will look at some of the terms used in the existing body of scholarly literature, *fundamentalism*, *integrisme* and *jihadism* and the problems associated with the use of these terms. The first section also looks at some historical background of Islamism and pays attention to the three phases of *revivalism, reformism* and *radicalism.* It is important to make this distinction because it hints at the fact that Islamism as a political ideology should not be viewed in monolithic terms and that some strands of thought are much more extremist than others. The second half of the chapter will look at Islamism in a more contemporary context and in this connection, the second half of the chapter will be focusing on the term, neo-fundamentalism, a term coined by French scholar Olivier Roy in his *Globalized Islam* (2004: 232–57). In the final section, there will be a discussion on how the new versions of Islamism differ from the earlier period.

The study of Islamism is important for both social policy and security reasons. This chapter is primarily for those who do not understand the distinction between Islam (religion) and Islamism (political ideology). This chapter has broad social policy implications since it aims to ease tensions that have arisen from erroneous assumptions about Islam based on Islamist ideology. Such a 'neo-orientalist' or hostile and unfavourable interpretation of Islam has been on the rise since the terrorist attacks of 11 September 2001 (9/11) and 7 July 2005 (7/7), after which many treated Islam and Islamism synonymously associating them both with fanaticism. A better understanding of Islamism could thus help in preventing the demonisation of Islam and enable the process of bridge building between Islam and the West.

This chapter is also important for security reasons. The rise of Islamism in the contemporary world needs to be studied within the broader framework of the New Security Agenda: recognising that in the post Cold War period, the concept of security has changed and instead of state aggression, Islamism and other new enemies have been identified as the main source of threat (Buzan 1998). In order to take pre emptive measures, it is important for analysts to be familiar with its causes or at least have some background knowledge of Islamism.

Defining Terms

Islamic fundamentalism is a vague term currently used as a catch phrase to describe the militant ideology of contemporary Islamic movements (Chouerri 1990: 9). It should be noted that both Muslim scholars and Western analysts have objected to the use of this term as a generic term since it is considered to be a dubious concept alien to the cultural heritage of Muslims. The term 'fundamentalism' emerged in a Christian American context as a reaction against modernity and the complications related to the modernisation process. The word first appeared in America, America being the showcase of modernity (Armstrong 2000a: 140). The equivalent term in Arabic is *usuliyah* coming from the word, *usul*, which refers to the fundamentals of the Islamic faith. Islamic scholars therefore refuse to recognise the term 'fundamentalism' arguing that it should not be imposed on an Islamic context since it has been taken from a Christian context, which does not respect the particularity of Islam. Other European terms like the French word, *integrisme* are also problematic. The term *integrisme* refers to a traditional tendency in contemporary Catholicism but now has been made synonymous with Islamist movements in France which have strong North African connections (Roberts 2003: 1). Similarly, it is a common mistake to use the word *jihadism* to describe these movements. The problem with this term is that it gives the impression that the word, *jihad* means to wage war against the infidel and the violence associated with it thereby ignoring the idea of the greater *jihad* which is to better oneself spiritually. The word *jihad* comes from the word *jahada*, which means struggle and endeavour. The idea of the original word is to struggle for peace and to better oneself spiritually and has a strong moral side to it. This is the idea of the *greater jihad*. The idea of the *lesser jihad* means to wage war against the infidel or non-believers but only for defensive rather than offensive reasons. The idea of the lesser jihad has been hijacked by Islamist ideologues who interpret the word in diverse ways. Because of the problems with these terms, earnest efforts have been exerted by scholars to come up with a more neutral designation deemed less tainted by European and American categories. Alternative options include, 'Islamism', 'Islamic resurgence', 'Islamic revival', 'radicalism' and 'political Islam'.

The word that is most commonly used these days is 'Islamism'. Islamism has been compared with other twentieth-century 'isms'. After Nazism, Marxist-Leninism and 'fascism' (Pipes 2002: 14), comes Islamism – a belief system of ordering power and wealth and regimentation of society (by imposition of *Sharia* law) according to a perceived plan but only this time with an Islamic orientation. Islamism banishes reason from religion and compassion from faith. Its main traits are revivalism, hostility to minorities, anti intellectualism, intolerance, arrogant insularity, intellectual bankruptcy and moral blindness (Noorani 2002: 65). Islamism is expressed through a rejection of rational discourse, pluralism, free speech and democratic governance. It advocates recourse to violence and is a worldwide response to the peculiar strains of the twentieth century.

There is a debate about the relationship between politics and Islamic movements. Some scholars prefer to use the term, 'Political Islam' but then the question may arise: is there an economic Islam and a social Islam? The whole issue of preferring one description to another relates not only to the phenomenon itself but also to the perspective of the analyst (Moussalli 1998). While the word, 'fundamentalism' to describe Islamic movements that seek to establish the Islamic state in accordance with Sharia law is subject to criticism, it has become part of the literature on Islamic thought and could safely be used as a descriptive term and not necessarily an evaluative term.

Islamism in a Historical Context

Scholars such as Youssef Choueiri (1990) and more recently Beverly Milton Edwards (2005) have looked into the historical side of contemporary Islamist movements. Choueiri has identified three major phases from the late eighteenth century onwards. The first phase he defines as 'Islamic revivalism', the second phase as 'Islamic modernism' or 'reformism' and finally he defines the third phase as 'Islamic radicalism'. Choueiri thinks Islamist movements are primarily political movements and Islamic systems of thought that emerged during the period of Islamic revivalism in the late eighteenth century in countries as far apart as India, Arabia, Indonesia and Nigeria (Choueiri 1990: 9). Because of the comprehensiveness of the Islamic movements and the diversity of their concerns, one may find that one description may fit a movement in Egypt or Algeria or Pakistan or Iran under certain circumstances or may account for an aspect of the movement in a specific period but the emphasis on the political aspect of such movements misses much of the significance of the other dimensions of the same movements. These movements are not limited to political action but deal with a diversity of issues that make them a way of life and philosophy at the same time as being able to critique them (Moussalli 1998: 3).

Islamism is a multifaceted phenomenon and each strand operates in different ways. When theorists try to explain Islamism they are basically explaining one particular strand of this multidimensional phenomenon, therefore the theory tends to apply only to a particular phase of the movement. Each phase is in constant flux and therefore theories also need to be revised in this connection. There will be both long term factors and some short term factors which lead to the outbreak of these movements but to analyse these movements and what causes them, we need to pin the movement down to its specific historical and geographical context and also to a particular time period. It is important to note that what acts as a long term factor or a trigger for one situation or one strand of Islamism may not apply to other Islamist movements located in totally different cultural contexts or other strands of the same movement. This is why specificities have become so important. Blanket theories which try to explain Islamism in the West, for instance in Britain will not apply to Islamist movements say in Pakistan, which are grounded in a totally different historical, cultural and geographical context.

Islamic Revivalism

Looking at the breakdown of Islamic movements into the three major phases of revivalism, reformism or modernism and radicalism, we see in the first phase that we are dealing primarily with movements that emerged in the peripheral regions of three empires: Ottoman Turkey, Safavid Iran and Mughal India. These movements emerged in the peripheral regions where the central authorities did not have much control and their social basis was predominantly a tribal formation (Choueiri 1990: 15–29). When we analyse these revivalist movements, we need to locate them in the background of disintegrating empires, when these three great Islamic empires were on the verge of collapse. The background is therefore one of political turmoil, agricultural stagnation and a time of demographic dislocations and dispersive movements, in other words, a phase of transition.

These Islamic movements arose as a response to the contemporary problems faced by Muslims and the idea was to reinstate Islam to its pristine glory. Revivalist thinkers in the Indian subcontinent were under the impression that Muslim societies were in a state of decline because of the corrupt influences of Hinduism and Sikhism and other religions of South Asia. Centuries of living next to Hindus and Sikhs had led to the polluting of the Islamic identity and erosion of what revivalists saw as 'purely' Islamic practices. The Wahabbi or Titu Mir's movement and Faraizi movemnt of Bengal in South Asia are classic examples of Islamic revivalism. Revivalist thinkers believe in the strict dichotomy of *Dar-ul-Harb* or *Dar-ul-Kufr* or land of the enemy/infidel and *Dar-ul-Islam* or land of the faithful or land of Islam. Revivalists insist Muslims to migrate from the enemy territory to the land of the faithful, that is, from *Dar-ul-Harb/Kufr* to *Dar-ul-Islam*. The idea was to imitate the prophet and in the process of this migration, popularly known as *Hijra* if there were obstacles on the way, then Muslims were permitted to fight and engage in defensive *jihad.* The year, 1749, is seen as the date of final consolidation of a political alliance struck between Mohammed Abdul Wahab and Mohammed Al Saud in central Arabia and this marks the beginning of the revivalist current. Ultimately, with the passage of time, revivalist movements failed to come up with suitable answers for the problems that Muslims were facing at the time and therefore they fizzled out creating a vacuum which paved the way for the second phase.

Islamic Reformism or Modernism

The second phase is called reformism or modernism. When we look at reformist movements, we need to locate these movements within the broader backdrop of European commercial expansionism and appreciate that these movements arose as a result of external pressure. Islamic reformism is primarily an urban phenomenon and we can trace the beginnings of this movement from the late 1800s to the beginnings of the twentieth century. In this phase we, see how the *ulema* or Muslim theologians, intellectuals and state officials brought themselves into a dialogue with European thinkers and philosophy and tried to use European philosophy and the European model of development to extricate the deplorable state Muslims were in at that time and they tried to arrest the process of what they saw as 'Islamic' decline (Choueiri 1990: 31–48). Thus we see that reformists or modernists were a lot more accommodating in their approach than their revivalist precursors. The reformers studied the pre-industrialised phase of Europe and firmly believed that European progress was because of intellectual factors rather than socio-economic ones. Mohammed Abduh, from Egypt is the chief ideologue associated with the second phase of reformism. Again, with the passage of time, these second group of movements failed to come up with consistent answers to the problems which Muslims were facing during the early half of the twentieth century and thus the vacuum that was created once reformism fizzled out, paved the way for the third phase called Islamic radicalism.

Islamic Radicalism

The third or final phase of Islamic radicalism is a post 1945 phenomenon and is a direct response to the rising tide of nationalism. The rise of nationalism as a force was seen to be dividing the worldwide Muslim community or the *ummah* and nationalist sentiments had fragmented the historic land of *Dar-ul-Islam.* Nationalist intellectuals had been educated in European style schools within the Muslim world and used the project of emancipation to thrust aside the religious establishment in pursuit of secular goals (Kepel 2002: 25). This phase again was an urban movement. Its constituency embraced recent rural migrants to the cities, peasants, merchants, artisans, shopkeepers, students, school teachers and other social groups. This phase of radicalism is, therefore, intrinsically associated with the tensions and ambitions of these different social groups and is also inextricably associated with the interrelated revolutionary changes that have been accompanied by the complex processes of modernisation and urbanisation. The third phase of radicalism is seen as the last attempt to create a totalitarian Islamic state. Its recruits came primarily from countries like Egypt, Iraq and Syria. Sayyid Qutb, again from Egypt is the main ideologue for the third phase of radicalism.

Sayyid Qutb's contribution to the contemporary Islamist debate is huge. Qutb realised that the Muslim world was culturally and politically besieged by the West and that the Muslim youth were increasingly getting sucked into the whole process of westernisation or 'McDonaldisation'. Qutb described this situation as the new *jahilya.* The original term, *jahilya* refers to the age of ignorance in pre Islamic Arabia, a time when people worshipped stones and idols-a period which is associated with primitive animism, polytheism and idolatry. Qutb took this word out of context with no consideration or respect for history or social circumstances and used the word to describe the present situation of cultural decay and Western influences in the Muslim world. He made *jahilya* synonymous with the whole process of westernisation and the evil cultural effects of westernisation on the Muslim youth.

Although Mohammed Abdul Wahab, Mohammed Abduh and Sayyid Qutb are seen as the three main ideologues for the three phases of Islamic revivalism, reformism and radicalism, the contributions of other thinkers and Islamists should not be underestimated. Islamism and Islamisation is an ongoing process. It is difficult to say when they started and when they will end. Some scholars trace the beginnings from the time of Ibn Taymiyyah (1263–1328). In a more contemporary context, contributions made by Mawdudi, founder of the Pakistani Jamat I Islami in the year 1941, An Nabhani, founder of the Hizb-ut-Tahrir in Jordan in 1953, Maullana Illyas, founder of the Tablighi Jamat in South Asia in 1926, Hasan al Bana, founder of the Muslim Brotherhood, Egypt in 1928, Ayatollah Khomeini, chief ideologue of the Iranian Revolution of 1979 and other pioneers of Islamic revival, should not be underestimated, for they have contributed just as much to the whole ongoing process of Islamisation. Also it should be remembered that it is not only Islamist ideologues who have contributed to this whole process but also major events and their ripple effects have only enriched and added to the whole process of Islamisation of Muslim countries. John Esposito's edited, *The Iranian Revolution-Its Global Impact*, shows very clearly that the revolution of 1979 had spill over effects throughout the Muslim world including places like Central Asia and South East Asia (Esposito, 1990: 203–33).

Throughout Muslim history, there were movements of reform or *islah* and renewal or *tajdid* which were often quite revolutionary. The Iranian Revolution, which brought an Islamic government to power, catapulted revolutionary Islam as a potent ideology on the international scene. The events since that date bear witness to the fact that Islam as a political force is not a passing fad. It appeals to the politically, socially and economically disinherited and provided a moral shield against the onslaught of Western 'anti-values' (Rahnema 1994: 2). Khomeini argued that the Islamic theologians or *ulama* should commit themselves to ousting corrupt officials and repressive governments which should be replaced by regimes led by Islamic jurists. He pressed for the subordination of political power to Islamic precepts and called on the *ulama* to bring about an Islamic state and to participate in its legislative, executive and judicial affairs and also offered a programme of action to establish an Islamic state.

An Islamic state requires an Islamic ruler who should know the *Sharia* thoroughly and must be absolutely just in its application. Shia's believe that *imams* were the ones who possessed these qualifications but in the absence of an *imam*, Muslims must find an alternative in order to avoid living in anarchy or under alien rule. Though lacking the infallibility and personal superiority of an *imam*, a just *faqih* is qualified to lead an Islamic state. Such jurists are also to oversee the actions of the executive and legislative branches of government. At its simplest, the *Vilayat-I-Faqi*, is the rule of the divine law as interpreted and applied by the just *faqih* (Sidahmed and Ehteshami 1996: 10). Since he does not rule according to his own will, but according to the divine law, the system is supposedly not dictatorial. What makes Khomeini's argument attractive is that it is simple and direct and derived from the first principles of Islam and therefore avoids convoluted religious arguments and is also conducted exclusively in traditional discussions with hardly any reference to Western or Western inspired politico ideological notions. Thus, there is no reference to nationalism, socialism and democracy.

Coming back to the three phases of Islamic revivalism, reformism and radicalism, in all three phases we see that there is constant tension, a battle between the 'forces of change' and 'forces of continuity'. 'Forces of change' refer to those elements in society who we would by and large label as progressive elements and by the term, 'Forces of Continuity' I am referring to reactionary, conservative elements in any society wanting to hold onto the status quo. As Karen Armstrong notes, any fundamentalist movement does not arise immediately as a knee jerk response to the advent of Western modernity but takes place when the modernisation process is quite advanced (Armstrong, 2000a: 140). At first religious people try to reform their traditions and effect a marriage between them and modern culture as we have seen Muslim reformers do. When Islamists cannot bring about reconciliation between modernity and Islamic tradition, some amongst them resort to more extreme methods and thus a fundamentalist movement is born. Today, conservative society is in trouble, either it has been effectively taken over by the Western ethos or it is undergoing the difficult transition from the conservative to the modern spirit and much of Islamism is a response to this painful transformation (Armstrong 2000b: 33). Islamists go back to a '*golden era*' before the irruption of modernity and are highly critical of secularism, socialism, capitalism and western notions of freedom and democracy.

When we look at the three phases, revivalism, reformism and radicalism we see that there are similarities between the phases and also areas of differences. It should be noted that all three of these phases are dealing with a transitional phase of change and societies are trying to cope with this changing situation. Fundamentalism is not simply the hallmark of fanaticism or traditionalism. It is an ardent endeavour imbued with an activist stance to grapple with overwhelming odds. Sayyid Qutb asserts that no Islamic ideology can exist without coming into a confrontation with other ideologies particularly other western ideologies. The explicit anti Americanism of the Iranian Revolution with demonstrators chanting, 'death to America', 'down with the great Satan' and burning US flags created the overwhelming impression that Islamism as represented by the Ayatollahs was primarily an anti Western revolution directed against American interests. In this ideological atmosphere, criticisms of US foreign policy are treated as displays of anti Americanism, which is used as a blind hatred for Americans and all secular aspects of US life, politics and culture (Ali 2002: 281).

Popular belief in the West tends to associate Islamism with the Iranian Revolution of 1979 and sees it as a movement of fanatics bent on harming western interests yet the oldest Islamist state, Arabia has been firmly allied with the West (Hiro 1989: 1–2). In Afghanistan, Western arms and funds played a crucial role in bolstering the Afghan fundamentalist camp in its war against the Marxist regime in Kabul. Islamism is also seen as a reaction against the encroachments made by Western capitalism into Islamic territory and a response against the various manifestations of 'godless' communism. Islamism postulates the qualitative contradiction between western civilisation on the one hand and the religion of Islam on the other. Islamists emphasise the all encompassing nature of Islam and any attempt to reconcile other belief systems or systems of thought with Islam is not only dismissed but condemned and in the process, Islamist ideologues try to emphasise the uniqueness and exclusivity of Islam, thereby trying to recapture what they see as the original territory of Islam. The Muslim Brotherhood of Egypt saw Islam as a total ideology encompassing society, politics and economics and came up with this theory when Egyptians were humiliatingly made aware of their servitude to an alien power. The movement coined an attractive slogan, 'The Qur'an is our constitution, the prophet our guide and the death for the glory of Allah is our greatest ambition'.

Today the Islamist response is both internal and external, that is, to release Islam from the scholastic cobwebs as well as to rid it of the ideas imbibed from the west. The Muslim Brotherhood of Egypt therefore refined their ideology in a way, which stressed the ability of Islam to become a total ideology since they declared their programme to be based on three principles: that Islam was a comprehensive, self evolving system and was the ultimate path of life in all its spheres; that Islam emanated from the Qur'an and the prophetic tradition; that Islam was applicable to all times and places (Enayat 1982: 85). However, Islamist violence is not simply directed at the West but also at Muslims 'who are not sufficiently pious' or more correctly, those Muslims who are not sufficiently pious according to certain imams and other Islamist leaders.

According to Islamist ideologues, the laws by which Muslims are ruled today are not by the laws of Islam but by the laws of unbelief and many of the Muslim rulers today are seen as apostates who have to be killed (Jansen 1997: 1–2). Islamists, therefore, found it necessary to reinterpret the Qur'an in the light of new circumstances. In its turn this exercise triggered the growth of modern and contemporary interpretations of the Qur'an in a form and content that was more accessible to contemporary Muslims and more suited to their needs. Because of their preoccupation with political activism, leaders of contemporary Islamism have been more concerned with emphasising segments of the Qur'an which serve their purpose than with interpreting the text itself. Consequently, the line of demarcation that sets the Islamist leaders and followers apart from their coreligionists is their political activism rather than a dogmatic or literalist attitude towards the Holy Scripture (Sidahmed and Ehteshami 1996).

Neo-fundamentalism

In this section, we will have a look at the term, 'neo-fundamentalism' exploring Islamism in a more contemporary context. There are clear problems with the term *fundamentalism* firstly because it has been taken from a Christian context and when imposed on an Islamic context, there is no appreciation for the peculiarities associated with the Islamic context and secondly because it gives the mistaken impression of the existence of a monolithic movement throughout the Muslim world without appreciating the variations which exist within Islamism. Despite the problems with the word, *fundamentalism,* the word is still widely used even by academics. The term, 'neo-fundamentalism' was coined by French scholar, Olivier Roy in his celebrated *Globalized Islam.* The term broadly refers to Islamist movements in a more contemporary scenario and a form of Islamism that is spreading rapidly through websites. Roy emphasises the de-territorialisation of these movements, that these movements have become supranational and that they are coping with the end of *Dar-ul-Islam* as a geographical entity (Roy 2004: 232–57). Neo-fundamentalism refers to a sort of uprooted activism which is dealing with westernisation that is at the core rather than at the periphery of the Islamic belief system. It is a common intellectual matrix that can be manifested in different political attitudes and can exist in differing, often opposing and contradictory contexts. Therefore, neo-fundamentalist versions of Islam exist from the *madrasas* in South Asia to the mosques and Islamic book shops in Paris and London. Neo-fundamentalism, Roy argues is a state of mind, a trend and is not a structured movement articulated around a coherent doctrine. Neo-fundamentalist groups often consider themselves to be the only true Muslims and do not recognise other categories within Islam and see themselves as the only 'pure' ones often using the word, *salafi*, meaning pure or the true ones of the Islamic faith.

Neo-fundamentalism broadly refers to two major strands of Islamic extremist thinking. In this connection, mention maybe made of Saudi Arabian Wahabism and South Asian Deobandism. Jocelyne Cesari, in her *When Islam and Democracy Meet*, very briefly, looks briefly at the differences between the two strands of

Islamism (Cesari 2004: 93). It should be remembered that not only are Islam and Islamism different categories but also within Islamism, there are certain strands of thought that are more extremist than others. The Deobandi model, for instance is a lot more accommodating and flexible than Middle Eastern Wahabism and Deobandism often incorporates mystical elements into its ideology whereas movements from the Middle East tend to reject all suggestions of mysticism. The name Deobandism comes from the Deobandi *madrasa* (Islamic centre of learning) in North India which came into existence during British rule. The term, Wahabism comes from the eighteenth-century revivalist thinker, Muhammad Abdul Wahab. The different strands of Islamism can also be distinguished from one another according to whether or not they rely on the achievements of the Islamic legal tradition, *fiqh*, or whether they reject them in favour of a direct relation with the Qur'an and *sunnah* or customs and practices of the prophet.

Deobandism is associated with the Islamic legal tradition or Islamic jurisprudence/*fiqh* and Wahabism relates itself more with the Qur'an and the *sunnah.* The differences between the two strands are therefore both theological and cultural (Cesari 2004: 93). The Taliban follows the Deobandi model and many other South Asian movements such as the Tablighi Jamat and the Jamat I Islami are also followers of the Deobandi model and many of the Middle Eastern movements follow the Wahabi tradition. Neo-fundamentalism has best adapted to globalisation than many other forms of Islam and uses globalisation to re-establish the *ummah* or the worldwide Muslim community on purely religious terms. Two of the main neo-fundamentalist movements, the Tablighi and the Wahabi had till the 1960s a limited territorial basis but now have gained a much wider audience through extensive propaganda and websites. Neo-fundamentalism is not a structured movement or organisation or even a precise school of thought. It is a trend, a state of mind and most importantly a dogmatic relation to the fundamentals of Islam. It thrives in very differing and often opposing contexts and has the capability to adapt to new situations (Roy 2004: 232–57). Examples of Islamist movements that would now fall into the neo-fundamentalist category include the Hizb-ut-Tahrir, Jamat I Islami, Tablighi Jamat, Ahl I Hadith and Ahl al Sunnah Wal Jamat.

Although these movements originated in one particular part of the Islamic belt, they have spread all over the world and make massive use of technology to spread their lesser *jihadist* message. They consider *jihad* to be a religious duty which is why they are also referred to as *salafi-jihadists*. Both the Tablighi Jamat and the Jamat I Islami had their origins in South Asia but now have their daughter organisations in Britain. The Tablighi mosque in Britain is at Dewsbury, Yorkshire, where it is believed by many that one of our London bombers, Mohammed Siddique Khan had been indoctrinated and the daughter institute of the Jamat I Islami is at Markfield, Leicestershire.

These are the prominent movements and groups that fall neatly into the neo-fundamentalist category. There are, however, independent and sometimes self taught preachers like Abu Hamza al Masari and Omar Bakri and also other lesser known preachers who have built their own constituency through websites.

Interestingly, many of these are converts (or 'reverts' as some Muslims would say since everyone is born a Muslim) to Islam in the West are often black.

The Tablighi Jamat launch short-term campaign tours by missionary teams comprising multinational lay preachers and they instruct their members to avoid entanglement with local politics, to promote the veiling of women, to close coeducational schools, to ban social interactions with non-Muslims all the while insisting on prayers and piety (Roy 2004: 232–57). The internet and written publications are not the main media of propaganda for the Tablighi, which is based on door to door personal contact. By contrast Saudi Wahabism is centred around a cluster of learned *sheikhs* who rarely leave the Gulf states and extend their influence through an intensive outpouring of *fatwas* and conferences and lectures, spread primarily through the internet, TV stations such as *Iqra* or via cheap booklets in Western universities. Through informal networks of disciples and former students they reach a lay audience far larger than the *madrasas* in which they teach. The Hizb ut Tahrir (HT) or the liberation party has become uprooted and deterritorialised with no thought of taking power in a given country. The Caliphate it wants to establish has no territorial basis. The HT uses pseudo Qur'anic terminology taken out of context with no consideration for history or social circumstances and its concept of the Caliphate has little to do with the historical Caliphate. The HT's Caliphate has no historical or sociological roots and has to be established as soon as possible for the whole *ummah* and not on any specific territory. This global and abstract conception of the *ummah* is typical of neo-fundamentalism. The HT and its development exemplifies how a former Islamist party has turned neo-fundamentalist.

Contemporary preachers usually produce video and audio tapes instead of books and do so in western languages in order to address much larger audiences, thereby transcending ethnic divides and to address a new generation of Western born Muslims. South Africans and Pakistanis who tend to be better in English than their Middle Eastern counterparts are spearheading this trend of translation work. In this connection, it is worth mentioning that the daughter institute of the Pakistani Jamat I Islami in Britain, which is the Markfield Institute of Higher Education in Leicestershire, has invested a huge amount of money in translating revivalist literature to make it available to the British Muslim youth. Good examples of such preachers would be South African mufti, Ahmed Deedat who writes in English and Hassan Iquoissen who writes in French in Europe and Abu Maryam Ishmaeel Alarcon in North America. The internet serves as a circulatory system of ideas that are reaffirmed by dint of repetition and the same set of references reappear again and again. The websites of student associations in Western universities are also a good vector for *salafi* propaganda. This strengthens the argument that British Universities are increasingly becoming a recruiting ground for Islamic radicalism and that in some of the Islamic societies in British Universities, we see the coexistence of Islam and Islamism. At some Universities like the University of Nottingham, pamphlets and books written by writers such as Mawdudi, founder of the Pakistani Jamat and Ahmed Deedat have regularly been on display when a talk or an event is organised by the Islamic society. When preachers and Islamic leaders are invited by the society to give presentations, there is always a mixture of radical speakers and moderate thinkers. With Nottingham as a case study, we can speculate that there are other British universities where Islam coexists with Islamism.

Neo-fundamentalist preachers stress the absolute unity of God or *tawhid* and they oppose any sort of innovation or *bida* and blind imitation or *taqlid.* Hence they reject all accretions to a strict literalist reading of the Qur'an and *sunnah.* Neo-fundamentalists are obsessed with the category of *bida* or innovation which for them amounts to heresy even if the novelty is of no consequence or importance. For example, there is a continuing debate on how to dress and brush one's teeth (Roy 2004: 232–57), and the observer is often surprised by the time neo-fundamentalist preachers spend discussing these apparently mundane issues. They are prone to imitate the prophet on all matters. Neo-fundamentalist preachers see religion as a code and life as a ritual and self purification is seen as a key concept. This sacralisation of daily life is to be found across the spectrum of neo-fundamentalists from the Tablighi to Al Qaeda terrorists. Neo-fundamentalist preachers are also in favour of the strict implementation of *Sharia* law with no concession for man made law and this pushes them to discard the modern state. They consider that there is nothing positive to be borrowed from the West and nothing to discuss with Christians and Jews except calling them to Islam or *dawa* although mainstream *salafis* agree that one should treat non-belligerent infidels leniently.

The main divide between Islamists and neo-fundamentalists is over state and politics. While in theory, neo-fundamentalists believe Muslims should live under an Islamic State, they reject the political struggle as a means of establishing such a state. They strongly believe that an Islamic State will result from re-Islamisation of the *ummah* through self purification and that the Islamic State should not be used as a tool for this process of re-Islamisation. In other words, political activism, according to neo-fundamentalists overshadows the need to reform the self. Islamists on the other hand, who strongly believe in, firstly the creation of an Islamic State, are advocates of a top-down approach whereas neo-fundamentalists believe in a bottom-top approach and that self purification will ultimately lead to the formation of an Islamic State. Neo-fundamentalists refuse to express their views in modern terms borrowed from the West. While Islamists consciously borrow concepts from Western political science terminology like ideology, revolution, vanguard, republic, neo-fundamentalists pretend that the West does not even exist and refuse to borrow anything from the West considering it to be *bida.* Therefore, mainstream neo-fundamentalists condemn the concepts of democracy, human rights and freedom whereas Islamists try to show how Islam represents the best forms of democracy, (through the conception of *shura* or consultation and *ijma* or consensus) and also the best protection of human rights including women's rights. Again, for neo-fundamentalists, the aim of action is salvation and not revolution and their objective is the individual and not society and the idea is that one should first return to the true path as an individual Muslim before taking any sort of political action, unlike Islamists.

However, it should be remembered that it is very difficult to draw a strict line of demarcation between Islamists and neo-fundamentalist preachers mainly because we are mostly looking at grey areas. In this connection, it is worth mentioning that there are many Islamists who have become disillusioned with power politics and participation in political affairs and have thus turned towards a more neo-fundamentalist approach, thereby focusing more on self purification. And at the same time, there are also neo-fundamentalist preachers who are nowadays actively participating in politics especially in situations where this approach can be used to further their own interest and consolidate their own position. One reason why neo-fundamentalism has become so popular is because it is seen as a tool for deculturation and provides the decontextualisation of religious practices.

Concluding Remarks

This chapter started off by looking at the term *fundamentalism* and analysing the problems associated with the usage of this term and others like *jihadism* and *integrisme*. It has looked at the three phases of Islamism identified by scholars when they looked at its historical context. The second half of the chapter looked at how Islamism exists in a more contemporary context. In some ways, Islamism today is a continuation of Islamic resurgence from earlier periods and in some ways they are of course different. Islamism is a multifaceted phenomenon which has different strands and each strand operates in different ways. Most theories which have tried to explain this multi dimensional phenomenon have come up with reactive explanations and argue that Islamism is a response to this or that, e.g., a reaction against modernity, communism, capitalism, racism in the West, nationalism, Western foreign policy in the Muslim world, poverty, oppressive political regimes and so on. Theories which try to explain Islamism in the developing world may not be useful whilst trying to explain Islamism in a Western context because the latter is grounded in a totally different sociological, political, geographical and cultural context. Islamism at earlier periods has strongly been linked with the complex processes of industrialisation, modernisation and urbanisation especially when these processes were at their initial stage. Islamism at earlier periods has also been strongly linked with colonialism especially when we look at the second phase of *reformism*. The earlier period was a time when these movements were confined to a particular territory but now these movements have become deterritorialised because of the extensive use of technology.

There seems to be unanimity amongst some scholars and analysts that the West has turned into the new epicentre of Islamic radicalism. In this connection, it is worth mentioning that some have even dismissed Britain as 'Londonistan' because of the presence of the large number of Islamist ideologues who are in exile in Britain. Since racism is seen to be one of the possible factors causing Islamism today in places like Britain, it is important for social policy workers and security analysts to do more collaborative work whilst dealing with the problem of Islamist terrorism. Present day Islamist groups are characterised by strong transnational networks and the idea of the *ummah* or the worldwide Muslim community has become increasingly important to some Muslims who have been born and brought up in the West and the *ummah* is seen as an important part of an Islamic collective identity. Recent technology has not only brought the *ummah* together but there is now a new and much stronger sense of inter connectedness. This has strong implications for Western foreign policy in the Middle East and other parts of the Islamic belt where the West has been actively involved politically.

Many of the earlier movements were reactions to colonialism and what theorists call 'modernity' or the arrival of modernity and we see how different forms of cultural nationalism merged with religious Islamism. In the present situation many of the contemporary movements are a response to Western foreign policy in the Muslim world although this is only one of the many explanations that have been put forward. Political events happening in the Middle East and South-Central Asia and the West's involvement in these regions are likely to affect some Western born Muslims for whom the idea of the *ummah* has increasingly become important. It could be safely argued that although Islamism had its beginnings at a much earlier period, in a more contemporary context, Western foreign policy has most certainly exacerbated the already strained situation. Islamism and Islamisation of different countries is an ongoing process and it is difficult to say when it started and when it will end. By and large, it can be said that in both the present situation and at an earlier time, we see a battle between the 'forces of continuity' and 'forces of change' although the present situation is a lot more complex than earlier times. Some of the sociological literature clearly shows that Islamism in the West should be analysed within the broader framework of identity issues. In Muslim majority contexts, on the other hand, much of Islamic revivalism is inextricably linked with power-politics. As we have seen during the time of general Zia-ul-Haq in Pakistan from 1978 till 1988, the political elite tried to use religion to suit their own needs especially when their power base lacked political legitimacy.

Bibliography

Ali, T. 2002. *The Clash of Fundamentalisms.* London: Verso.

Armstrong, K. 2000a. *Islam: A Short History.* London: Weidenfeld and Nicolson.

Armstrong, K. 2000b. *A Battle for God.* London: HarperCollins.

Buzan, B. 1998. *Security: A New Framework for Analysis.* London/Boulder: Lynne Rienner Publisher.

Cesari, J. 2004. *When Islam and Democracy Meet.* Basingstoke: Palgrave Macmillan.

Chouerri, Y. 1990, *Islamic Fundamentalism.* London: Pinter.

Dekmejian, R. 1985, *Islam in Revolution.* New York: Syracuse University Press.

Edwards, B. 2005. *Islamic Fundamentalism since 1945*. London: Routledge.
Enayat, H. 1982. *Modern Islamic Political Thought*. London: Macmillan.
Esposito, J. 1990. *The Iranian Revolution: Its Global Impact*. Florida: Florida International University Press.
Hiro, D. 1989. *Islamic Fundamentalism*. London: Paladin.
Jansen, J. 1997. *The Dual Nature of Islamic Fundamentalism*. London: Hurst.
Kepel, G. 2003. *Jihad: The Trail of Political Islam*. London: I.B. Tauris.
Moussalli, A.S. 1998. *Islamic Fundamentalisms: Myths and Realities*. Reading: Ithaca Press.
Noorani, A.G. 2002. *Islam and Jihad*. Dhaka, London: Zed.
Pipes, D. 2002. *Militant Islam Reaches America*. New York, London: W.W. Norton.
Rahnema, A. 1994. *Pioneers of Islamic Revival*. London: Zed.
Roberts, H. 2003. *The Battlefield Algeria 1988–2002: Studies in a Broken Polity*. London: Verso.
Roy, O. 2004. *Globalized Islam*. London: Hurst.
Sidahmed, A.S and Ehteshami, A. 1996. *Islamic Fundamentalism*. Boulder/Oxford: Westview.

Chapter 3
God, the State and War

Rosemary Durward

> The practice of politics is greatly influenced by the images the politicians entertain.
> (Waltz 1959: 225)

Kenneth Waltz, in *Man, the State and War* (1959), advocated a realist position in inter-state relations based on a balance of power strategy to secure the national interest in a fundamentally anarchic world. During the Cold War when Waltz was writing, religion was given little conscious consideration as a dynamic in international affairs. Yet the index to Waltz's book contains references to the doctrine of 'original sin' formulated by St Augustine (354–430 AD); discussion of Christian pacifism; an example of Christian political activism from nineteenth century Richard Cobden who campaigned against the Crimean War as well as twentieth century theologians, Reinhold Niebuhr (1892–1971) and Karl Barth (1886–1968).

On the causes of war, Waltz observes that 'The practice of politics is greatly influenced by the images the politicians entertain' (Waltz 1959: 225). Christianity has exercised significant overt and covert influence on the minds of politicians and on war. However there is no single Christian position on war with views ranging from Christian pacifism through to militarism drawn from scripture, doctrine, theological reflection, human experience and political, social, economic and cultural context. The first impression might be of chaos but the unifying element to them all is Christ and the diversity of responses to war is accounted for by different understandings of who Christ is. Christian thinking about war involves a dialectic relationship between considerations of the nature of God's righteousness in Christ and the ethical problem of war, leading to a variety of truth claims that link, operate in parallel and sometimes even in opposition with each other. Theology, defined here in St Anselm's celebrated phrase as 'faith seeking understanding' (Migliore 2004), calls for dialogue between those claims which itself encourages the ability to stand outside and critique them. Christians should be at ease in the post-modern world precisely because of that tradition of dialogue, which itself contributes to a culture of pragmatism in foreign policy.

There has been much speculation about whether President Obama is Niebuhrian (Julian 2009: 1–9), a description which aligns him closely with his predecessor and successive American Presidents of both Republican and Democratic loyalties, within a 'good and evil' paradigm. Obama may be influenced by this dominant culture, but he shows the pragmatism of a post-modern Christian who is orientated towards reconciliation with others, representing a radical alternative to the dualism that has characterised recent political discourse. To move away from dualism, a new paradigm is needed, not only to inform state behaviour and strengthen reconciling tendencies within the international system, but to give a moral underpinning to strategies for state and peace building within the state.

Images the Politicians Entertain

Today there is a political assumption that religion is incompatible with post-Enlightenment rationalism, and that it is best kept as a private matter. Belief in the separation of church and state meant the West was ill-prepared for the religious undercurrents in the civil war in the Balkans (1991–2001). Neither did it anticipate the religiously motivated backlash of Islamist terrorism that germinated after US troops deployed to Saudi Arabia in 1991, following Iraq's invasion of Kuwait. In reality, religious wars have been a continuous feature of the international system over the last 100 years and more. The West has been both a bystander and participant in carnage in the Middle East between Jew and Muslim, over land imbued with symbolic religious value, and between Muslim and Muslim over the fundamentals of their faith (Fisk 2005).

Military intervention in Afghanistan (October 2001) and Iraq (March 2003), intended as a response to the 9/11 attacks, provoked Muslim zealots to take up arms. The 'enemy without' became an 'enemy within' born of latent distrust of Islam and alarmism about a situation where the sympathies of many Muslims in the West were with those of the same faith who were struggling against foreign military intervention. In the slip stream of 9/11, the image of violent religious fundamentalism dominates politics but, pointing a finger at enemies, self righteously ignores both the depth of despair and anger that leads people to violence and the potential for violence from Christians.

Although early Christians were pacifist, Christianity is unlikely to have spread so rapidly if it were not for the victory in battle of Emperor Constantine (AD 306–337). Constantine attributed his success to seeing a vision of Jesus in advance of battle and issued an edict of toleration that enabled Christianity to evangelise openly, beginning an uneasy relationship between church and state that has both benefited and compromised Christian teaching.

History is full of evidence of Christian religious zeal mixed with political ambition resulting in violence and war. The pre-Enlightenment era is associated with religious wars between Christians and Muslims during the eleventh to the thirteenth centuries over the boundaries of Christendom (Hindley 2003), and in the sixteenth and seventeenth centuries amongst Christians in Europe during the Reformation period (Lindberg 1996). Religious zeal extended also to persecution and capital punishment for thousands of people accused of witchcraft. The Gunpowder Plot (1605) constitutes a religiously motivated act of violence intertwined with political objectives against the state. Collaboration of state and religion in Christian missionary activity alongside European states' race for colonial expansion in the eighteenth and nineteenth centuries has left a legacy of unease at the way in which ends became more important than means (Wilson 2002: 493). In Northern Ireland the seeds of violence lay in Roman Catholic and Protestant identity and it was sectarian conflict along a religious divide that prompted British military intervention in Northern Ireland in 1969, and much of the bloodshed after that (O'Brien 1973).

If someone wanted to find endorsement for war in the Bible, they would certainly find it (see Marsden, Chapter 5). The act of warfare was not a problem for the Ancient Israelites, except when they lost (Hobbs 1989a: 292). Peace came only with total annihilation of the enemy, and on many occasions, no mercy was shown so that by today's standards, the Ancient Israelites would be accused of genocide (Rodd 1995: 5). God is good but there are circumstances where God appears as vengeful and pitiless, endorsing punishment. The Book of Isaiah is quoted, 'they shall beat their swords into plowshares …' (Isaiah 2:4), underneath the statue outside the United Nations headquarters in New York gifted by the Soviet Union in 1959 as a symbol of a universal hope for peace. Yet that is reversed in the Book of Joel with the words, 'Beat your plowshares into swords' (Joel 3:10).[1] Alongside contradictory texts advocating love the ethics of the Old Testament are 'chaotic' (Barton 1983: 113).

In the New Testament, Jesus modelled a peaceful life but he used military imagery ('I bring not peace but a sword' (Matthew 10:34)), in the context of a cosmic battle that runs through the Gospels between Jesus and Satan (Mark 1:13; 24–27; 34). The last book of the New Testament, the Book of Revelations, makes 70-odd references to 'armies of heaven', 'blood', 'conquer', 'slaughter', 'battle', 'torture', and derivatives of 'fight', 'defeat' and 'death'. Miroslav Volf explains Gilles Deleuze's reasoning that the dream of the New Jerusalem is more sinister than political dictatorship because under God, people are forced to 'interiorise' the judgements of the final arbiter, making it indistinguishable from hell. Hence, modernity's reason and Christianity's absolute God are two sides, secular and sacred, of the same system of terror (Volf 1996: 286–7). Volf records Deleuze's proposition that the Apocolyptic vision in Revelation 'is not the concentration camp (Antichrist); it is the big military police, and civil security of the new state (heavenly Jerusalem)' (Deleuze 1980: 114). Pagels' study of the political circumstances of Jesus' crucifixion and the Gospel writers, proposes that the devil and Satan in the New Testament are themselves allegories for the military domination of Rome and the resistance to it by a Jewish minority, recorded after the desecration of the Temple (Pagels 1995: 3–34).

How Biblical text is interpreted says a great deal about the condition of humankind, its hopes and limitations at any particular time. The Hebrew Bible and New Testament feed the human imagination about the possibilities of a transcendent God with a promise of a heavenly kingdom in the future where

1 Bible references are taken from the New Revised Standard Version.

there is no more war. The Hebrew Bible's commandment 'You shall not murder' (Deuteronomy 5:17), and both the Hebrew Bible and the New Testament command 'You shall love your neighbour as yourself' (Leviticus 19:17–18, Matthew 22:39) are dominant Christian themes today, having resonance in contemporary Western values that uphold the sanctity of life, and in other faiths.

The Church in the World

Today, the Christian faith is represented by a diverse Church, spanning Roman Catholicism, Eastern Orthodoxy, Pentecostal, Assyrian and Protestant churches, the Anglican Communion and many more. The Nicene Creed (325 AD) agreed the fundamentals of Christian faith in a statement of belief that is common to Judaism and Islam, namely, 'I believe in one God, maker of heaven and earth …'. But Christianity stands out from the other monotheistic religions in its profession of faith in the Trinity, in which one God is also understood as the 'three-in-one' of Father, Son and Holy Spirit (George 2006). There are exceptions, however, in Christian Quakers and Unitarians who reject the idea of the Trinity and there are many cults on the edge of Christianity that do not subscribe to the Nicene Creed at all. The adoption of the Nicene Creed was preceded by intense debate and disagreement and the way in which the Christian Churches attempted to re-affirm the fundaments of faith during the Reformation, split and re-shaped again, mirrors similar patterns of renewal in the Islamic faith (Armstrong 2001), described by Kunal Mukherjee (Chapter 2).

Christian Perspectives on War

Diversity in churches appears, at first glance, to be replicated in the diversity of Christian perspectives on war. Some Christian organisations lobby both against preparations for war and military intervention, whilst others support a robust military posture. After World War II, Christians appeared to be polarised between a movement known as Christian realism, under the guidance of Reinhold Niebuhr (Lovin 1995), which advocated a strong defence posture to sustain a stable balance of power, and Christian idealism or utopianism, a phrase coined by E.H. Carr in 1939 (Dougherty and Pfaltzgraff 2001: 65). During the Cold War, when the Soviet Union and United States deployed around 12,000 nuclear warheads each, realists judged proposals to unilaterally disarm to be idealistic and irresponsible. Realists supported a strategy of nuclear deterrence, the threat to annihilate the adversary with nuclear weapons, to keep the peace in Europe. The idealist camp was on the 'other side', urging unilateral nuclear disarmament, supported by an active peace movement embracing pacifist Christian organisations such as the Quakers, Mennonites, and Pax Christi working with secular organisations like the Campaign for Nuclear Disarmament (CND) in the UK, the European Nuclear Disarmament

Campaign (END) and the American Freeze Campaign. The peace movement used a variety of tactics including non-violent direct action (Rose 1985).

Christian pacifism involves non-violence as a particular form of witness to Christ's life and teaching. Jesus taught his disciples to 'love one another' (I John 3:11–23), and he rejected violence and coercion, even when arrested by Roman soldiers under false charge, tried and nailed on a cross to die. Christ's life and teaching in the Beatitudes that begins 'Blessed are the peacemakers …' (Matthew 5:3–11) led theologian Stanley Hauerwas to say, 'I am a pacifist because I cannot imagine being anything other than a pacifist in light of the gospel of Christ' (White 2003).

The pacifist impulse is motivated by the desire to model Christ's teaching and example, in the hope of ushering in God's kingdom. Much of the non-violent direct action during the nuclear debate was still of a coercive kind that created physical barriers to the proper functioning of defence institutions and to provoke a disproportionate response from the state. This can be distinguished from pacifism that witnesses to the life of Christ and his divinity. That kind of pacifism is non-coercive and better found in the refusal of conscientious objectors to take part in war, and in Christian martyrdom that accepts violence, suffering and even death from those that exercise physical power over them (Harries 1986: 105–21).

The image of martyrs is normally associated with early Christians who were persecuted under Roman rule. During the Reformation, Christians persecuted each other. A translation of the Bible into common languages by characters such as William Tyndale, beginning in the sixteenth century, came about only because of the determination to face the punishment of death if caught (Lindberg 1996: 313–15). Today, in Burma, India, North Korea, Somalia, Eritrea and parts of Nigeria religious freedom is suppressed and Christians as a minority are marginalised, persecuted and die for their faith. Typically, accusations of insulting Islam and of Christian evangelism precede arrest or spontaneous acts of violence, including public stripping, beatings, stabbings and burning. Political factors often contribute to the marginalisation and persecution of Christians. In China, for example, multiple Christian denominations influenced by European and American missionaries, were funnelled into Protestant and Catholic state controlled churches in 1949. During the Cultural Revolution, these churches disappeared altogether along with all other expressions of Chinese culture (Tang 2000: 55–70), in a drive against perceived Western interference. Today, there is still some harassment of Christians, particularly those worshiping in house groups, but the numbers of worshipping Christians, along with people of other faiths, has grown. The Chinese government admits to 21 million Christians, including Protestant and Catholic (Grim 2008), but there are some unverifiable estimates putting them at between 25 and 100 million. The flourishing of Christianity and other religions in China may be seen as a barometer of the health of the country in economic, political and social terms. If this notion is extended to Afghanistan, where the crime of apostasy (Dalacoura 2003: 47–8) is still on the statute books in a context where religious freedom is anathema and personal freedom the preserve of a minority, then the diagnosis is one of extreme ill-health.

Debates about military intervention in Kosovo on humanitarian grounds, and in Iraq on the technicalities of a UN Resolution and a latent threat, have highlighted the significance of Christian just war tradition as a legitimising tool (Guthrie and Quinlan 2007). *Jus ad bellum* principles of just cause; legitimate authority; balance of consequences; likelihood of success; last resort; and *jus in bello* principles of proportionality and discrimination denote a particular way of Christian moral thinking, which includes a pacifistic orientation, in other words, one which has an aversion to war. In *The City of God*, when under the might of Roman rule, St Augustine (354–43 AD) wrote of the 'horror and cruelty' of war and argued that 'a man who experiences such evils, or even thinks about them, without heartfelt grief, is assuredly in a far more pitiable condition, if he thinks himself happy simply because he has lost all human feeling' (St Augustine 2003: 862).

International law on the use of force has also been informed by Christian thought. Hugo Grotius (1583–1645), father of international law, drew on Christian tradition and Roman rhetoric in his formulation of natural law. In *The Rights of Peace and War* (1625), Grotius resisted the notion that self defence could mean anything more than defence against imminent attack (Grotius 2005: 417). Reference to Grotius sends a clear message of moral condemnation against George Bush's doctrine of 'anticipatory self defence' (Bush 2002), prior to a possible terrorist attack. Grotius insisted that force can be used to avert an imminent disaster but 'to pretend to have a Right to injure another, merely, from a Possibility that he may injure me, is repugnant to all the Justice in the World: For such is the Condition of the present Life, that we can never be in perfect Security' (Grotius 2005: 417). Grotius was also a proponent of the moral necessity of intervening to protect weaker neighbours, particularly citizens living under tyrannous rule. He justified his case using the example of Constantine who went to war to stop the persecution of Christians (Grotius 2005:1161).

In recent years, Christian influence has been most visible in the area of peace and reconciliation in the aftermath of conflict, made famous by Desmond Tutu's Peace and Reconciliation Commission. The Commission has brought victims and persecutors in the apartheid system together to confess their sins and ask for forgiveness. The work of the Peace and Reconciliation Commission is based on the understanding that there can be no reconciliation or progress to a more stable and productive future, without penitence and forgiveness first. This model is being mirrored at grass roots level in Northern Ireland, Rwanda and other places where there is a desire for recovery after violence and civil war (Helmick et al. 2001). The beginning of the twenty-first century has also seen a concerted effort at inter-faith dialogue and the growth of fora where people of all faiths and none can work towards the goal of reconciliation. Tony Blair's Faith Foundation is reportedly working to encourage people of different faiths at grassroots level to work together on fighting malaria (Landau 2009), encouraging collaboration instead of differences in doctrine and belief.

Christian groups also work independently to advance human security. The Mother's Union in the Democratic Republic of the Congo, for example, helps women who have been raped as a weapon of war. Behind this is a concern for the persecuted and vulnerable. In other places, such as in South America, the goal of justice has inspired many Christians working towards freedom from military dictatorship in the 1970s and 1980s. These themes have strong Judeo-Christian roots, told in the narrative of the Jewish exodus from Egypt to escape slavery. The sharing of the Jewish Passover is offered to all who are in need, with eyes on the land of Israel, a symbol of the hope of redemption and freedom (Woodhead 2004: 395–401). Christianity is associated too with a martial spirit that has contributed to the ethos of Western armed forces, based on Christian principles of service, integrity and moral courage. The idea of sacrifice also plays a part so that Services of Remembrance of the deaths of soldiers in both world wars and subsequent conflict give thanks for those who were prepared to lose their lives for others' tomorrow, mirroring the Christian claim about the saving purpose of Christ's death. For the Christian, suffering is evident in God's creation and the whole human experience and part of the apostolic mission is to be witness to Christ's suffering by being a suffering community (O'Donovan 1996: 178).

Dietrich Bonhoeffer's predicament as a German pacifist confronted with Hitler, shows how the pacifist urge, symbolic of Christ's acceptance of his suffering, raises a moral predicament when it impacts on the lives of millions. Bonhoeffer was arrested and executed for taking part in the plot to assassinate Hitler, seeing each Christian as the cross-bearer, forced in certain circumstances to carry the burden of guilt that others might live (Bonhoeffer 2001). In this sense, soldiers prepared to defend their country and protect the weak, occupy a moral high ground.

Shake the Devil Off

The Medieval Christian paradigm of 'good and evil' has shaped Western thinking about war based on a polarisation between the just and the unjust, the aggrieved and the aggressor, the moral and the immoral, the weak and the powerful. During the Cold War, Republican President Ronald Reagan's choice of the term 'evil empire' in 1983 (Reagan 1983) to describe the Soviet Union was indicative of the polarised positions of East and West in which the West occupied a self-righteousness moral high ground. The expression used by President George W. Bush of an 'axis of evil' (Gaddis 2002) in his January 2002 State of the Union Address strengthened the impulse towards military intervention in Afghanistan and Iraq to eliminate evil, and bolstered a sense of moral supremacy over the enemy, having resonance within cultures that understand the paradigm of good and evil, and provoking a response. There is a sense in which the imperatives for intervention rest not only on the realities on the ground but on images of evil.

The 'good and evil' paradigm affirms self worth and over inflates the wickedness of the other. It is deeply embedded in Western culture with European and American literature and film confirming the process of enculturation. C.S. Lewis's *The Lion, the Witch and the Wardrobe*, for example, is an allegory of Jesus' battle with Satan, where the White Witch battles with Aslan. She kills Aslan but he comes alive again to defeat her. The film *Star Wars* portrays a more complex picture of the Jedi as peacekeepers and diplomats who commit the sin of intellectual, moral and spiritual pride that leads to their downfall.[2]

The Christian roots of this paradigm go back to Apostolic times and St Paul's insight that 'all have sinned and fallen short of the glory of God' (Romans 3:23). The Hebrew Bible contains a number of fall narratives such as that of Adam and Eve, Samson, Job, Saul, David and the fall of Israel at the hands of the Babylonians and a great many stories of redemption, notably in the journey to the promised land of the ancient Israelites. St Augustine's doctrine of 'original sin' has been particularly influential based on the notion that God created good and then good fell from its perfect state in rebellion against God (Vardy 1992: 175). Augustine saw evil as defection from good (Hick 1966: 52–54) and he separated the *Civitas terrena* in the realm of sin from the *Civitas Dei*, setting firm lines between the secular and the spiritual (Millbank 2006: 413). It is not axiomatic that a dualist psychology need develop from St Paul or St Augustine's insights about sin, since if 'all have sinned' there can be no moral distinction between 'them' and 'us'. On this basis, everyone is compromised. But the idea of sin, combined with the possibility of living a heavenly life in the realm of the *Civitas Dei* by being a disciple of the resurrected Christ, served to encourage the notion, at least in Medieval Europe, of the complicity of the 'fallen' in a worldly 'lust for domination' (Augustine 2003: 5).

The Enlightenment challenged St Augustine's doctrine of 'original sin' on grounds that humanity could be improved by reason in the pursuit of truth. Human imagination about the location of hell in the bowels of the earth and heaven above the clouds was discredited by advances in human knowledge. From the period of the Enlightenment evil wrought by natural disaster became explicable through science and moral evil through human causes. Nietzsche wrote about the death of God in the nineteenth century (Nietzsche 1976: 56–71), and it was explored in Fyodor Dostoevsky's play, *The Brothers Karamazov*, completed in 1880. Contemplation of stories of evil and cruelty caused Ivan to argue that if God allows suffering, then he is not the sort of God he wanted to worship (Wright 2006: 7). But the rise of fascism and communism in the twentieth century was also proof of the suffering caused when God is killed off as a moral agent and the distinction between good and evil is blurred (Vardy 1992: 171).

2 The themes of 'good' and 'evil' are addressed in an original way in an unpublished MA dissertation, by Martin Dryden, 'Niebuhr, Downfall and Star Wars: An Exploration into How the *Star Wars* Films Reflect Themes of Downfall Through the Thinking of Reinhold Niebuhr', submitted in 2008 to Sarum College, Salisbury.

Perhaps for that reason, St Augustine's division between the City of God and the earthly realm of sin has persisted. If the anarchical system is the *Civitas terrena* where evil pervades, militarists use the tools of the *Civitas terrena* to create order and justice in anticipation of a heavenly kingdom. Pacifists, on the other hand, occupy the heavenly space, as living witness to a heavenly kingdom already arrived. To caricature the result, militarists view the pacifist position as ignoring the evil around them, and pacifists view the militarist position as having sold out to the devil. Determination to face down evil has often overridden Christian themes of justice and love of neighbour that provide moral underpinnings for military intervention.

The Moral Dimension of Military Intervention

Association with St Augustine's just war principles means Christians are caught up in the War on Terror through association. Yet lip service has been paid to just war criteria, particularly the principles of proportionality and discrimination. Decisions about military intervention in Iraq centred on the legality of the action, based on estimates of an Iraqi threat from nuclear weapons and prior UN resolutions. Just war criteria were ticked off, and the just cause of self defence against imminent attack slipped to 'anticipatory self defence' against an imagined threat. However, it is interesting to speculate to what extent the Chicago principles, contained in Blair's 'Doctrine of the International Community' and delivered in a speech to an audience in Chicago (22 April 1998), may have influenced the government in its decision to support militarily intervention in Iraq.

The Chicago principles were designed to test the certainty of a humanitarian need in Kosovo and step around obstructions in the UN Security Council (Kempfner 2003). Critically, the Chicago principles abandoned the need for legitimate authority, and introduced the national interest as a reason for intervention. Applied to humanitarian intervention, the national interest is an innocuous principle signifying the operating conditions of statehood, but for the purposes of responding to a threat where evidence of the threat could not be found, it takes on a more sinister aspect. The additional requirement set by the Chicago principles to be prepared to deploy for the long term does imply some sense of moral responsibility in military intervention. However, the Chicago principles fall far short of the kind of moral enquiry that the just war tradition invites. The debacle over the military intervention in Iraq points to the need for a re-examination of the moral underpinnings of the just war tradition, as well as for imaginative thought about how threats are judged.

A major feature of the pre-2003 debate on military intervention was the demonisation of the enemy. Attention turned from Al Qaeda, which was responsible for the attack on the New York World Trade Centre and the Pentagon, to Saddam Hussein who took on ever more fearful clothing. Behind such dualism is the fear which induces aggression and a dynamic that can spread violence impersonally and indiscriminately. Martin Buber describes the effect in his theory of 'I-thee' and 'I-it' (Buber 2002). Dualism depends on occupying the moral high ground. However, problems in carrying out a targeted and proportionate military intervention and the inevitability of being implicated in suffering in war, makes occupying the moral high ground hard in war. If 'the other' is evil, then Americans and the British are uncomfortable with being tainted with the same label. When belief in the capacity of 'good' to confront evil unravels, the legitimacy of force is undermined and the strategy of military intervention is threatened.

George W. Bush failed to face down the evil of terrorism without an unacceptable opportunity cost to the US image overseas. The United States' reputation was affected adversely by its alleged endorsement of the torture of prisoners in Abu Ghraib, and indefinite detention of so called enemy combatants at Guantanamo Bay. These factors contributed to the large-scale withdrawal of American public support for Bush's 'war on terror'. There is a sense in which, by electing Barack Obama as President of the United States, the people were expressing a yearning for an alternative vision. But a radically different vision for the United States will not materialise without shaking off the 'good and evil' paradigm. 'Shake the devil off', is the title of an African-American gospel song. Shaking the devil off is not just about shaking off evil, as an existential reality, by responding to it robustly. It is also about minimising evil in the response.

Barack Obama and Niebuhr

Inevitably, given President Obama's confident admission of his Christian faith, there has been speculation about his theology. Despite his training in political activism and awareness of racial and social inequality, there is little evidence of liberation theology shaping Obama's political philosophy since he has always operated within the law and the constraints of the political system. Barack Obama's own success in rising from a minority black candidate to President, in a country where race and skin colour have sifted out aspirant candidates, has redemptive qualities that resonate with the Christian narratives in the Hebrew Bible (Amos 5:24 and Isaiah 40:4–5) and New Testament's resurrection story. Martin Luther King set out a vision of a 'promised land' to which black Americans could say they had finally come home. Obama's election feels like the fulfilment of that hope. Speculation has arisen, also, about the influence of Christian realist and political theologian Reinhold Niebuhr (1892–1971) on Obama's politics. In the Spring of 2007, Obama was linked to Niebuhr when a *New York Times* columnist, David Brooks, asked him if he had read anything by him. Reputedly, Obama said that he was his favourite philosopher and that he had extracted the idea that serious evil exists in the world (Julian 2009: 7).

A pacifist in World War I, Niebuhr came in World War II to endorse Christian realism based on a rejection of pacifism and the need to match force with force. Influenced by the successful military intervention of the United States against

Axis aggression and the Cold War arms race, he adopted a robust attitude towards the Soviet Union, consistent with mainstream thinking about war and nuclear deterrence, on the grounds that war was not the worst thing that could be imagined. Only over the Vietnam War did Niebuhr question government policy, and his sense of duty and loyalty to government meant that he found this opposition personally troublesome. From World War II, Niebuhr believed that pacifists failed to take the presence of sin seriously enough. Waltz (1959: 28) quotes Niebuhr writing '"political strategies" invariably involving "the balancing of power with power", are made necessary by "the sinful character of man"' (Niebuhr 1940: 4). Niebuhr was critical of what he saw as the pacifist's denial of dualism. He believed that we cannot act in an evil world as if the kingdom were already here. Niebuhr's motivation was social justice nationally and internationally, seeing a Christian imperative to contain power and tyranny over the weak (Harries 1986: 114).

Current US strength and its leadership role are, arguably, precisely because realism was dominant during the Cold War. A degree of realism is necessary today in navigating threats to security, and Niebuhr's influence can be seen in Obama's recognition of the world as a dangerous place, his insistence on realism about the failings of humankind, and hope in the capacity of humankind to change things for the better. But, as a strong advocate of social change, Obama's record shows, additionally, strong reconciling tendencies, including a preparedness to recognise the failings of the United States and extend a hand of friendship to those that are prepared to 'unclench their fist' (Obama 2009). There is none of the polarising effects of Bush's rhetoric in Barack Obama's speeches and policy statements. Indeed, his election success was, in large part, because he resists the polarisation of his predecessor's politics that set the United States on a trajectory towards war.

Engaging with Theology for a New Paradigm

Despite the influence of the doctrine of original sin on Christian thinking about war and the causes of war, the idea that theology could inform politics is counter cultural. Richard Dawkins' portrayal of Christianity as out of touch and out of place is a more dominant claim on the European imagination today (Dawkins 2006). Like Nietzsche and Dostoevsky before him, Dawkins offers a vision of no God. From the starting point that there is no scientific evidence for God there is an inner logic to his arguments but he is undertaking a different task to the theologian.

Philosophically, if God is not at the beginning of all things, then nothing good can be deduced from Him. He is merely contingent on human imagining. From radically different starting points, Richard Dawkins and theologians might feel comfortable together discussing, as Aristotle did, what it is to be good since human beings experience good in different ways, whether believing in God or not. They might continue in conversation to ask what it is to be human. Scientists analyse human neuro-physiology to answer this question. The centre in the brain which responds to religious stimuli causing a physical response points to religious experience being a human characteristic. A sociologist studies human behaviour in society and finds the human being to be a naturally social animal. An anthropologist observes that the identification of self as human comes through knowledge of the other, starting in the infant, and that human beings are motivated strongly by love. Belief in God satisfies that human need. But the theologian and Christian finds the answer to what it is to be human in a relationship with God, revealed in Scripture through Jesus Christ. Indeed, it is belief in Christ that draws the pacifist and Christian realist together.

With Christ as the starting point for his reasoning, twentieth century political theologian Karl Barth set aside the paradigm of good and evil on the assertion that in Christ, evil is already defeated. He wrote in 1939 in the past tense, 'It was on the truth that God is one that the "Third Reich" of Adolph Hitler made shipwreck' (Gorringe 2005: 117). Whereas Niebuhr had been impressed by the exercise of American power in overcoming Nazi aggression, and had focused on who to blame for the outbreak of war in Europe, Barth's concern was to put humankind back under the authority of God from which, he believed, it had rebelled (Barth 1966: 104–5).

The outbreak of World War I highlighted for Barth how morality had become detached from politics because God had been detached as a moral agent by Christian liberalism and atheism (Barth 1960: 39). He believed theology was compromised by the way it projected human concerns and interests onto God and defended a totally other, totally transcendent omnipotent God revealed in Christ, that could not be manipulated by humanity for its own ends. For Barth, God was the benchmark for what is good, and not people's feelings which can be set off course by events. This is an important point when reflecting on decisions about military intervention taken in the aftermath of 9/11. It is important, too, in the training of armed forces to give them the tools to resist what Aquinas called 'disordered passions' in war, typically resulting in retaliation and indiscriminate violence.

Barth's context, from the Kaiser through two world wars and the Cold War, was the same as Niebuhr's, albeit with different experiences. Barth was expelled from Germany in 1935, after signing the Barmen Declaration that resisted the authoritarianism of the Third Reich, and insisted on obedience to Christ as Sovereign Lord. He lived and worked in Switzerland thereafter. Whereas Niebuhr joined forces with the American establishment during the Cold War, Barth was rejected by the establishment because of his opposition to the anti-communist rhetoric and policies of the Cold War. His criticism of the Western condemnation of the Soviet Union's invasion of Hungary in 1956 caused particular hurt. Whereas Niebuhr was in the dualist Antioch tradition, which accepted the two-natures of Christ, Godhead and manhood, Barth was in the monist Alexandrian tradition that believed in the divine descent of Christ in the incarnation, and the unity of Christ with God. This monism was evident in Barth's castigation of Western ethics, philosophy and theology for re-casting 'Eastern collective man' into an 'angel of darkness' and for consecrating 'Western collective man' into an 'angel of light' on the basis of mythology and metaphysics (Gorringe 2005: 120). For Barth, anti-communism was a greater evil than communism itself because of its basis in myth; and he saw the Church's urgent task was to remind nations and governments that war is not a product of 'hell' but of individuals, their decisions and actions.

Barth's theology does not deny the necessity of the use of force but his ethics of war challenges those that revel in dualism, the supporters of 'muscular Christianity' that advocate the aggressive assertion of military power (Albright 2006: 158). Barth opposed pacifism, supporting instead military involvement, on a case-by-case basis, under God's authority vested in the state. Barth saw the supreme task of Christian ethics 'to recover and manifest a distinctive horror of war and aloofness from it' (Barth 2004: Vol III.4: 456 (hereafter CD)). Barth saw peace as 'the real emergency' (CD III.4: 458), which it was everyone's responsibility to nurture and sustain, not just governments'. Barth's was not anti-state but saw the Church's task to set 'frontiers' for the state (CD III.4: 469). Barth's 'No' to war, was always tempered with the unknowingness of God and what we can know and as such, his theology sits in opposition to political ideologies that seek order by imposing rigid rules on society.

Barth was an early supporter of humanitarian intervention, naming certain situations where it might be necessary to disregard the integrity of state borders, for example, on behalf of ' weaker neighbours' (CD III.1: 462). That this gives legitimacy to the emerging 'Responsibility to Protect' norm in the wake of NATO's intervention of Kosovo would not have been of much interest to Barth, since on his terms, theology is not there to endorse policy but to have a distinctive voice. If the practice of politics is greatly influenced by the images that politicians entertain, context and prevailing norms censor images that are uncomfortable. Barth's voice was prophetic in that it refused to accept the logic of the Cold War and was censored because of it.

Barth's Doctrine of Reconciliation is founded upon a Trinitarian relationship in which he described 'love which meets us in reconciliation, and then retrospectively in creation' as 'real love, supreme law and ultimate reality, because God is antecedently love in Himself' (CD I.I: 484). For Christians, the Trinitarian relationship of self-giving love is self perpetuating. It is expressed in the words of the Eucharist: 'Take, eat, this is my body given for you'. Noticeably, it involves no coercion, whether active or through denial but loving generosity. Barth's doctrine of reconciliation points to all of humanity being in varying stages of rebellion and a turn to God must be conscious. During the Cold War, to use the language of reconciliation was unrealistic. Détente meant a relaxation of tension, and was a poor imitation. Yet reconciliation was a necessary part of the rebuilding of post-war Germany and Japan. Today, it is seen as an essential feature of recovery in the aftermath of war, without which the seeds of war germinate and take root. It has been an essential part of the transition from apartheid rule to democracy in South Africa through the Truth and Reconciliation Commission and is being explored in Bosnia-Herzegovina (Goodwin and Lang 2006) and other places that have endured conflict.

Barth challenged Christian exceptionalism that reinforces the image of 'them' and 'us' because for him, Christ and God are one and God is beyond sectarianism' (Ticciati 2006: 436). As such his reconciling theology reverses the inevitability of a 'Clash of Civilizations' forecast by Samuel Huntington in the political realm. It is essentially optimistic about the future, since Barth believed that in Christ, the battle with evil is already completed. The story of the rise of Christianity in China today out of a barren land, in which all religious and cultural life was supposedly wiped out during the Cultural Revolution is redolent of that.

Barth is postmodern, to the extent that he invites the reader to step into his theological frame of reference and try it out. He is also contemporary because his theology points to a new paradigm that is more appropriate to the challenges of intra-state conflict and war today. For the religious, Barth's doctrine suggests an image of God at the centre of human activity and life, and to whom all of humanity is ultimately reconciled. This image signifies that within each individual there is a choice to be far from or nearer God. With the strength of a centripetal force, there is a sense in which good as a moral agent must prevail. Barth would not accept an exact equivalence between good and God, since God's omnipotence puts him out of human control and rivalry. Nevertheless, 'good' is good enough, as a starting point, to put flesh on the moral underpinnings of just war criteria. To confer real legitimacy to military intervention, just war might also have in mind a 'good war'. That is not a war fighting for good over evil, but one that opens up a much needed debate about the meaning of a 'force for good'. Certainly, the notion of a just war might include the principle of whether military intervention has reconciliation as an objective.

The nature of warfare today, defined by General Rupert Smith as 'war amongst the people' (Smith 2006: 3), presents new challenges to armed forces. The temptation to give in to the desire to take revenge and punish, which American troops succumbed to in Abu Ghraib, can be resisted by reference to knowledge of what is essentially good. Soldiers face a moral dilemma when they face threats to their life from child soldiers. In this context, the debate should consider what good means not just for states, but for different constituents, particularly civilians, and amongst them, women and children. Wars where children are coerced into carrying weapons and acts of savagery, and women live amongst warriors as sex slaves, as they do in the Democratic Republic of the Congo, puts the responsibility for evil into the hands of human beings and not some metaphysical cause. Such wars prevent also an absolute demarcation of good from evil. The use of force can only contain violence, so that political, social and economic mechanisms can be put in place that put relationships, communities and nations onto a stable footing. Hence, as much, if not more, effort needs to go into other forms of investment, professionally organised, as into military activity.

Any attempt to shed the paradigm of 'good and evil' will be open to the criticism that to do so is idealistic and not in touch with the real world. But a paradigm that polarises is out of touch with understandings today about security where human, state and international security are conceived of as integrated. A monist, as opposed to a dualist paradigm that relies on good as the present and end goal of the human condition, encourages flexibility in approaches to the use of force, at one time reconciling, at another time robust depending on the circumstances, but always with an underlying aversion to the use of force. Importantly, a monist paradigm encourages consideration of the consequences of the use of force, not just for the protagonists, but those caught up inadvertently in war and its fallout.

The rejection of fundamentalism does not imply rejection of faith. It means continuing to seek truth, recognising the virtue in being on the path to truth, rather than truth being settled. It requires holding in balance the image of power being vanquished in weakness alongside a responsibility to protect the weak. And it holds an image of God's love for all humankind. A Christian way should, necessarily, reject religious fundamentalism. A Christian way of being does not prescribe particular political affiliations or policies as a point of principle. It is pragmatic about next steps, able to operate within the real world, holding onto a vision of a 'peaceable kingdom' (Haeurwas 1983) without imagining it is already here. It is firm about God as the starting point for all reason, leading to a relationship that is secure, that is not contingent and that engages human emotion and spirituality. A Christian way should be able to reflect ethically about the use of force, insisting on considerations of wider consequence as well as national interest.

This description of the Christian way might explain the enigmatic style that President Obama displays as he navigates his way through the political minefields of Capitol Hill and the international arena. Political commentators who find similarities between Obama and Niebuhr should consider the possibility that he has probably picked what suits him from a range of theologies, ideologies and political perspectives including Niebuhr. If theology is 'faith seeking understanding' then Obama does theology. In an interview in the *Chicago Sun-Times* in 2004 he said, 'I'm rooted in the Christian tradition', and 'I believe that there are many paths to the same place' (Falsani 2004). Obama's rhetoric has been persuasive and he has already begun to usher in a change of style. His Christian faith and experience played a role in developing his character and style. President Obama's success in making the world feel at ease, suggests that character and style can contribute a great deal to the dynamics of conflict. In Europe, Christianity's influence is minimised. Yet in matters of peace and war, it has never gone away.

Bibliography

Albright, M. 2007. *The Mighty and the Almighty: Reflections on Power, God, and World Affairs*. Basingstoke/Oxford: Pan Macmillan.

Armstrong, K. 2001. *The Battle for God: Fundamentalism in Judaism, Christianity and Islam*. London: HarperCollins.

Augustine, St 2003. *The City of God*. London: Penguin Classics.

Barth, K. 1960. *The Humanity of God*. London: Collins.

Barth, K. 1966. *Dogmatics in Outline*. London: SCM Press.

Barth, K. 2004. *Church Dogmatics: The Doctrine of the Word of God*, Vols 1–VI. London/New York: T. and T. Clark.

Barton, J. 1983. Approaches to Ethics in the Old Testament. In J.W. Rogerson, (ed.) *Beginning Old Testament Study*. London: SPCK.

Bonhoeffer, D. 2001. *Letters and Papers from Prison*, ed. E. Bethge. London: SCM Press.

Bonney, R. 2004. *Jihad: From Qur'an to bin Laden*. New York/Basingstoke: Palgrave Macmillan.

Buber, M. 2002. *Between Man and Man*. London/New York: Routledge.

Bush, G.W. 2002. The National Security Strategy of the United States of America. Online 17 September. Available at: http://www.whitehouse.gov/nsc/nss.html (accessed 18 April 2009).

Dalacoura, K. 2003. *Islam, Liberalism and Human Rights: Implications for International Relations*. London/New York: I.B. Taurus.

Dawkins, R. 2006. *The God Delusion*. London: Transworld Publishers.

Doughterty, J.E. and Pfaltzgraff Jr, R.L. (eds), 2001. *Contending Theories of International Relations: A Comprehensive Survey*, 5th edn. London/New York: Longman.

Dungan, D. L. 2006. *Constantine's Bible: Politics and the Making of the New Testament*. London: SCM Press.

Deleuze, G. 1980. *Kleine Schriften*, translated by K.D. Schacht. Berlin: Minerva.

Falsani, C. 2004. Obama: I Have a Deep Faith. *Chicago Sun Times*, interview. Online 5 April. Available at: http://www.suntimes.com/news/falsani/726619, obamafalsani040504.article (accessed 18 April 2009).

Fisk, R. 2005. *The Great War for Civilisation: The Conquest of the Middle East*. London: HarperCollins.

Gaddis, J.L. 2002. A Grand Strategy of Transformation. *Foreign Policy* 133, November–December, 50–57.

George, T. 2006. *God the Holy Trinity: Reflections on Christian Faith and Practice*. Grand Rapids MI: Baker Academic.

Goodwin, S.R. 2006. Fractured Land, Healing Nations: A Contextual Analysis of the Role of Religious Faith Sodalities: Towards Peace-building in Bosnia-Herzegovina. *Studies in the Intercultural History of Christianity* 139.

Gorringe, T.J. 2005. *Karl Barth: Against Hegemony*. Oxford: Oxford University Press.

Grim, B. 2008. Religion in China on the Eve of the 2008 Beijing Olympics. Pew Forum on Religion in Public Life, Pew Research Centre Publications. Online 2 May. Available at: http://pewresearch.org/pubs/827/china-religion-olympics (accessed: 22 June 2009).

Grotius, H. 2005. *The Rights of War and Peace*, Book II. Indianapolis: Liberty Fund.

Guthrie, C. and Quinlan, M. 2007. *Just War: The Just War Tradition: Ethics in Modern Warfare*. London: Bloomsbury.

Haeurwas, S. 1983. *The Peaceable Kingdom: A Primer in Christian Ethics*. Notre Dame: University of Notre Dame Press.
Hauerwas, S. and Pinches, C. 2001. Courage Exemplified. In J. Berkman and M. Cartwright (eds), *The Haeurwas Reader: Stanley Haeurwas*. Durham/London: Duke University Press.
Harries, R. 1986. Reinhold Niebuhr's Critique of Pacifism and his Pacifist Critiques. In R. Harries (ed.) *Reinhold Niebuhr and the Issues of Our Time*. London/Oxford: Mowbray.
Helmick, R.G., Petersen, S.J. and Petersen, R.L. (eds) 2001. *Forgiveness and Reconciliation: Religion, Public Policy and Conflict Transformation*. Philadelphia/London: Templeton Foundation Press.
Hick, J. 1966. *Evil and the God of Love*. London: Macmillan.
Hindley, G. 2004. *A Brief History of the Crusades: Islam and Christianity in the Struggle for World Supremacy*. London: Constable and Robinson.
Hobbs, T.R. 1989a. Reflections on the 'Poor' and the Old Testament. *Expository Times* 100, 291–4.
Hobbs, T.R. 1989b. *A Time for War: A Study of Warfare in the Old Testament*. Wilmington, DE: Michael Glazier.
Julian, L. 2009. Niebuhr and Obama. *Policy Review*, April/May, 1–9.
Kempfner, J. 2003. *Blair's Wars*. London: Free Press.
Landau, C. 2009. Blair's Faith Foundation. *BBC Radio 4 Broadcast*. Online 14 April. Available at: http://www.bbc.co.uk/programmes/b00jmv21 (accessed 18 April 2009).
Lindberg, C. 1996. *The European Reformations*. Oxford: Blackwell.
Lovin, R.W. 1995. *Reinhold Niebuhr and Christian Realism*. Cambridge: Cambridge University Press.
Migliore, D.L. 2004. *Faith Seeking Understanding: An Introduction to Christian Theology*. Michigan: Wm. B. Eerdmans.
Millbank, J. 2006. *Theology and Social Theory: Beyond Secular Reason*. Oxford: Blackwell.
Niebuhr, R. 1940. *Christianity and Power Politics*. New York: Charles Scribner's Sons.
Nietzsche, F. 1976. *Beyond Good and Evil: Prelude to a Philosophy of the Future*. Harmondsworth/Baltimore: Penguin.
O'Brian, M. and O'Brian, C.C. 1973. *A Concise History of Ireland*. London: Thames and Hudson.
Obama, B. 2007. Renewing American Leadership. *Foreign Affairs*. Online July/August. Available at: http://www.foreignaffairs.com/articles/62636/barack-obama/renewing-american-leadership (accessed: 16 April 2009).
Obama, B. 2009. President Barack Obama's Inaugural Address. *The White House Blog*. 21 January. Available at: http://www.whitehouse.gov/blog/inaugural-address/ (accessed 3 April 2009).
O'Donovan, O. 1999. *The Desire of the Nations: Rediscovering the Roots of Political Theology*. Cambridge: Cambridge University Press.

Pagels, E. 1995. *The Origin of Satan*. London: Penguin Books.
Reagan, R. 1983. Speech to the National Association of Evangelicals. Orlando, Florida. Online 8 March. Available at: http://www.hbci.com/~tgort/empire.htm (accessed 18 April 2009).
Rodd, C.S. 1995. The Use of the Old Testament in Christian Ethics. In C.S. Rodd (ed.), *New Occasions Teach New Duties? Christian Ethics for Today*, Edinburgh: T. and T. Clark.
Rose, C. 1985. *Campaigns Against Western Defence: NATO's Adversaries and Critics*. London/Basingstoke: Macmillan.
Sills, J. 2004. The United Nations and the Formation of Global Norms. In J.E. Krasno (ed.), *The United Nations: Confronting the Challenges of Global Society*. Boulder/London: Lynne Reinner.
Smith, R. 2006. *The Utility of Force: The Art of War in the Modern World*. London: Penguin.
Tang, E. 2000. The Second Enlightenment: The Spiritual Quest of Chinese Intellectuals. In T. Murayama and W. Ustorf (eds) *Identity and Marginality: Christianity in North East Asia*. Frankfurt am Main: Peter Lang.
The New Interpreter's Study Bible 2003. New Revised Standard Version. Nashville: Abingdon Press.
Ticciati, S. 2006. Scriptural Reasoning and the Formation of Identity. *Modern Theology* 22 (3), July.
Vardy, P. 1992. *The Puzzle of Evil*. London: HarperCollins.
Wright, N.T. 2006. *Evil and the Justice of God*. London: SPCK.
Volf, M. 1996. *Exclusion and Embrace: A Theological Exploration of Identity, Otherness and Reconciliation*. Nashville: Abingdon Press.
Waltz, K. 1959. *Man the State and War: A Theoretical Analysis*. New York: Columbia University Press.
White, J. 2003. General in a Small Army: Hauerwas Battles for Pacifism. *Religion News Service*. Online 17 March. Available at: http://www.baptiststandard.com/2003/3_17/pages/hauerwas.html (accessed 15 April 2009).
Wilson, A.N. 2002. *The Victorians*. London: Hutchinson.
Woodhead, L. 2004. *An Introduction to Christianity*. Cambridge: Cambridge University Press.

PART 2
Religious Influences on Military Intervention

Chapter 4
Religiously-Motivated Political Violence in Iraq

Rebecca Glazier

Violence in Iraq has been a consistent problem since the US invasion in 2003. In 2006, at the height of what many termed a civil war (NIC 2007), daily news reports reinforced the dire nature of the conflict with tallies of the ever mounting death toll and reports on the increasingly sectarian nature of the violence. Lt General Ricardo S. Sanchez went so far as to call the situation in Iraq 'a nightmare with no end in sight' (Cloud 2007). Since the high water mark of the violence, some progress has been made towards increased security and stability. Despite the relative success of the peaceful trifecta of the surge, the Sunni Awakening, and Moqtada al-Sadr's cease-fire, the religious undertones of the conflict in Iraq persist. Many clerics are emerging as political leaders (Nakash 2006), the dangers of religious violence endure, and a government divided along sectarian lines reveals conspicuous weaknesses in the plan for political unity in Iraq.

Little academic research has been done on the role of religion in the conflict in Iraq, and even the most recent books on the topic reflect confusion over who the insurgents are and what motivates them (Mowle 2007). Much of the evidence we do have points to religion at the heart of at least some of the violence in Iraq. Those that participate in sectarian violence, both Sunni and Shi'a, see the conflict in religious terms and use religion to identify targets and to define threats (Duffy Toft 2008). Additionally, both sects have appealed for help from their religious compatriots outside of Iraq (Duffy Toft 2008; Associated Press 2007). The empirical evidence indicates that religion is an important factor in the conflict in Iraq, but many questions remain unanswered. What exactly is the role of religion, for which groups does it have the most influence, and how can understanding the effects of religion help us in countering the violence? This chapter is a first attempt at addressing these questions, and it brings the analytical power of political science to the problem by utilising a new conceptual tool for understanding how religion motivates political behaviour.

In this chapter, I argue that, in order to truly understand the effects of religion, we must examine the *nature* of religious beliefs, the *content* of religious beliefs, and how these beliefs are *connected* to real events in a way that motivates believers to take political action. These three steps comprise the providential beliefs model, which will be applied in this chapter to the case of Iraq. Thus, the goal of this chapter is threefold: first, to identify the categories of violent participants in the conflict in Iraq and their objectives; second, to use the conceptual tool of providential beliefs to describe how religion influences each of these groups; and third, to apply this knowledge in order to find potential solutions to the religiously motivated violence in Iraq.

Religion and Violence in Iraq

From 2003 through the end of 2007, terrorist acts of violence steadily increased in Iraq, as did descriptions of the violence as sectarian in nature. In 2006, a leaked chart from a classified Central Command briefing showed Iraq descending into chaos, largely attributed to rising sectarian conflict (Gordon 2006). The marked increase in sectarian violence began with the bombing of a Shiite shrine in Samarra in February, 2006. Looking back at the data over this period of time, the number of deaths attributed to terrorism reflects a trend that is precipitously upward. Although the levels of violence have decreased in recent months, Iraq is far from a stable country.

Iraqis, and the foreign fighters in Iraq, participate in the violence for a number of reasons, many of which have their roots in religion. In his analysis of suicide bombings in Iraq, Mohammed Hafez (2007b) argues that there are two insurgencies underway in the country. The first insurgency is made up of nationalists who use religion to encourage resistance against coalition forces. The second is the more radical insurgency, composed of ideological Ba'athists and jihadist Salafis. Whereas the first insurgency aims to extricate coalition forces in order to allow Iraqis to govern themselves, the second insurgency is less concerned with the nation of Iraq and instead aims to collapse the state to further its own interests (Little and Swearer 2006). Included in the latter group are middle to high level Ba'ath party members, composed almost exclusively of Sunni Muslims, who believe that they will be unable to compete in any type of a democratic system, and so seek instead to make Iraq a failed state where their paramilitary power will hold more sway. Religion is only important to the Baathists insofar as it can be used to foster a civil war and lead to a system wide collapse.

The more radical jihadists, who are also counted as members of the second insurgency, truly have religious motivations at the heart of their actions. They are interested in creating an Islamic state and a regional base from which to carry out *jihad* (Hafez 2007b). Since 2003, these jihadists have been crossing into Iraq along the unprotected border with Syria to take part in what they see as a religious war (Foulk 2007), and have been swelling the ranks of al-Qaeda in Iraq. Additionally, this radical insurgency has sought to provoke a civil war between the rival Muslim factions and has been blamed for the 2006 bombing of the mosque that inspired sectarian reprisals on a massive scale throughout Iraq (Haynes 2007). Thus, this more radical insurgency is a dangerous hybrid of the local Sunni insurgency and al-Qaeda elements that have grafted themselves onto the movement and significantly heightened the bloodshed (*Economist* 2008a).

Outside of the delineating borders of these insurgencies, I would add two additional groups that engage in violence in Iraq. First, as in any conflict area, there are opportunistic violent criminals. Although these individuals rarely engage in the type of violence that leads to massive casualties, like suicide bombings, they are responsible for a number of kidnappings and extortion schemes. These criminals, although not motivated by religion, do contribute to the general sense of chaos and hopelessness in Iraq.

Second and more importantly, are religious individuals that have organised themselves into armed militias in response to what they see as an increasingly sectarian conflict. These people were not actively participating in the violence in the early years of the war, but as sectarian attacks and their almost inevitable reprisals increased, formerly peaceful Iraqis have also turned to violence (Maples 2006). As the internal tensions in Iraq grew into what some characterised as a civil war, these groups facilitated the growing religious nature of the conflict in Iraq in part by appealing to their co-religionists outside of Iraq. From the east, weapons and support from Iran came into Iraq, often with the purpose of assisting the Shi'a insurgents with attacks against coalition forces (Associated Press 2007) and of assisting the Shi'a militias in their sectarian reprisals. The addition of sectarian fighters to the chaos in Iraq is one major reason the death toll increased at such a dramatic rate from 2005–2007 (Maples 2006).

There are a number of violent groups contributing to the conflict in Iraq, motivated by a number of different factors ranging from authentic religious beliefs to sheer greed to revenge. This chapter is primarily interested in the role of religion in the Iraqi conflict, and so it focuses on those groups that are motivated at least in part by religion: religious nationalists, radical jihadists, and sectarian combatants. The characteristics of these groups, along with the other violent groups in Iraq, are displayed in Figure 4.1 with their sectarian affiliations, level of religious commitment, goals, and common tactics.

	Religious sect	**Religious commitment**	**Goals**	**Major tactics**
Nationalists	Mostly Sunni, but also Shi'a	Moderate	Drive the US out of Iraq	Attacking military targets and US supporters
Baathists	Sunni	Minimal	Collapse Iraq	IEDS, mostly against civilians and Iraqi police
Radical jihadists	Sunni	Extreme	Establish Islamic government and a base for jihad	Suicide bombings; attacks on civilians
Sectarian combatants	Mostly Shi'a	Great	Protect in-group; retaliate	Roving death squads
Criminals	All	Minimal to non-existent	Personal monetary gain	Robbery; kidnapping

Figure 4.1 Violent groups in Iraq

Providential Beliefs

Although violence has at times seemed pervasive in Iraq, the majority of the population does not choose to strap on a suicide vest or to torture and shoot members of another religious sect. What then is the motivation of the relatively few individuals who do? In Iraq, we have to understand the potential power of religion in order to answer this question. Utilising a model that has proven valuable in other studies (Glazier 2009a, 2009b; Cleary and Glazier 2007), I propose three steps to understanding how religious beliefs motivate political action in Iraq. The first step is distinguishing among the different *natures* of religious beliefs, the second is determining the *content* of the belief system, and the third is ascertaining the *connection* between the content of the belief system and actual political events.

Although religious beliefs could be grouped according to an almost infinite number of characteristics, at the most basic level we can divide them into two major types, providential and non-providential, depending on the *nature* of the beliefs. Providential beliefs, as I am defining them, have two important components. The first is that the adherent believes in a divinely-authored inevitable future state for humanity. This is often thought of as 'God's plan'. People who hold religious beliefs that are providential in nature believe that they know God's will, or know the inevitable path that history will take, and this lends a profound certainty to their beliefs and their actions.

The second important component that identifies the nature of a belief system as providential is the notion that believers have a role to play in carrying out the plan. God does not want them to sit idly by, but instead requires their action. People who hold beliefs of this nature are much more likely to engage politically, because the idea of actively helping to bring about God's plan is an important component of their belief system. The presence of these two components, the belief in a plan and in one's role in it, classifies the nature of the belief system as providential. The distinction between providential and non-providential believers forms the first step in a process of understanding how the behaviours of these two groups differ. Individuals who believe that they are working towards an inevitable end point with divine assistance will behave very differently from those who do not. Providential beliefs are powerful forces that can motivate and even compel action.

Identifying the nature of belief is a critical first step, but knowing what kinds of issues a providential believer cares about – that is, knowing their providential content – provides additional insight into possible political actions. Thus, the second step in understanding religiously-motivated political action is identifying the *content* of the belief system. Content is defined as the specific beliefs the adherent holds about the world and about God's will for it. Content is likely to vary greatly from one religion to another, from one mosque to another, and from one believer to another. Indeed, religious content is constantly shifting and being redefined, both by leadership and by believers. Thus, specific religious texts or dogmas should not be interpreted as applying to every adherent of a particular faith in the same way, if at all.

After the first two steps, we are left to conclude that there are ostensibly millions of people in the world who believe that they have a role to play in God's plan, and who also believe in a variety of doctrinal specifics. Why do these people take action when they do? Why do their religious beliefs come into play for decisions that may not be objectively religious? The explanation lies in the *connection*, or framing, of political reality in terms of religious content – the third step in the providential beliefs explanation of how religion can influence politics.

In order for beliefs to serve as an impetus to action, a connection must be made between that particular belief and some aspect of reality. This connection is most often made through the process of framing (Druckman 2001; Snow et al. 1986; Tversky and Kahneman 2000). The connection may be an exogenous one – motivated by a foreign occupation or the death of a loved one. The connection may be made by a religious leader – calling the faithful to action in a sermon or fatwa, or pointing out the religious significance of an exogenous event. Or the connection may be a personal one – reached in a moment of contemplative meditation or personal prayer. But it is this connection between content and reality that tells the believer that *now* is the time to act as well as the action that needs to be taken. The connection makes the current event or state of reality religiously, and therefore personally, meaningful. This compels the believer to action. How can this theoretical framework help us understand religiously motivated violence in Iraq? In the next section, I will discuss how the providential nature of Islam, together with malleable content regarding martyrdom and *jihad*, make violent religious frames more acceptable to the believers in Iraq. Following this discussion, I present specific evidence of religious frames in Iraq and their political ramifications.

Providential Beliefs and Providential Content in Iraq

In countries all over the Middle East, motivated individuals have left their families, crossed borders, and even given their lives for the purpose of helping their Iraqi 'cousins' and fulfilling Allah's commandment to undertake *jihad* (Sedgwick 2004). Within Iraq, terrorist organisations and local religious leaders alike have encouraged violent actions in the name of religion, and many individuals have answered the call. In order to understand and potentially counter these acts of political violence, we need understand the real religious motivations driving them. The common thread connecting the religious nationalists, jihadists, and sectarians in Iraq is their identification with the Muslim faith.[1] Thus, I turn to Islam as a starting point for understanding how religion motivates individuals to violent political behaviour in Iraq because it is the dominant lens through which Iraqis understand religion.

1 The fact that these individuals identify with Islam and also participate in the violence is not an indictment of Islam; it is simply a fact that most Iraqis are Muslim.

The first step is to determine if Islam is a providential religion or not. The two most important components that identify the nature of a religious belief system as providential are first, that the adherent believes in a divinely authored plan, and second, that the adherent believes that she or he has a role to play in it. Inherent in this concept, and in the more generally understood definition of providentiality, is the notion that God will intervene in helping believers to accomplish this plan and/or that believers will be rewarded in the life to come for their efforts on God's behalf. According to these standards, Islam is a providential religion. Evidence for this claim is found in religious texts, the words of religious leaders, and common religious practices.

Both the overarching message of the Koran, as well as individual stories within it, reflect the notion that Allah has a plan and that He requires certain behaviours from faithful Muslims. The Koran is filled with stories about the triumphs of the Prophet and his followers, including how Allah has intervened on the behalf of believers to help them achieve victory.[2] These stories communicate a message of divine intervention and providentiality to Muslim believers (Cook and Allison 2007).

Additionally, Islam adheres to a doctrine that considers human life from an eternal perspective – the period on earth being but one piece of a divine plan authored by Allah. Parts of this plan will be carried out on earth, like the notion that the entire world will convert to Islam and be governed by the laws of *sharia*, but other parts discussed include how the providential nature of Islam, is cosmic or heavenly (Juergensmeyer 2003).

Another piece of providential doctrine is the concept of *tawhid*, or the notion that there is only one true God. Islamic scholars say that the effect of *tawhid* is to 'focus our awareness of divine demands and consequent human responsibilities' (Pinault 1992: 15). *Tawhid* causes believers to focus on carrying out the will of God – a very providential idea. These messages are continually reinforced by religious leaders – from the moderate to the extreme. Every mosque teaches that Islam will eventually cover the earth and the righteous will be ruled by a global caliphate. Every mosque and Muslim family teach the providential stories of the Koran.

The religious practices of the Muslim faithful are also providential. For instance, dreams have a special place in the faith of devout Muslims. Allah communicates directly to the faithful through visions and dreams, as he did with the prophets Abraham and Mohammed. 'Many Muslims today, when facing tough decisions, rely on a prophetic tradition that urges them to undertake prayer for guidance (*istikhara*) in which they hope God would reveal to them the correct

2 A particularly potent example is the battle of Badr, the first major battle between the Muslims of Medina and the invading Meccan army. Despite the fact that the Muslims were outnumbered 1,000 to 314, they were ultimately victorious in the battle, in part because God sent angels from heaven to fight alongside the faithful, an explicit instance of divine intervention. Excerpts from the Koran reiterate this: 'So you slew them not but Allah slew them …' (Verse 8:17).

choice in a dream' (Hafez 2007a: 109). Not only do the faithful believe that God has a plan and will inform them of it, but they are actively seeking to know God's will so that they can carry it out.

Thus, in both personal religious moments and in widely taught religious doctrines, believers in Iraq are reminded of the providential nature of their faith. This reinforcement keeps at the forefront of believers' minds the fact that God has a plan and that they have a role to play. In such a frame of mind, the believers are ready and even searching for their roles, and political frames rooted in religion are more likely to resonate and motivate action.

The things that will be the most compelling are those that resonate with religious content (Snow et al. 1986). Now, the content of any given religion is virtually endless. For the purposes of this analysis, I focus on content that is most likely to be used to motivate the violence in Iraq. Religious concepts relating to issues of war and peace have always had a place in the content of Islam. But some concepts have been adapted and redefined by those who would use religion to justify and motivate political violence. Two specific cases of this are the concepts of *jihad* and the actions that deem one worthy of the title of martyr.

Jihad as an active and violent concept is a fairly new interpretation of *jihad*. Historically, Muslim jurists have distinguished between the greater *jihad*, or the struggle within one's self against temptation, and the lesser *jihad*, or the physical struggle with an external enemy in the cause of God (Heck 2007). Examples of the more activist notion of *jihad* are found more regularly in recent Islamic history. Dr Abdullah Yusuf 'Azzuam of Saudi Arabia, for instance, exhorted the students at his university, including Osama bin Laden, to undertake violent *jihad* as a duty of all Muslims, saying: 'Jihad and the rifle alone. No negotiations, no conferences, no dialogues …' (cited in Aslan 2005: 86). This shift in emphasis came about in large part as a result of the efforts of radical Islamic scholars like Muhammad 'Abd al-Salam Faraj, the author of the pamphlet 'The Neglected Duty', which outlines the duty all faithful Muslims have to active and violent *jihad*. This emphasis on the lesser *jihad* represents a new interpretation of the concept, and is an example of the general malleability of religious content, as well as the ability of a relatively small number of religious scholars to further their own religious interpretations.

The concept of martyrdom is another doctrinal component of Islam that can be used either for conflict or for peace. Martyrdom has traditionally held particularly important sway in the Shi'ite sect of Islam,[3] but the concept of martyrdom as

3 A central component of the Shi'a belief system is the martyrdom of Husayn at Karbala, which is still mourned by Shi'ites today (Pinault 1992; Hyder 2006) and represents a key moment in their religious history. Husayn was the Prophet Mohammed's grandson and, as a blood relative, Shi'ites past and present believed him to be the rightful leader of Islam. In 680, he was martyred on the road to Karbala by an opposition faction of Muslims that supported the Umayyad rulers (Cook 2007). This historical wrong represents the prototype of every struggle for justice and every suffering undergone by the Shi'ites (Moghadam 2007).

a political weapon, has more recently been adopted by Sunnis throughout the Muslim world (Burdman 2003). Today, Hezbollah, a nationalist Shi'a organisation thought to be behind the original Beirut barracks bombing, has decreased its usage of the tactic of suicide terrorism (Cook and Allison 2007), often referred to as 'martyrdom operations' by radical Muslim groups, and the current proponents of the tactic are largely drawn from the ranks of Sunni Muslims.

This shift is largely attributable to the growing popularity of martyrdom amongst fundamentalist Sunnis. The fundamentalist movement of Salafi jihadists, emerging from the Sunni sect of Islam and finding particularly fertile ground in Saudi Arabia, has found great use in the Shi'ite concept of martyrdom. Today, many of the themes of self-sacrifice and martyrdom that have traditionally been a staple in the Shi'ite tradition are also reflected in the content of the more radical Sunni sects (Moghadam 2007). The radical religious elements of the Sunni sect of Islam have been growing over the past decade or so, even at a time when Shi'a radicalism, seen in groups like Hezbollah and reflected in the use of suicide terrorism, has been on the decline (Nakash 2006). Martyrdom has always had a place in the religious content of Sunnis, but it has not been until more recent times when it has been emphasised so forcefully, by the more radical religious leaders in particular. In the constant shifting and redefining of content, martyrdom as a political concept has become central for religiously extreme Sunnis, and has risen to the forefront of the violence in Iraq.

The specifics of this religious content is important because it is the raw material from which individuals and organisations are drawn from in order to create political frames that motivate violence in the name of religion. The specifics of how this is being accomplished in Iraq are presented in the next section.

Providential Religious Connections in Iraq

Throughout history, radical Islamic leaders have tried to connect salient religious content to current reality by recalling earlier episodes when Islam was threatened and connecting these important religious events to modern political situations. Muslim revolutionaries and political figures throughout history have attempted to employ religious symbolism in support of their cause, sometimes even using direct passages from the Koran as political slogans (Heck 2007). Evidence of the use of Islam as a 'master frame' (Snow et al. 1986) to motivate political movements is also present in the literature (Cleary and Glazier 2007). Thus, it is not surprising to see Islam used to motivate political violence in Iraq.

Baathists, jihadists, nationalists, sectarians, and thugs have all engaged in violent activities in Iraq, many of them motivated by religion. Nationalists use the rhetoric and content of religion to motivate individuals to resist what they see as a foreign occupation; jihadists have a broader agenda of establishing a global caliphate and seek to collapse the country of Iraq in order to do so; some sectarians are religious radicals, but many of them can be thought of as 'reluctant sectarians' – turning to violence as a means of protection and retaliation in an increasingly chaotic world divided by religious beliefs. These differences were first summarised and compared in Figure 4.1.

For each of these groups, religiously motivated political violence became an option as a result of the precipitating events of the 2003 invasion. The invasion created the situation against which nationalists currently rail, the chaos and the convenient targets which jihadists are gladly taking advantage of, and the shift in the sectarian balance of power that has unleashed centuries of hostility and disagreement in a self-perpetuating cycle of violence and reprisals.

Radical jihadists, typified by al-Qaeda, employ the most overt religious frames in their attempts to connect the conflict in Iraq to religious considerations. In particular, they have worked to portray the military engagements in Iraq and Afghanistan as attacks against Islam as a whole and therefore requiring an active and violent *jihad*. 'To the average Arab the toppling of the Taliban in Afghanistan appeared as an act of revenge on the people of Afghanistan, and the invasion of Iraq appeared as an unprovoked attack on a long-suffering people whose only crime was to be Arab and Muslim' (Sedgwick 2004: 803). Osama bin Laden called the occupation of Iraq '... but one link in a chain of attacks' (cited in Heck 2007: 19), reinforcing the notion that the US is on a crusade against Islam. The perception that Islam is under attack has served as a powerful motivating force for combatants in Iraq. 'It was as a result of these perceptions that during 2003 volunteers crossed the Syrian border to help their Iraqi "cousins"' (Sedgwick 2004: 803). Thus, al-Qaeda takes grievances from around the world – against the US, against Israel, against the West, against unrighteous Muslim leaders – and weaves them together in a narrative about the threat to Islam and the religious duty to respond with violence (*Economist* 2008b).

Indeed, what makes al-Qaeda so deadly is that it brings together an uncompromising worldview and a set of real, local grievances and religious conflicts waiting to be inflamed. 'Like a parasite, al-Qaeda moves between the conflicts in the Islamic world, deriving sustenance from genuine, often well-founded local anger and grievances' (Reuter 2004: 153). Terrorist organisations like al-Qaeda make it their goal to connect content with reality in order to gain both supporters for and participants in their cause. Moving into Iraq after the invasion, al-Qaeda in Iraq has been the single most violent terrorist group in that country, claiming responsibility for more than 200 individual attacks since 2003 (MIPT website, accessed 8 November 2007), many of these attacks have been suicide attacks or 'martyrdom operations'. Along with other, more nationalistic groups, al-Qaeda has been very successful in establishing connections between their radical Islamic worldview and the experiences of local populations. The insurgency was able to recruit of large number of adherents from the ranks of Baath Party members and Iraqi soldiers who, after the US invasion, suddenly found themselves out of a job and angry (Ricks 2006). It proved only too easy to connect this anger with the religious content of *jihad* against a foreign invader.

Thus, the US invasion of Iraq provides a ready-made connection that can motivate violence from radical jihadists for years to come (Rogers 2006). Although the events are exogenous, the connection made between the events and religious content is often articulated and reinforced by religious leaders. For instance, Sheik Abdul Salam al-Kubaisi, a Sunni religious leader, stated that the invasion of Iraq by the US was a conspiracy to eliminate the faithful (Foulk 2007). Other clerics have called resistance to the occupation a 'religious duty' (Sheik Yusuf al-Qaradawi, cited in Foulk 2007: 167). But al-Qaeda is not the only group to use religious frames. Iraqi nationalists have turned to religion and violence in response to some of the actions taken by coalition forces, particularly in the early months of the war. When soldiers abuse and humiliate prisoners like at Abu Ghraib, accost or even touch Muslim women, and indiscriminately arrest Iraqi civilians, the notion that Islam is under attack becomes more personal and salient for the people of Iraq (Foulk 2007; Ricks 2006). The killing of civilians at Haditha (West 2006), for instance, turned the local populations against coalition forces, and reinforced the concept of Western oppression and imperialism. Both religiously motivated Iraqi nationalists and radical jihadists are likely to react strongly and violently to situations of abuse and humiliation described above, especially when such a reaction is connected to God's will for the individual or the community. Only recently has American leadership come to the realisation that 'for every innocent Iraqi killed or wounded by an American, ten new insurgents [are] recruited' (Foulk 2007: 17).

The political and security situation in Iraq also lends itself well to religious frames that are sectarian in nature. Increasing numbers of civilian deaths, whether from suicide attacks or coalition raids, contribute to a general sense of threat and chaos, which leads people to retreat to the relative safety of their 'in-group' (Allport 1979). Under these conditions, sectarian violence is likely to emerge. Additionally, the invasion of Iraq and the ousting of Saddam Hussein's government had the added effect of changing the balance of power between the Sunni and the Shi'a sects of Islam (Nasr 2004). Regime change removed not only Saddam, but also the minority Sunni leadership, which had ruled Iraq for over 70 years. Suddenly, the Shi'a majority found themselves with political clout in the move towards a more democratic form of government, and the Sunni minority found themselves threatened and weakened under this new arrangement. The tension between the sects is manifest in the Sunni refusal to participate in the 2005 elections, unevenly distributed public goods like electricity, and evidence of formerly mixed neighbourhoods dividing along religious lines (Mowle 2007).

In the years following the invasion, most Sunnis were disenfranchised and saw no place for themselves in a democratic government. Newly weakened by the ousting of Saddam and fearful of the formerly oppressed Shi'a majority taking revenge, these Sunnis saw civil war as an acceptable option (Mowle 2007). Thus, some nationalist Sunnis are also fighting to preserve their religious identity, which they believe is threatened by a Shi'ite-run, and thereby apostate, government (Hyder 2006). Sunni content declares the Shi'a sect an impure form of Islam, and the Shi'a people thereby not truly Muslim. This content, connected with political advances by the Shi'ites, is enough to motivate some Sunnis to violent action.

The more radical jihadist elements in Iraq recognised that inflaming religious conflicts could contribute to their goals of state collapse and an unregulated base of operation, and set out to use targeted suicide attacks against Shi'ites to provoke a sectarian civil war (Bremer 2006; Brym 2008; Little and Swearer 2006). During the early years of the conflict, al-Qaeda was able to move into more moderate Sunni areas because the Sunni Muslims were afraid of Shiite militias. Al-Qaeda played on this fear to gain a base for operations and support from the local population (Anderson 2007: 3–13). In a letter to bin Laden, Abu Musab al-Zarqawi, the leader of al-Qaeda in Iraq, wrote that if they could succeed in dragging the Shi'a 'into the arena of sectarian war, it will become possible to awaken the inattentive Sunnis as they feel imminent danger' (quoted in Bergen 2006: 363). The notion that a holy war is afoot is reinforced by sectarian violence, including violence supported by co-religionists from Iran and Saudi Arabia, a warning sign that violence could spread beyond Iraq.

Shi'ites are also motivated by sectarian religious frames, although they do have a stake in the new government and therefore do not want to facilitate the type of chaos that some Sunni groups do. As the big winners in the 2005 elections, Shi'ites have moved forward with their own religious agenda, thus further alienating the already threatened Sunnis (Little and Swearer 2006). This political organisation has been facilitated by the extensive network of mosques that held clandestine Friday prayers under the Saddam regime. The Sadr Movement utilised these networks in order to organise the militia and in order to organise politically (Cole 2003). Thus, instead of rejecting the new political situation, the Shi'a are embracing it. Even Moqtada al-Sadr and his followers have joined the political process (Nakash 2006).

Whereas some Sunni groups were motivated by religious frames about the necessity of *jihad* or the dangers of an apostate sect ruling the country, the Shi'ites were more likely to respond to frames based on a religious mentality of 'us versus them', leading to the development of militias for protection as well as for revenge. The Shi'ite militias are more narrowly motivated by in-group protection and revenge (Cook and Allison 2007) than their violent Sunni counterparts. Iraq's Shi'a population was particularly shaken by a series of political assassinations directed again its leadership during 2003–2004 (Nakash 2006) and the bombing of the Golden Mosque in Samarra. This helped set the stage for strained relations between the sects, and contributed to a political reality in which violent religious reprisals were seen as justified.

Although religious frames have motivated the great deal of violence in Iraq, they can work in the other direction as well, and perhaps provide some hope for the future of Iraq. In the fall of 2007, a number of factors came together to bring a degree of stability to Iraq. The surge of US troops, the ceasefire declared by Muqtada al-Sadr, and the Sunni Awakening all contributed to decreases in violence and some small political steps forward. The Awakening was perhaps the most surprising and consequential of these developments. As violence spun out of control in 2006, many Sunnis who had previously supported the insurgency grew tired of the bloodshed and particularly the indiscriminate killings by the radical jihadists. Led by local tribal leaders, thousands of fighters were recruited to turn against the insurgency and begin fighting al-Qaeda and other radical elements in return for a salary (Haynes 2007). Although economic concerns certainly played a role in the willingness of the Sunnis, many of whom were former insurgents, to turn against al-Qaeda, religious concerns were also present. One tribal sheik described the Awakening as: 'not just an awakening of force but an awakening of heart and spirit, an awakening from sectarian hatred' (Rubin 2007: A23). The Awakening does not mean that the Sunnis are pleased with the occupation, but many seem to have decided that the coalition soldiers represent the lesser evil. Al-Qaeda, with their indiscriminate killing of civilians, efforts to foment sectarian conflict, and imposition of strict interpretations of Muslim law, has become the greater threat (*Economist* 2007).

Thus, as the radicals and militias from either sect go too far, religious frames can lead support for them to drop. For instance, one Shi'ite man's brother was killed by the local militia, known as the Jaish al-Mahdi, who was supposed to be protecting his neighbourhood from the radical Sunnis. Enraged by the death of his brother, the man began a massive providential campaign of revenge, saying, 'God wants me to kill these people. It is *haram* to kill cats, but it is good to kill the Jaish al-Mahdi' (Anderson 2007: 70). It took some time for the citizens of Iraq to realise the damage the radical jihadists were doing to their country, and sometimes it took personal experience with the bloody tactics of al-Qaeda for the population to turn against them, but once a personally and religiously meaningful connection is made, the result is a committed effort to fight the radical religious insurgency (Raghavan 2008).

Despite this recent success, the problems in Iraq are far from over. In fact, the formation of Sunni militias to combat al-Qaeda has fuelled some Shi'a fears of a potential resurgence in sectarian violence. Many are concerned that the Awakening Councils have been infiltrated by militant groups like al-Qaeda (Haynes 2007) and represent 'wolves in sheep's clothing' (Rubin and Cave 2007: 1). The growth of what are perceived as sectarian Sunni militias may spur a resurgence of Shi'a militias, eventually restarting the cycle of violence once again (Rubin and Cave 2007).

How Providential Beliefs Can Inform Policy in Iraq

In order to have a chance at true success in fighting the violence in Iraq, policymakers have to recognise the role of religion in the conflict. What the providential beliefs approach provides is an explanation of religiously motivated political violence that identifies and explicitly addresses the religious roots of the violence. Building on the concepts of the approach, there are three major ways to address religiously motivated political violence. The first is to change the nature of the beliefs. If the adherents do not believe God wants them to act to carry out a plan, the impulse to take part in the violence will not be nearly so great. The second option is to change the content. If calls to violence do not resonate with the believers' content, they will not take action. The final option posited by providential belief systems is to change the opportunity for connections, or the frames that are available. In this case, even if the believer still has violent content, if this content is not connected to some aspect of reality in the world, they will see no reason to act. A frame has to resonate with prior content, come from a reliable source, and make sense in terms of the political climate in order for it motivate violence in the name of religion (Snow et al. 1986; Druckman 2001).

Taking each of these ideas in turn, we see first that, although it is theoretically possible to attempt to convince believers that God does not actually have a plan and/or that they do not have a role to play in God's plan, this is unlikely to be successful. It is hard to imagine approaching a devout Muslim who believes God's will for his life is to become a martyr in the battle against the infidel invader, and successfully convincing him that there is no God, or that God does not request his services in bringing His plans to pass. The vast majority of people in the world profess a strong commitment to some spiritual faith (Gill 2001), and are not likely to turn away from that faith at the request of an outsider. Additionally, efforts in this vein may fuel fears that the US presence in Iraq is part of a crusade to destroy Islam.

Thus, the second option, changing or reinterpreting religious content, is more feasible than the first. Religious content is never static. In both the lives of individuals and in the more formal constructs of organised religion, content is constantly shifting. This dynamism provides the opportunity to inject new ideas about content into the debate. As discussed earlier, the two concepts that have been at the heart of the violence, both in Iraq and elsewhere, are *jihad* and martyrdom. In the past, there have been debates over whether or not suicide bombers qualify for martyrdom benefits in the eyes of Allah (Pedahzur 2006; Hafez 2006; Cook and Allison 2007; Moghadam 2007). A revival of these debates may decrease societal support for such attacks, as well as change the payoff matrix for those who would consider carrying them out. A shift in emphasis away from the need to wage *jihad* against the American invaders and towards the evils of killing innocent Muslims is what helped turn the tide among the Sunni population and led to the Awakening. Similarly, an emphasis on *jihad* as an internal struggle, even in the face of an external enemy, might discourage some from turning to violence in the name of religion. A broader renunciation of violence from within the radical Islamic community is already beginning, a phenomenon that has been referred to as the 'rebellion within' al-Qaeda (Wright 2008).

The fact that content can be changed, however, does not mean that input from just any source will result in an immediate modification of content. Shifts in content are the most effective when they make sense in the context of the individual believer's life, and/or when they come from a trusted source (Druckman 2001).

In a country like Iraq, where personal relationships are everything, adjustments to content should be made by trusted religious and community leaders (Foulk 2007). The strategy of gaining the support of local leaders has met with some success in Iraq (Colvin 2007), particularly in the case of some Sunni tribal sheiks turning against al-Qaeda (Raghavan 2008).

Another possibility is that the United States can attempt to affect content anonymously, via the Internet, for instance, a tactic that is currently being utilised to combat extremism in Saudi Arabia (Yehoshua 2006). The medium of the Internet is widely used by extremist groups to spread their message. 'In order to counter this in an effective way, Western government should also enter the discourse without using pejorative terms like terrorist, but instead injecting doubt about the religious justification for suicide bombing' (Cook and Allison 2007: 107). Hopefully this will encourage debate about these important religious concepts within the Muslim community, and may also prove useful for dispelling some false portrayals of U.S. forces as an apostate invading army intent on destroying the Muslim religion and culture.

This brings us to the final, and perhaps most readily available, tactic: reducing the possibilities for connections between content and reality and injecting new frames into the political discussion. Of course, this may not be particularly effective with some of the groups engaging in violent activities in Iraq. Al-Qaeda type groups will find connections no matter what the circumstances. For these types of highly committed groups and individuals, there is little one can do to combat them outside of military and intelligence tactics. For the Sunni nationalists and 'reluctant' sectarians, however, reducing or eliminating current connections may reduce the appeal, or the perceived necessity, of violence. The pattern of the insurgency at its height suggests the importance of substantial community support (Rogers 2006); unradicalised, local supporters are the most susceptible to efforts to shift content or eliminate connections. If the community support for the insurgency can be eroded, the country of Iraq can take a significant step towards peace and stability, as has been illustrated recently by the Sunni Awakening movement.

I close this chapter on a cautiously optimistic note. A recent reduction in violence, combined with Sunni participation in elections in 2009, provides reason for hope (Goodspeed 2009). Keeping the Sunnis invested in their country is one way to thwart providential frames that are based on facilitating civil war. Despite the fact that much progress has been made in Iraq, it is fragile and easily reversible. Although sectarian violence is down, this may be attributable to successful religious 'cleansing' and the fact that the separation of the sects is nearly complete (*Economist* 2009b). In fact, sectarian fears remain a problem; in recent months some members of the Awakening have resisted Iraqi government control and expressed fear that they are being treated unfairly by the Shi'a majority government (Haynes 2007). The process of disbanding the militias is proving difficult and meeting with sectarian suspicion (Chulov 2009), leading some former insurgents to question if it was the right choice to turn away from al-Qaeda in the first place (*Economist* 2009a).

The problem of religious violence in Iraq is a real one, and it can only be understood and resolved by recognising and analysing the real religious roots of the violence. This chapter has been a first step towards identifying the various motivations underlying religious violence in Iraq, with the hope that it will inspire future work on the topic by academics and policymakers alike. This is a problem that deserves more attention; not only because the future of Iraq and US foreign policy is at stake, but also because sectarian divisions in Iraq may spread sectarian conflict across the Muslim world (Ricks 2006). Providential beliefs can help us recognise *how* the nature of Islam, the particular content of the different Muslim sects, and the connections that are made between content and real events, come together to motivate religious violence. This information brings us one step closer to stopping it.

Bibliography

Allport, G.W. 1979. *The Nature of Prejudice*. New York: Basic Books.

Anderson, J.L. 2007. Inside the Surge: The American Military Finds New Allies, But at What Cost?. *The New Yorker* 83 (36).

Aslan, R. 2005. *No God But God: The Origins, Evolution, and Future of Islam*. New York: Random House.

Associated Press 2007. Crackdown on Shia Militia; Joint Force Arrests Militants Suspected of Smuggling Weapons from Iran; Gun Battle, Air Strike Kill Others. *Newsday*, 6 January.

Bergen, P.L. 2006. *The Osama bin Laden I Know: An Oral History of Al Qaeda's Leader*. New York: Free Press.

Bremer, L.P. 2006. *My Year in Iraq: The Struggle to Build a Future of Hope*. New York: Simon and Schuster.

Brym, R.J. 2008. Religion, Politics, and Suicide Bombing: An Interpretive Essay. *Canadian Journal of Sociology* 33 (1).

Burdman, D. 2003. Education, Indoctrination, and Incitement: Palestinian Children on their Way to Martyrdom. *Terrorism and Political Violence* 15 (1), 96–123.

Chulov, M. 2009. Iraq Disbands Militia that Helped Defeat Insurgents; Gamble May Renew Sectarian Tensions. *The Guardian London*, 2 April.

Cleary, M. and Glazier, R. 2007. Contemporary Islamism: Trajectory of a Master Frame. *American Journal of Islamic Social Science* 24 (2).

Cloud, D.S. 2007. Ex-Commander Calls Iraq Effort 'a Nightmare'. *The New York Times*, 13 October.

Cole, J. 2003. The United States and Shi'ite Religious Factions in Post-Ba'thist Iraq. *Middle East Journal* 57 (4).

Colvin, M. 2007. Sunni Sheikhs Turn their Sights from US Forces to Al-Qaeda. *Sunday Times*, 9 September.

Cook, D. 2007. *Martyrdom in Islam*. Cambridge: Cambridge University Press.

Cook, D. and Allison, O. 2007. *Understanding and Addressing Suicide Attacks: The Faith and Politics of Martyrdom Operations*. Westport, CT: Praeger Security International.

Druckman, J.N. 2001. On the Limits of Framing Effects: Who Can Frame?. *Journal of Politics* 63, 1041–66.

Duffy Toft, M. 2008. Why Islam Lies at the Heart of Iraq's Civil War. *Christian Science Monitor*, 2 June.

Economist 2007. I Want to Kill You, But not Today. 6 October.

Economist 2008a. Hearts and Minds. 19 July.

Economist 2008b. How to Win the War within Islam; Al-Qaeda's Global Jihad. 19 July.

Economist 2009a. Bad Blood Again; Iraq's Former Insurgents. 4 April.

Economist 2009b. Still Tread Softly. 28 March.

Foulk, V. L. 2007. *The Battle for Fallujah: Occupation, Resistance and Stalemate in the War in Iraq*. Jefferson, NC: McFarland and Company.

Glazier, R. 2009a. Bringing Religion into International Relations: Providential Beliefs and US Foreign Policy. Dissertation, Political Science Department, University of California Santa Barbara.

Glazier, R. 2009b. Religion and US Foreign Policy: An Experimental Study. Paper to the International Studies Association Annual Conference, New York.

Goodspeed, P. 2009. Secularism Prevails in Crucial Iraq Vote. *National Post*, 4 February.

Gordon, M.R. 2006. US Central Command Charts Sharp Movement of the Civil Conflict in Iraq toward Chaos. *The New York Times*, 1 November.

Hafez, M.M. 2006. Dying to be Martyrs: The Symbolic Dimension of Suicide Terrorism. In A. Pedahzur (ed.) *Root causes of suicide terrorism: the globalization of martyrdom*. London: Routledge.

Hafez, M.M. 2007a. Martyrdom Mythology in Iraq: How Jihadists Frame Suicide Terrorism in Videos and Biographies. *Terrorism and Political Violence* 19 (1), 95–115.

Hafez, M.M. 2007b. *Suicide Bombers in Iraq: The Strategy and Ideology of martyrdom*. Washington, DC: United States Institute of Peace Press.

Haynes, D. 2007. New Attack on Mosque Sparks Wave of Revenge Bombings. *The Times (London)*, 14 June.

Heck, G.W. 2007. *When Worlds Collide: Exploring the Ideological and Political Foundations of the Clash of Civilizations*. Lanham, MD: Rowman and Littlefield.

Hyder, S.A. 2006. *Reliving Karbala*. Oxford: Oxford University Press.

Juergensmeyer, M. 2003. *Terror in the Mind of God: the Global Rise of Religious Violence*. Berkeley: University of California Press.

Little, D. and Swearer, D.K. (eds) 2006. *Religion and Nationalism in Iraq: A Comparative Perspective*. Cambridge, MA: Harvard University Press.

Maples, M.D. 2006. The Current Situation in Iraq and Afghanistan. SAS Committee. Washington, DC.

MIPT 2007. Al-Qaeda Organization in the Land of the Two Rivers. *Terrorism Knowledge Base*. http://www.tkb.org (accessed 8 November 2007).

Moghadam, A. 2007. Mayhem, Myths, and Martyrdom: The Shi'a Conception of Jihad. *Terrorism and Political Violence* 19 (1), 125–43.

Mowle, T. (ed.) 2007. *Hope Is Not a Plan: The War in Iraq from Inside the Green Zone*. Westport, CT: Praeger Security International.

Nakash, Y. 2006. *Reaching for Power: The Shi'a in the Modern Arab World*. Princeton, NJ: Princeton University Press.

Nasr, V. 2004. Regional Implications of Shi'a Revival in Iraq. *The Washington Quarterly* 27 (3), 7–24.

NIC 2007. *Prospects for Iraq's Stability: A Challenging Road Ahead*. Washington DC: National Intelligence Council.

Pedahzur, A. (ed.) 2006. *Root Causes of Suicide Terrorism: The Globalization of Martyrdom*. London: Routledge.

Pinault, D. 1992. *The Shiites: Ritual and Popular Piety in a Muslim Community*. New York: St Martin's Press.

Raghavan, S. 2008. A New Breed Grabs Reins in Anbar: US-backed Sheiks Reshaping Own Areas and, Potentially, the Future of Iraq. *The Washington Post*, 21 October.

Reuter, C. 2004. *My Life is a Weapon: A Modern History of Suicide Bombing*, translated by H. Ragg-Kirkby. Princeton, NJ: Princeton University Press.

Ricks, T.E. 2006. *Fiasco: The American Military Adventure in Iraq*. New York: Penguin Press.

Rogers, P. 2006. *Iraq and the War on Terror: Twelve Months of Insurgency, 2004/2005*. London: I.B. Tauris.

Rubin, A.J. and Cave, D. 2007. In a Force for Iraqi Calm, Seeds of Conflict. *The New York Times*, 23 December.

Rubin, T. 2007. A Powerful Awakening Shakes up Iraqi Politics. *The Philadelphia Inquirer*, 12 December.

Sedgwick, M. 2004. Al Qaeda and the Nature of Religious Terrorism. *Terrorism and Political Violence* 16 (4), 795–814.

Snow, D., Benford, R., Rochford Jr, B. and Worden, S. 1986. Frame Alignment Process, Mircomobilization, and Movement Participation. *American Sociological Review* 51, 464–81.

Tversky, A. and Kahneman, D. 2000. *Choices, Values, and Frames*. Cambridge: Cambridge University Press.

West, B. 2006. The Road to Haditha: How Did the Heroes of Fallujah Come to Kill Civilians in Haditha? *The Atlantic Monthly*, 95–100.

Wright, L. 2008. The Rebellion Within; An Al-Qaeda Mastermind Questions Terrorism. *The New Yorker* 84 (16).

Yehoshua, Y 2006. Reeducation of Extremists in Saudi Arabia. *Inquiry and Analysis Series* 260, 18 January.

Chapter 5
God, War and Iraq

Lee Marsden

In order to justify warfare, kings, despots and politicians have throughout history appealed to divine providence to guide their actions and deliver victory over their enemies. Military chaplains provide support and succour to troops in the field while church leaders host parades and church services to honour the bravery of returning troops after the successful conclusion of campaigns. At the same time a long established Christian tradition of pacifism emphasises divine antipathy to warfare. Both traditions appeal to biblical interpretation and religious tradition in support of their differing interpretations of divine will. This chapter examines the approach of Christian churches to warfare, analysing biblical accounts of warfare, exploring the pacifism of the early church and the emergence of Just War theory. A brief history of the relationship between church and warfare provides a background to consider the Iraq war as a case study. The chapter analyses the differing interpretations of God's will proffered by American Christendom before considering the impact of such interpretations on support for going to war against Iraq, the conduct of the war, and attitudes towards military personnel fighting the war.

War in the Bible

The starting point for any claims about the role of God in warfare made by religious actors must be those scriptures used to justify their interpretations of the divine will. In particular, as this chapter seeks to critically examine the roles of Christian leaders, organisations and their followers in the impulse to war with Iraq, the conduct of the war and the subsequent occupation, biblical understandings provide a starting point to situate the debate within a wider discussion of just war theory. As with all other sacred texts the Bible[1] is the site of contention between literal and liberal interpretation. Opposing viewpoints appeal to their favoured verses, ignoring contradictory verses or differentiating between verses as illustrative or literal, historical or allegorical, contextual or universally applicable. Warfare is a recurring theme from Genesis to Revelation providing subsequent generations

1 All Bible references in this chapter are taken from the International Bible Society (1983), *New International Version Holy Bible*, Colorado Springs: International Bible Society.

of believers with a formidable array of passages to determine the divine will. The New International Version of the Bible records 137 references to war, 426 to killing and 237 to destroying.

According to the Book of Revelation war begins in heaven even before the creation of humanity with a palace coup leading to war between Satan and God. This results in the exile of Satan and one third of the angels, whereupon Satan sets himself on a course to wage war against humanity in revenge (Revelation 12). The story ends with yet another bloody war between Satan and God with the ultimate destination of unbelievers to be the lake of fire (Revelation 17–22). In the intervening period the writers of the Bible portray a capricious and vengeful God revealing himself as a mighty warrior (Zephaniah 3:17). He is credited with destroying his enemies (1 Samuel 15:8), slaying Egypt's firstborn (Exodus 13:15), and insisting on ethnic cleansing and genocide as the inhabitants of the promised land are driven out to make room for the Israelites (Numbers 25, 31; Joshua 8; Esther 9:5). God's commitment to his chosen people is revealed through leading them to destroy their enemies or removing his protection and allowing them to be defeated in war in order to discipline them for disobedience (Ezekiel 9). The Old Testament does, however, also provide glimpses of a more peaceful age when swords will become ploughshares (Isaiah 2:4; Micah 4:3).

These glimpses are reflected in the New Testament portrayal of God as revealed through the earthly ministry of Jesus, as Jewish messiah, Son of God and God incarnate. Jesus exhorts his followers to love their enemies and pray for their persecutors (Matthew 5:44; Luke 6:27, 35) thereby overcoming evil with good (Romans 12:17–21; 1 Peter 3: 8; 1 Thessalonians 5:15, 22). He discourages the use of force even against evildoers and forbids Peter to use force to save him from arrest (Matthew 5:39; 26:52). Jesus describes peacemakers as blessed and children of God (Matthew 5:9) and his disciples urge fellow believers to pursue a lifestyle of peace (Romans 12:18; 14:19; 1 Peter 3:11). Where the Old Testament detailed bloody conflict the New Testament describes spiritual battles waged with prayer rather than human weapons (Ephesians 6:12; 2 Corinthians 10:4). However, echoes of Old Testament warfare continue with Jesus informing his followers: 'Do not suppose that I have come to bring peace to the earth. I did not come to bring peace, but a sword' (Matthew 10:34). Neither was Jesus averse to causing division (Luke 12:51).

Pacifism in the Early Church

The early church was overwhelmingly influenced by a peace rather than a war narrative from the time of Jesus until the conversion of Constantine to Christianity. This coincided with the reversal of the Diocletian persecution and the Edict of Milan in 313, which extended religious toleration to Christians throughout the Roman Empire (Hoekema 1986; Bainton 1960). Early Christians lived with the constant expectation of the imminent return of Christ and as a minority sought to lead peaceable lives with no compulsion or desire to serve in the military. As time went on and the first generation of Christians died out the realisation dawned that there was no guarantee when the second coming would occur. In such uncertainty believers were to consider the world a pilgrimage with the opportunity to resist evil and witness to the hope of Christ and the pacifism highlighted in Isaiah 2:4 as an alternative to the violence all around them (Reichberg et al. 2006: 60–61). As the Church grew in number so conversions began to reflect the socio-economic and political demographics of the time, which included soldiers and bureaucrats within the Roman imperial machinery. From c.170, Reichberg, Syse and Begby and James Turner Johnson suggest that Christians started to become active participants within the armed forces (Reichburg et al. 2006: 61; Johnson 1987).

The appeal of the New Testament and messianic prophecies in the Old Testament to pursue peace rather than warfare were supplemented by the writings of early church leaders including Ignatius of Antioch (c.107), Justin Martyr (c.100–165), Clement of Antioch (c.150–c.210), Tertullian (c.160–c.220), Origen of Alexandria (c.185–c.254 and Lactantius (c.250–c.325). Ronald Musto in his excellent work *The Catholic Peace Tradition* (1986) details the contribution of the founding fathers to the pacifism of the early church. Ignatius of Antioch typified this understanding of the early church that 'nothing is better than peace, by which all war of those in heaven and those on earth is abolished'. Justin Martyr presented a church that preferred to die under persecution for its faith rather than fight back or recant. Clement of Alexandria in his message in *Exhortation to the Gentiles*, *Miscellanies*, and *Christ the Educator* emphasised that Christian believers were only to be armed with the word of God (Musto 1986: 34–8). Tertullian reinforced this message arguing consistently in his many works that the pacifist tradition was an integral part of the Christian life. In Chapter 19 of *On Idolatry* he argued that 'the Lord, by taking away Peter's sword, disarmed every soldier thereafter' and in *On the Crown* he advised military converts to leave the army (Reichberg et al. 2006: 63). Those that remained could do so on the condition that they did not kill anyone (Kurtz 1998). In his later writings too, the sword is anathema to the Christian and they should suffer death rather than kill anyone. Hippolytus (c.160–c.236), who laid down conduct for the church, established the Apostolic Tradition which went further than Tertullian in actually excommunicating Christians who joined the army (Musto 1986: 34–8).

Tertullian's torch was passed on to Origen of Alexandria who led the next generation of Christians in a clear pacifist witness refusing to fight for Rome despite being condemned for not doing so by the Greek intellectual Celsus. In his reply, *Against Celsus*, Origen argues that:

> Christians fight through their prayers to God on behalf of those doing battle in a just cause and on behalf of an emperor who is ruling justly in order that all opposition and hostility toward those who are acting rightly may be eliminated. (Reichberg et al. 2006: 65)

The appeal to the spiritual warfare of Ephesians 6:11 and the ploughshares of Isaiah confirms opposition to any form of violent conduct. In *Homilies on Joshua*, Origen presents the wars of the Old Testament as allegorical rather than literal (Reichberg 2006: 65), an argument used by Christian pacifists ever since. The Church in the latter part of the third century experienced great persecution under Emperor Diocletian before the accession of Constantine and subsequent *Peace of the Church*, reconciling church and empire. The *Peace of the Church* was partly written by Lactantius and reveals that the pacifist tradition was to remain among at least part of the church as it became increasingly entwined with the empire and its wars:

> God prohibits killing … and so it will not be lawful for a just man to serve as a soldier – for justice itself is his military service – not to accuse anyone of capital offence, because it makes no difference whether you kill with a sword or with a word, since killing itself is forbidden. And so … no exceptions ought to be made to the rule that it is always wrong to kill a man, whom God has wished to be a sacrosanct creature. (Musto 1986: 38)

The peace tradition finds renewed expression during the reformation in the form of the Anabaptists and historic peace churches including the Religious Society of Friends, the Brethren and the Mennonites. These not only refused to fight in wars but also called on other Christians to lay down their arms, an historic witness that continues to the present day. Other groupings including the Fellowship of Reconciliation between German and British Christians during the First World War and the Women's International League for Peace based their pacifism on the experience of the early church and reading of the New Testament (Daryl Charles 2005: 55; Kurtz 1998). Stanley Hauerhaus, among other Christian writers, reaffirmed this tradition in the early 1980s with his *The Peaceable Kingdom* (1983) and *Against the Nations* (1985), which asserted that all Christians should be pacifist in keeping with the ethic of Jesus. More recently their claims have been met with claims from Nick Rengger who posits that 'the only fully coherent pacifism is a Christian pacifism' (Rengger 2002).

Just War Tradition

As the church became absorbed into the imperial system the need to defend war and safeguard its own position and expand its membership and influence became more important. Ambrose (c.339–397) legitimates warfare, supporting Constantine but arguing that war must be fought without cruelty (Kurtz 1998; Reichberg et al. 2006: 69). Augustine (354–430) develops a theoretical basis in the *City of God*, *Against Faustus the Manichean*, *On True Religion* and in his letters. He argues that war can be justified in defence of Christianity where war is proclaimed by rightful authority, where there is just cause such as responding to a wrongful attack or injury, and where the intentions are to oppose brutality or domination. Such wars must respect the sanctuary offered by churches. Augustine initially sought to confine the limitations of war to the defence of religion but after Donatist violence, he justified war to spread the Christian message (Reichberg et al. 2006: 85). Thomas Aquinas (c.1225–1274), one of the most influential medieval scholars, further shapes just war thinking in a number of chapters in *Summa Theologiae*, in particular 'On war', 'On peace', and 'Killing in self-defence'. Following on from Augustine he reaffirms the principles of legitimate authority, just cause and right intention. For Aquinas the practicality of warfare excludes the participation of priests and condemns killing the innocent. Rather than regard warfare as a necessary evil of last resort Aquinas seeks to identify offensive warfare as laudable when it seeks to advance the common good. A positive peace is advanced rather than regarding it as simply being an absence of conflict (Reichberg et al. 2006: 187).

Just war tradition was firmly established by Augustine and Aquinas within a Catholic tradition and was used to justify the wars of empire, the Crusades between the eleventh and thirteenth centuries, imperial conquest, Reformation and Counter Reformation. Hugo Grotius (1583–1645) in *On the Law of War and Peace* (1625) and the posthumously published *On the Law of Prize and Booty* (1604–1606) Grotius provides a synthesis on just war thinking, arguing in *On the Law of War and Peace* that from the 'first principles of nature there is nothing which is opposed to war, rather, all points are in its favour' (ch. 2, § 1, point 4). The next point, however, emphasises that right reason overrules the nature of society because it does 'not prohibit all use of force, but only that use of force which is repugnant to society' (Reichberg et al. 2006: 394). Grotius and his predecessors incorporate aspects of *jus ad bellum* and *jus in bello* delineating the right circumstance in which states may go to war and the right conduct during warfare. More recently the US Conference of Catholic Bishops in 1983 and 1993 re-examined just war principles rejecting Aquinas' defence of offensive warfare.

In *The Challenge of Peace: God's Promise and Our Response* (US National Conference of Catholic Bishops 1983) the Catholic Bishops set out their understanding of church teaching based on five key principles:

1. Catholic presumption against war and for the peaceful settlement of disputes with some exceptions;
2. the right of self defence against unjust aggression;
3. that offensive war of any kind is morally unjustifiable;
4. the intentional killing of innocent civilians and non-combatants is always wrong;
5. war must be within limits of proportionality.

With the background of nuclear weapons to focus their attention the Bishops argued that to be justified there must be just cause such as confronting a real danger, to protect lives or secure basic human rights. War must be declared by a 'competent authority' for the common good, such an authority will usually be a legitimate government and although revolutionary warfare is not ruled out, the same tests must apply. Any move to war must weigh the issue of comparative justice, in other words: 'Do the rights and values involved justify killing?' The principle of right intention must proceed from the just cause. War must be a last resort after all peaceful alternatives have been pursued and exhausted, and the Bishops re-emphasised Pope Paul VI's wish for the United Nations (UN) to be used more to establish world order. There must be a probability of success even though this is difficult to establish. Warfare must be bound by the principle of proportionality, measuring the good that can be achieved against the harm that would remain if no action was taken. This must take into account the interdependency of the world and the corresponding effect on other nations. The Bishops also emphasised that conduct during warfare must take account of the issues of proportionality and discrimination, a particular problem regarding nuclear, biological and chemical weapons (US National Conference of Catholic Bishops 1983).

On the tenth anniversary of the conference the US Catholic Bishops revisited *The Challenge of Peace*. The later conference re-emphasised the presumption against the use of force and redefined some of the statements on *jus ad bellum*. The order of the seven principles was slightly altered but still included: just cause, comparative justice, legitimate authority, right intention, and probability of success, proportionality and last resort. In *The Harvest of Justice is Sown in Peace* (1993), the Bishops insisted that 'to override the presumption against the use of force the injustice suffered by one party must significantly outweigh that suffered by the other' and no longer are revolutionaries afforded the same legitimacy as 'duly constituted public authorities' who alone may use deadly force.

The Bishops confirmed that *jus in bello* is subject to taking into account non-combatant immunity, proportionality and right intention. The overwhelming emphasis is that civilians and non-combatants must not be subject to direct attack and that indiscriminate and vengeful attacks are not permissible (US National Conference of Catholic Bishops 1993). Michael Walzer in his seminal text *Just and Unjust Wars* (1977) also makes the case effectively for non-combatant immunity.

Late twentieth century and early twenty-first century discussion in the West at least, around warfare are bounded by differing interpretations of just war. The pacifist stream within Christianity has been marginalised and overwhelmed by a plethora of comment from just war theorists both within and without a religious tradition. Modern debate focussed on the legitimacy of waging warfare in the nuclear age with particular attention paid to specific engagements such as the Vietnam War in which writers such as Paul Ramsey sought to present war that had a clear political objective as being a moral activity (Ramsey 2002). Ramsey argued that just war theorists had the same presumption against violence as pacifists, except of course that those presumptions did not preclude the resort to war (Ramsey 1988). Since the end of the Cold War the impulse to intervene militarily in other nations on humanitarian grounds or in order to promote democracy has increased interest in just war theory. According to leading just war theorist James Turner Johnson contemporary just war theory focuses on defence rather than justice, unlike in the classical tradition where the sovereign's responsibility was to maintain justice. Johnson argues that in the light of international law and its emphasis on justice there is a need to rethink the contemporary discourse (Johnson 2008). The Iraq War provided politicians and religious bodies the opportunity to do just this.

The Iraq War

Following an easy initial victory in Afghanistan in 2001, neo-conservatives and the Christian Right saw an opportunity to link the war on terror to unfinished business in Iraq. President Bush was certainly amenable to such encouragement and although his father's advisors had cautioned against invading Iraq because of the danger of the country disintegrating and increasing the influence of Iran, Turkey and Syria the risks were far outweighed by the prospects of projecting American power in the region. A successful invasion could result in establishing permanent bases, controlling oil resources, removing a human rights-abusing dictator who had defied US hegemony and establishing a free market democracy. Added to the mix was the defiance and lack of cooperation shown by Saddam Hussein to the UN in its fruitless search for the weapons of mass destruction that American and British intelligence insisted must be there. For the neo-conservatives, Iraq represented a wonderful opportunity to send a message to Iran, Syria, North Korea and other states they did not approve of that pre-emption was the new *modus operandi* and that they had better reform or they would be next. For the Christian Right, Saddam Hussein's missile attacks on Israel during the first Gulf War and his support for Palestinian resistance groups and suicide bombers made Iraq an obvious next target. George Bush himself had a personal score to settle because of a failed assassination attempt by Iraqis on his father. For Vice President Dick Cheney and the corporate backers of the Republican Party, Iraq represented a wonderful opportunity to open up the oil industry to US companies, boost the arms industry and award lucrative reconstruction contracts to supporters. *Jus ad bellum*.

The one problem was the lack of legitimate reasons to go to war with Iraq. The regime was being contained, US/UK control of a no-fly zone over Iraq and selective strikes against air defences and military targets over the previous ten years had rendered Iraqi defences ineffective, and UN inspectors were being given access, albeit reluctantly, to Iraqi weapons and chemical facilities. In the effort to justify invading Iraq and the overthrow of the regime, the Bush administration sought any scrap of information that would confirm their hypothesis that Iraq had weapons of mass destruction and was prepared to use them against other countries including Israel. If Saddam Hussein's regime did not use such weapons itself then there was the possibility that it would pass them on to terrorists who would attack America or its allies. Using information from Iraqi defectors anxious to impress their new benefactors, and from intelligence services eager to deliver what their employers were looking for, misinformation was accumulated and distributed via 'dodgy dossiers' and UN briefings. It was a clear attempt to abrogate international law, which rules out regime change. In the process the Bush administration, with the loyal assistance of the British government, succeeded in misleading sufficient numbers of their electorates and foreign governments into believing that Iraq had weapons of mass destruction, to garner support for an invasion.

In reality, the decision to attack Iraq had been made in the weeks following 11 September and by 21 November 2001, Bush had instructed Donald Rumsfeld to start planning for war with Iraq (Woodward 2003, 2004; Clarke 2004). The driving force propelling America to war with Iraq was Vice-President Cheney and a cabal of neo-conservatives within the administration. As the commitment to regime change in Iraq became more public, key figures within the Christian community were eager to provide theological justifications for and against the war to discern divine will and to inform fellow believers and secular audiences whether this was a just or unjust war. On 13 January 2003 Pope John Paul II addressed the diplomatic corps declaring '"*NO TO WAR*"! War is not always inevitable. It is always a defeat for humanity' (John Paul 2003). The pontiff set his objection to war in the context of just war theory's insistence on last resort:

> War is never just another means that one can choose to employ for settling differences between nations. As the Charter of the United Nations Organization and international law itself remind us, war cannot be decided upon, even when it is a matter of ensuring the common good, except as the very last option and in accordance with very strict conditions, without ignoring the consequences for the civilian population both during and after the military operations. (John Paul II, 2003)

The Pope was not the only Christian leader commenting on the imminent prospect of war. In a report by Religion News Service on 19 March 2003 a further twenty four statements from churches were compiled. All but two of the statements opposed the war and the majority urged peaceful methods to resolve the conflict. Interestingly ten of the statements referred explicitly or implicitly to just war theory, nine urging President Bush to halt the rush to war. Presiding Bishop Frank Griswold of the Episcopal Church urged Bush to 'exhaust all diplomatic and multilateral initiatives as the alternatives to waging war" and to "act only in concert with the United Nations Security Council.' The Lutheran World Federation's executive committee condemned the Bush administration for seeking war without Security Council approval stating that 'the "just war" criteria … were designed to constrain – not justify – the resort to war. Indeed, they stand in clear opposition to a preemptive war for the purpose of "regime change"'. The board of elders of the Metropolitan Communities Churches appealed to principles of just cause, comparative justice and right intention when arguing that 'war will only increase unrest and suffering in the world, deepen the distrust that already divides America and Britain from Iraq and its allies, and divert international attention … from world poverty, a rapidly deteriorating ecological structure and oppression of too many of the world's peoples' (RNS 2003).

The United States Conference of Catholic Bishops spoke out against war in a 'Statement on Iraq' on 13 November 2002. The Bishops were troubled over the unilateralist approach adopted and the argument for pre-emptive or preventive use of force. While any connection between Saddam Hussein and Al Qaeda would activate the self-defence justification for just war, they doubted whether this was the case. The justification for humanitarian intervention would be valid if it had not already occurred in the Kurdish area of Iraq. The Bishops made the point that arguments on the grounds of material breaches of ceasefire resolutions need to differentiate between 'efforts to change unacceptable behavior of [Iraq] and efforts to end that government's existence'. If force was to be used then, along with the Vatican, they proposed that the UN alone represented legitimate authority for the use of force, taking into account the outcome for the Iraqi people and their regional neighbours. The Bishops also expressed concern about proportionality and the probability of success, given previous experience of the unintended consequences of military action. The prospects for peace and stability in the Middle East and for the civilian population in particular following military intervention were poor (US Conference of Catholic Bishops, Statement on Iraq, 13 November 2002).

By way of contrast there was also considerable support among the Christian Right in America for military action. Richard Land, President of The Ethics and Religious Liberty Commission of the Southern Baptist Convention wrote a letter dated 3 October 2002 stating that a pre-emptive military strike on Iraq would be legitimate under just war theory. The letter was co-signed by other leading members of the Christian Right (Anderson 2002). Land stated that Hussein's pursuit and development of weapons of mass destruction fell within the just war tradition:

> In just war theory only defensive war is defensible; and if military force is used against Saddam Hussein it will be because he has attacked his neighbors, used weapons of mass destruction against his own people, and harbored terrorists from the Al Qaeda terrorist network that attacked our nation so viciously and violently on September 11, 2001. (Land, 2006)

Secondly, Land argued that there was just intent to support 'political and economic liberty in a unified Iraq'. Thirdly, the last resort stipulation of just war was met for Land by Hussein's defiance of UN Security Council resolutions since the end of the first Gulf War. For Land it was the US government rather than the UN that represented the legitimate authority as American citizens, even though Bush was praised for trying the UN first. Fifthly, the principle of limited goals and reasonable expectation of success were met for the Christian Right leaders by the stated goals of removing weapons of mass destruction and 'liberating' the Iraqi people. Land was confident that the US military would not target non-combatants and the civilian population. Finally, the letter argued for immediate action rather than later so that less human lives would be lost and as far as Land was concerned, this dealt with the issue of proportionality. Land and his fellow leaders of the

Christian Right urged the president to take action confident that they had the support of their constituency.

As we have seen this advice was contradicted by almost every other religious leader in the United States and more importantly, for the 25 per cent of the US population who are Catholic, by Pope John Paul II who declared that 'war is never just another means that one can choose to employ for settling differences between nations' (John Paul II 2003). Bush refused to see a delegation from leading ministers from mainstream denominations, including his own United Methodists, opposing the war (Wallis 2005: 133). Land, Robertson, Falwell and other leading members of the Christian Right played an important role in reducing the impact of the Pope's and traditional churches opposition to the war, enabling Bush to claim to be on the right side of a Manichean struggle between the forces of good and evil. Although not a member of the Christian Right, James Turner Johnson nonetheless provided academic endorsement for their position arguing that: 'The traditional just war idea of just cause allows the use of force to punish evil, and this surely applied in the case of Saddam Hussein and his regime' (Johnson 2005: 63).

Christian Right backing for the Iraq war and linkage with the war on terror was loud and consistent enough for Bush's core constituency in the conservative evangelical churches to embrace conflict enthusiastically. In March 2003 on CNN's *Larry King Live*, John MacArthur of the Grace Community Church, Sun Valley, California was one of four clergymen discussing 'What would Jesus do about war with Iraq?' MacArthur's position was the default position for the Christian Right. War with Iraq was justified and would be approved of by Jesus. Taking Bible passages out of context, MacArthur claimed Jesus' approval for war in Luke 14:31 and Luke 22:36. Although he specifically stated that the war was not a Christian war he emphasised that Bush was a Christian president and that Saddam Hussein prayed to the wrong God, that Muslim beliefs were wrong and that they would be condemned to an eternal hell with eternal punishment. For MacArthur there was no issue of legitimacy since the war against Iraq started with Saddam Hussein's nonexistent involvement in the events of 11 September.[2]

Jus in Bello

Throughout the build up to war with Iraq and in the following years of the Bush administration it was the Christian Right's leadership and conservative evangelicals sitting in church or in front of Christian television that were the most vociferous and enthusiastic supporters of the war. Support was strengthened by calls to see the conflict in spiritual terms of a battle between good and evil. As in life, where believers are exhorted to wage a constant and vigilant battle against the forces of evil, so the war on terror (and Iraq) was going to be long and difficult. Whenever support for the war was strained the president and his speech writers

2 CNN *Larry King Live*, What would Jesus do about war with Iraq?, broadcast at 9 pm EST on 11 March 2003.

were able to rely on language that would resonate with supporters and stiffen resolve. A president who did not seek advice from his father, Bush Senior, but rather appealed to a 'higher father' was a president conservative evangelicals could call their own (Woodward 2004: 421). A president who could tell, then Palestinian Prime Minister Mahmoud Abbas that 'God told me to strike at al-Qaeda and I struck them, and then he instructed me to strike at Saddam, which I did, and now I am determined to solve the problem in the Middle East', was speaking in terms the Christian Right related to and could appreciate.[3]

The just war tradition relies on far more than claims from President Bush to have heard God's voice on Iraq. In actual combat, war needs to be conducted in the right manner providing non-combatants immunity from the conflict. Despite Land's confidence this seems to have been misplaced in Iraq and at year end 2008 civilian deaths in the conflict according to the *Iraq Body Count* were recorded at just fewer than 100,000.[4] There have been some democratic gains but for those who have lost loved ones and live in fear for their safety can these justify the harm caused? The misrepresentation of the case on the issue of weapons of mass destruction and association with Al Qaeda challenges even the most supportive just war theorists to legitimate the conflict. Once the lack of evidence and human costs of the war became apparent support for the war ebbed in America apart from among the Christian Right.

Regular visitor to the White House and a leading advocate for war, Richard Land considers that Bush's policies resonate with conservative evangelicals. For Land, and the Southern Baptists he represents, the only answer to 'Islamic jihadism' is modernity and representative governments. Evangelicals appreciate that democracy and religious freedom provide the best opportunity to spread the Christian message, including the right to change faiths.[5] The conservative evangelical experience in leading US opposition to human rights abuses in Sudan and the fight to achieve the International Religious Freedom Act gave the Christian Right considerable influence in ensuring that religious freedom was included within the post-Saddam Iraqi constitution. Religious freedom is evangelical shorthand for being able to evangelise within ostensibly Muslim countries and the military conflict encouraged a rush of missionary activity and training to witness to, and share their faith with Muslims in Iraq.

The urge to promote democracy and evangelise in Iraq has parallels with the crusades, a comparison Bush has been eager to avoid. Tertullian, Origen, Clement and Lactantius had steered the early church away from promoting Christianity with the sword but contemporary just war apologists in the Christian Right enthusiastically embraced the opportunity. Glenn Miller, interviewed on the *700 Club* said that the war in Iraq had nothing to do with oil but rather was concerned

3 Road Map is a Life Saver for us: PM Abbas tells Ha'aretz, 26 June 2003, as cited in Esther Kaplan's *With God on their Side* (2005: 9).

4 Iraq Body Count, http://www.iraqbodycount.org/, accessed 14 December 2008.

5 Richard Land, interview with the author 19 July 2007, Washington DC.

about Jehovah God breaking the 'power of deception' exercised by the 'false God Allah' over 1.2 billion Muslims.[6] The military battle was also being fought in the spiritual realm and represented an opportunity to share 'the good news of salvation'. A plethora of evangelistic organisations either sprang up or were revitalised by war in the Middle East determined to harvest for souls in the 10/40 window (the area of North Africa, the Middle East and Asia 10 degrees to forty degrees north). Esther Kaplan records that the Southern Baptist Convention had one thousand missionaries in the 10/40 window and were distributing food boxes with John 1:17 in Arabic stating that 'the law indeed was given through Moses; grace and truth come through Jesus Christ'. According to her research Samaritan's Purse allocated $194 million to send missionaries to Iraq and In Touch Ministries, Atlanta circulated a pamphlet entitled 'A Christian's Duty' to thousands of US troops in Iraq (Kaplan 2005: 14–16).

By 2004 the *Los Angeles Times* reported that there were 30 evangelistic missions operating in Iraq.[7] After three years of conflict in Iraq, despite the resources that had been provided to faith-based organisations their attempts to convert Muslims to Christianity proved futile and half the indigenous Iraqi Christian population have fled the country. Christian proselytisers are unable to operate as a result of the Iraqi resistance who have targeted Iraqi Christians and their churches.[8] The identification of Christianity with the occupation by coalition forces has been strengthened by presidential language that only just stops short of describing US actions as a crusade. In George Bush's notorious 'Mission Accomplished' speech, aboard the *USS Lincoln*, 1 May 2003, he told troops that they 'carry a message of hope – a message that is ancient and ever new. In the words of the prophet Isaiah: 'To the captives, come out, and to those in darkness, be free'.

The appointment of General Jerry Boykin as Deputy Under Secretary of Defense for Intelligence, in charge of the hunt for Mullah Omar, Bin Laden and Saddam Hussein, is reflective of the extent to which conservative evangelicals are involved at the highest levels in the US military. In a series of in-uniform speeches and sermons at churches in 2002 and 2003 the general recounted his earlier service in Somalia in 1993. He described a dark mark on a photograph he took of Mogadishu from an army helicopter as being a demonic presence, which God had revealed to him as the real enemy in Somalia. He recalled one of Aidid's lieutenants saying on CNN that the Americans could not get him because Allah would protect him. Boykin pointed out that he knew 'that my God was bigger than his. I knew that my God was real and his was an idol'. He also told a congregation in Oregon that faith in God caused special operations forces in Iraq to be successful and warned the congregation that 'Satan wants to destroy this nation, he wants to destroy us as a nation, and he wants to destroy us as a Christian

---

6 http://www.gnn.tv/headlines/2725/Stations_of_the_Cross_The_Emergence_of_Faith_Based_news, accessed 4 March 2006.

7 US Christian Missions in the Middle East, *Los Angles Times,* 18 March 2004.

8 In 20 years, there will be no more Christians in Iraq, *The Guardian*, 6 October 2006.

army'. In answering the question, 'Why do they hate us?' Boykin told churchgoers in Sandy, Oregon in June 2003 that it was because they are a Christian nation. 'We are hated because we are a nation of believers. Our spiritual enemy will only be defeated if we come against them in the name of Jesus' (Arkin 2003; Rennie 2003). Boykin came under intense criticism from politicians and the media. Bush refused to criticise the general's comments but Boykin was shortly afterwards transferred from his sensitive post.

Jerry Boykin reflects a growing assertiveness of conservative evangelicals in the military. Buoyed by the Bush presidency born again Christians are actively evangelising within the Pentagon and occupying senior positions. A video produced in 2006 by the Christian Embassy, a conservative evangelical targeted towards converting and sustaining diplomats, government leaders, and military officers, demonstrates the extent of Christian Right influence in the Pentagon. The video showed interviews conducted inside the Pentagon with interviews with senior officials and high-ranking officers in uniform. The Embassy organises bible studies attended by some forty generals, discipleship groups, prayer breakfasts and outreach events. The Flag Officer Fellowship provides an opportunity for fellow Christians to meet and be seen by fellow officers. The video has interviews with four generals and two colonels based in the Pentagon. Major-General Jack Catton shares his faith with fellow officers and believes this is making 'a huge impact because you have many men and women who are seeking God's council and wisdom as we advise the Chairman and the Secretary of Defence, Hallelujah!'[9]

The influence of the Christian Right also extends to the battlefields of Iraq. Over the past few years conservative evangelicals have taken over fifty percent of the military chaplaincy posts, an integral part of the US military, which is a ripe recruiting ground as bullets and missiles fly. One Southern Baptist chaplain at Najaf even offered soldiers the chance to swim in the swimming pool, if they were willing to convert and be baptised. Soldiers receive DVDs of their home church services, attend church services, prayer meetings and bible classes (Hedges 2007; Layklin 2003; Beaumont 2007). This is neither surprising nor necessarily wrong but it does reflect a US military made up disproportionately of conservative evangelicals who see themselves as being a Christian army. The combination of intense patriotism, American exceptionalism and born again Christianity is hardly conducive to cultural sensitivity and respect for faiths they are taught to regard as inferior, false or satanic.

The shortfall in recruitment from mainstream Christian churches to serve as military chaplains, caused by falling numbers entering the priesthood and

---

9 A copy of the video was posted on YouTube, http://www.youtube.com/watch?v=uT2BE5RS01E&eurl=, accessed 21 December 2006, the video keeps being taken down and resubmitted. Information is also available from Questionable Mission: A Christian Embassy campaign at the Pentagon test constitutional boundaries, *The Washington Post*, 6 January 2007. See also Chris Hedges, America's Holy Warriors, http://alternet.org/story/46211/, accessed 16 February 2007.

opposition to the Iraq war, has created an opportunity for Christian Right churches to dominate the chaplaincy. The agenda is clear to use the opportunities provided by war to evangelise within the military and beyond to those of different faiths in the combat zones (Goodstein 2005; Lampman 2007a, 2007b).

Traditionally, volunteer recruitment to the military comes disproportionately from the southern and western states where there are a higher proportion of evangelicals. In these areas of America support for the war by conservative evangelical pastors and congregations encourages recruitment and retention. Christian Right leaders have remained unwavering in their support for the conflict. In 2004 Jerry Falwell considered the Iraq war a 'worthy pursuit' and reminded believers that:

> Many present-day pacifists hold Jesus as their example for unvarying peace. But they ignore the full revelation concerning Jesus pictured in the book of Revelation 19, where He is depicted bearing a 'sharp sword' and smiting nations, ruling them with 'a rod of iron'. (Falwell 2004)

Two years later Richard Land was asked to reconsider his support for the Iraq war, which he was pleased to do reaffirming just war principles (Land 2006). Similarly a poll conducted among one hundred evangelical church leaders representing sixty denominations in February 2008 reflected a desire to 'stay the course' in Iraq 'until the job is done'. Most leaders supported the Just War theory and one unnamed leader explained that: 'Iraq represents the existential threat we have from global Islamic Jihadists. We must defeat it in Iraq, Afghanistan and then act preemptively to destroy it where ever it emerges' (NAE 2008). The enthusiasm to justify war by the Christian Right, despite the Republican defeat in the 2008 elections, appears undiminished approaching the seventh year of conflict in Iraq and the increase in US troop presence in Afghanistan.

Conclusion

The just war tradition largely formulated by Augustine, Aquinas and Grotius has dominated Christian thinking on warfare since Constantine converted together with much of the Roman empire early in the fourth century. The noble peace tradition promulgated by the early church disappeared amidst the *realpolitik* of church-empire relations as the church fathers and medieval followers abandoned pacifism for a church militant prepared to fight for faith and country to propagate Christianity and support state rulers. The twentieth century and early twenty-first century refocused attention on the principles of just war in contemplating warfare in an age of total war, age of nuclear weapons and humanitarian intervention in the post-Cold War era. The events of 11 September 2001 and subsequent attacks on Afghanistan and Iraq have again moved the debate forward to consider the justifications for pre-emption and preventive warfare. Christians, including leaders of the Christian Right and academics, have abandoned pacifist alternatives to warfare and sought to stretch the just war tradition to breaking point in justifying an Iraq War that was without just cause, comparative justice, legitimate authority, right intention, proportionality, last resort or immunity for non-combatants.

The refusal to contemplate warfare in order to convert unbelievers adopted by the early church fathers was usurped during the latter period of the Roman Empire, continued throughout the crusades, imperial adventures, Reformation and Counter-Reformation, great wars, and today is adopted in Iraq. The invasion of Iraq in the name of humanitarian intervention, weapons of mass destruction and democracy promotion has been a twenty-first century crusade, which the Christian Right effectively exploited as their members came to dominate the US military chaplaincy and higher echelons of the armed services. The war was undertaken in spite of overwhelming opposition from mainstream churches, citing just war and pacifist objections from the traditional peace churches. The New Testament readings of Jesus and church as peacemaker has given way to the Christian Right's version of muscular Christianity with the Jesus of Revelation and the warrior God of the Old Testament, as spiritual battles become physical and American troops become the advance guard in efforts to convert Muslims to Christ. In such an era, Just War is in the eye of the beholder, while pacifist alternatives are condemned to the pages of history.

Bibliography

Anderson, D. 2002. Conservative Protestant Leaders Back Bush on Iraq. *Religion News Service*. Online. Available at: http://pewforum.org/news/display.phpNews ID=1600 (accessed 6 August 2007).

Arkin, W. 2003. The Pentagon Unleashes a Holy Warrior. *Los Angeles Times*, 16 October.

Bainton, R. 1960. *Christian Attitudes Towards War and Peace*. New York: Abingdon Press.

Beaumont, P. 2007. Providing a Place of Sanctuary and Solace for the Faithful on the Frontline. *The Guardian*, 21 February.

Clarke, R. 2004. *Against All Enemies*. London: Free Press.

Daryl Charles, J. 2005. *Between Pacifism and Jihad*. Downers Grove, IL: InterVarsity Press.

Falwell, J. 2004. God is Pro-War. *WorldNetDaily.com*. Online 31 January. Available at: http://www.worldnetdaily.com/index.php?pageId=23022 (accessed 9 December 2008).

Goodstein, L. 2005. Evangelicals Are a Growing Force in the Military Chaplain Corps. *New York Times*, 12 July.

Hauerhaus, S. 1983. *The Peaceable Kingdom*. Notre Dame, IN: University of Notre Dame Press.

Hauerhaus, S. 1985. *Against the Nations*. Minneapolis: Winston Press.

Hedges, C. 2007. America's Holy Warriors. *Truthdig*. Online. Available at: http://alternet.org/story/46211 (accessed 16 February 2007).

Hoekema, D. 1986. A Practical Christian Pacifism. *Christian Century*, 22 October, 917–19.

John Paul II. 2003. Address of his Holiness Pope John Paul II to the Diplomatic Corps, 13 January. Online. Available at: http://www.vatican.va/holy_father/john_paul_ii/speeches/2003/january/documents/hf (accessed 28 July 2007).

Johnson, J.T. 1987. *The Quest for Peace*. Princeton, NJ: Princeton University Press.

Johnson, J.T. 2005. *The War to Oust Saddam Hussein: Just War and the New Face of Conflict*. Lanham, MD: Rowman and Littlefield.

Johnson, J. 2008. The Idea of Defense in Historical and Contemporary Thinking About Just War. *Journal of Religious Ethics* 36 (4), December, 543–56.

Kaplan, E. 2005. *With God on their Side*. New York/London: The New Press.

Kurtz, L. 1998. *Encyclopedia of Politics and Religion*, 2 vols, ed. R. Wuthnow. Washington, DC: Congressional Quarterly, Inc., 783–9.

Lampman, J. 2007a. US Army Looking for a Few Good Chaplains. *The Christian Science Monitor*, 12 April.

Lampman, J. 2007b. Building God's (Christian) Army. *The Christian Science Monitor*, 19 October.

Land, R. 2006. A Christian Defense of the War in Iraq. Beliefnet.com. Online. Available at: http://www.beliefnet.com/News/2006/03/A-Christian-Defense-Of-The-War-In-Iraq.aspx (accessed 9 December 2008).

Layklin, M. 2003. Water Shortage Works to Chaplain's Advantage. *Miami Herald*, 7 April.

Musto, R. 1986. *The Catholic Peace Tradition*. Maryknoll, NY: Orbis Books.

NAE. 2008. Evangelical Leaders Survey, *National Association of Evangelicals*. Online February. Available at: http://www.nae.net/index.cfm?FUSEACTION=editor.page&pageID=509&idCategory=1 (accessed 9 December 2008).

Ramsey, P. 1988. *Speak Up for Just War or Pacifism*. University Park: Pennsylvanian State University Press.

Ramsey, P. 2002. *The Just War: Force and Political Responsibility*. Lanham, MD: Roman and Littlefield.

Reichberg, G., Syse, H. and Begby, E. (eds) 2006. *The Ethics of War: Classic and Contemporary Readings*. Malden, MA: Blackwell.

Rengger, N. 2002. On the Just War Tradition in the Twenty-first Century. *International Affairs* 78 (2), 353–63.

Rennie, D. 2003. God put Bush in Charge, Says the General Hunting bin Laden. *The Daily Telegraph*, 17 October.

RNS. 2003. *Religious Groups Issue Statements on War with Iraq*, 19 March, *Religion News Service*. Online. Available at: http://pewforum.org/docs/index.php?DocID=21 (accessed 13 December).

US National Conference of Catholic Bishops of Catholic Bishops. 1983. *The Challenge of Peace: God's Promise and Our Response*. Washington DC: Office of Publishing Services, United States Catholic Conference.
US National Conference of Catholic Bishops of Catholic Bishops. 1993. *The Harvest of Justice is Sown in Peace.* Online. Available at: http://www.usccb.org/sdwp/harvest.shtml (accessed 13 December 2008).
Wallis, J. 2005. *God's Politics: Why the American Right Gets it Wrong and the Left Doesn't Get It*. Oxford: Lion Hudson.
Walzer, M. 1977. *Just and Unjust Wars*, 4th edn. New York: Basic Books.
Woodward, B. 2003. *Bush at War*. London: Simon and Schuster.
Woodward, B. 2004. *Plan of Attack*. London: Simon and Schuster.

Chapter 6
Trust Me! Jesus Would Go to War Too

Sandy Mergenschroer-Livingston

Sorting out the Questions, Actors and Agendas

In the previous chapter, Lee Marsden explicated the modern biblical justifications and arguments that support just war theory, which in turn has been distilled down to the religiously oriented masses in order to promote aggressive US foreign policy agendas. This chapter follows with an exploration of how these justifications and arguments have come to be ferociously supported by a particular arm of the Religious Right Movement, the Southern Baptist Convention. Thus, an investigation of how this protestant denomination transformed from a pacifist oriented organisation to a collection of revenge seeking supporters of aggressive military action is ascertained.

The question that persistently importunes this chapter is who created and maintains the religious identity that continues to appear in American policy rhetoric. Is it the voice of the religious or is it the voice of policymakers, and does American foreign policy eventually lead the Southern Baptist Convention (SBC) in how it interprets theological imperatives and the role of religion? This chapter demonstrates the political relationship between the SBC, via the Religious Right, and the Republican National Convention (RNC) as less of a progressive political coup by religion and more a use of theo-political constructs that shape discourse, binaries, hegemony and identities in order to promote support for party and state agendas. Important eschatological terms used in Religious Right political discourse are examined, leading to a brief glimpse at SBC history. This includes information on foreign policy support up to the 1970s, Republican political actors and agendas, the designation and formation of the Moral Majority and the fundamentalist take over of the SBC. Finally, SBC shifts in theological imperatives based on eschatological interpretations that support aggressive US foreign policies are discussed.

In the last half of the twentieth century, Southern Baptists have exerted a great deal of political influence. It is the largest Protestant denomination in America, and was instrumental in developing a number of the largest lobbying groups in Washington DC. Some of modern history's most politically powerful and influential people have been Southern Baptists, including Harry Truman, Jimmy Carter, William (Bill) Clinton, Al Gore, Newt Gingrich,[1] Tom Delay, Trent Lott,

1 Newt Gingrich recently converted to Catholicism.

Bill Moyers, Billy Graham, Jerry Falwell and Pat Robertson. Unfortunately, there has been a lack of serious research on the denomination and its involvement in politics. Therefore, this chapter attempts to illuminate how Southern Baptists have utilised their politically contentious heritage to transform political alliances and religious rhetoric via cultural hegemony, binary systems and discourse formation.

For many, the issue of religion in politics has been a somewhat shallow pool. Researchers simply seem to accept current religious engagement in politics without questioning how or when the modern religious viewpoint was formulated. An article by Josef Braml, *The Religious Right and US Middle East Policy* (2008), displays just how policies are directly affected by religious right interest groups. However, he neglects to pursue the question of how these religious organisations developed stances on issues of foreign policy in the first place. Another example is *The New Christian Right* (1983) by Robert Liebman and Robert Wuthnow. These researchers explore the development of Religious Right influence, but they neglect to look underneath the meticulously organised façade to discover how agendas are generated. One of the foremost researchers on Southern Baptists is Nancy Ammerman, *in Baptist Battles: Social Change and Religious Conflict in the Southern Baptist Convention* (1995), explores the ideological and theological war that broke out within the SBC during the 1980s but does not provide an adequate political summation of why this battle was engaged. Therefore, the mission of this chapter is to delve into the origins of religious agendas on US policies and demonstrate how re-interpreted SBC history and religious beliefs as well as restructured theological debates and imperatives are used to buttress religious constructions of foreign policy.

Understanding Theo-political Discourse of the SBC

In order to comprehend the brevity of religious identity and discourse constructs, one must understand etymological interpretations of today's political situations. The language framing how religious constituents interpret international situations is born out of theological insights expounded by Church Fathers or directly from the Bible which are then elucidated by today's SBC clergy who applies the information to current and future scenarios, sometimes even providing past and current examples. This chapter explores SBC religious identity and discourse in disseminating foreign policy agendas to its members. Thus, the following terms must be appreciated when identifying the seemingly ubiquitous nature of religion in the aggressive foreign policy context of Southern Baptists.[2] It is important to

2 Since the standard texts for Systematic Theology courses at Southern Baptist Seminaries are *The Evangelical Dictionary of Theology* edited by Walter Elwell, *Systematic Theology: An Introduction to Biblical Doctrine* by Wayne Grudem, and *Systematic Theology: Church/Last Things* by Norman Geisler, the following terms are defined based on the interpretations and usages provided within these texts in the construction of SBC

keep in mind that explanations of the following concepts are based on SBC usages of the terms; therefore, some continuity issues arise but further demonstrate the use of theology to justify political agendas.

Eschatology, or 'The End Times', resurged after World War II in Southern Baptist circles. This is the branch of theology concerned with events that bring about the end of the world and includes several fundamentals which are discussed below. Southern Baptists operate within the context that the Earth has a predetermined number of years for existence and that Christ will return to signal its end. Consequently, theological inquiry and layman fascination with the philosophy, history and interpretations of *eschatology* has caused it to become important elements of Sunday worship, Sunday morning and evening teaching sessions, weekly bible studies, news articles and word games; and *End Times* theology has been used to emphasise the limited time Earth has to exist, the limited capabilities of humanity to change the world, the limited time Christians have to evangelise people around them and the completion of God's creation.

Premillennialism is the belief that Christ will return to establish His literal Kingdom for 1000 years once the *tribulation* and *rapture* have occurred. The important factor in this theory is the nation and state of Israel. Jerusalem is also important because of its ties with the Abraham's Covenant and King David, who established Jerusalem for God. Accordingly, the city and state of Israel are integral to fulfilling the covenant promising Abraham's descendants dominion over Israel forever. Because Jews prevented Christ from establishing His Kingdom 2,000 years ago, He created the Church as a substitute; and all promises and prophesies surrounding Abraham and David applies to the Church. Another important aspect of *Premillennialism* is that it requires global wars and chaos, genocide, environmental and ecological destruction, and unbridled famine and poverty. Hence, the resurgence of *Premillennial* theological debates in clerical training has shifted the perception of war from that of pacifism to that of justifiable force, which has nurtured a revenge mindset amongst believers (Connolly 2005). This has allowed SBC leaders such as Richard Land to bucolically construct discourse based on a judicious acceptance of aggressive American military action (ERLC 2002).

Dispensationalism is the division of human history into seven dispensations.[3] Never a fashionable way of interpreting eschatology due to its complex views, it gained popularity after World War II when the nation-state of Israel was being formed and another more radical resurgence after the formation of the Moral Majority in the 1970s. Because this theory stresses the literal interpretation of

---

eschatology, unless otherwise cited. This chapter does not provide a comprehensive discussion of eschatological imperatives in theo-political discourse; rather, it highlights the relationship that has developed between the two.

3 The Earth has seven dispensation periods. For today's theological purposes, the Earth is believed to be nearing its final dispensation. Although Darby conceived of more than seven, the SBC generally accepts seven as being the limit.

promises made to Israel in the Old Testament, advocates believe all promises made to Israel must be fulfilled for the current, ethnic nation of Israel in the contemporary, established state of Israel. Therefore, Israel and Jews are central figures in the fulfilment of all 'end time' prophecies. Without them in position to receive Abraham's and David's promises, Christ cannot return to claim His Kingdom or His Church. Thus, premillennial dispensationalism produces a cultural hegemony in the form of the 'true Church' populated by 'true Believers' who must acknowledge global chaos as a means of fulfilling prophesies.

Since the 1980s' conservative shift in the SBC, the concept of progressive dispensationalism has taken hold of eschatological analysis. This is the belief that all events foretold in the Bible are being fulfilled today and that Jews and the Church are co-receivers of the covenant and promises God made to Abraham and David. The most important factor of this position is ensuring the nation-state of Israel is occupied and controlled by the ethnic nation of Israel. Thus, events that occur in the Middle East summons the hopes and fears of Southern Baptists in a desire to see New and Old Testament prophecies fulfilled.

The 'Tribulation' is the seven year period prior to Jesus' return that, according to premillennial theory, will be a difficult time for Christians. This period will usher in global anarchy and turmoil for all inhabitants of the planet. Environmental, ecological, political, social, economic and military instability will lead to famines, environmental destruction, governmental upheaval, genocide and wars which will allow the 'Anti-Christ' to emerge to provide an illusion of peace. This period of difficulty must come to pass in order for Christ to return and demonstrate His power and glory by defeating, punishing and destroying the Anti-Christ, the 'Harlot' and their armies. When considering the impact of the Tribulation on opinions of foreign policy, the significance is the expectation and necessity of global chaos and human destruction. Thus, nations or political leaders who call for greater regulation of environmental issues or eradication of poverty are viewed as those who will oppose Christ's return and who want to hinder his reclamation of His Church. Meanwhile the Harlot is used as a way of labelling politically or socially vocal women, such as Hillary Clinton or Nancy Pelosi, since the Harlot is the commander of the Anti-Christ's armies.

The *Rapture* has three points of occurrence: pre-tribulation, post-tribulation and mid-tribulation. There is conjecture on when it will occur in the eschatological timeline, but that is unimportant since the message of the rapture does not change: those who are Christians will be raptured. This is the event that shows the entire world who is Lord in order to inaugurate His rule on earth. SBC discourse on the *rapture* requires that God's Temple must be rebuilt upon the Temple Mount in Jerusalem, the original site of David's Temple, thus maintaining Israel's integral part in international relations and policies. Also, Jews of the world must be reassembled in Jerusalem/Israel since this event hinges on the fulfilment of Abrahmic and Davidic covenants with the ethnic nation of Israel. Christ will enter His resurrected Temple in Jerusalem to accept His place as Earth's literal King. Obviously, the possession of Israel is the central concept for this outlook.

Without it, none of the necessary events can occur; and Christ will be without His Kingdom, again.

'Armageddon' is the ultimate final battle between God and the evil social and political forces ruling this world. These forces will be embodied in the Anti-Christ, the Harlot and their armies; and the battle will take place outside Jerusalem on a mountain called Megiddo. In order for this battle to occur, the world must be in utter turmoil while providing an illusion of peace and unification. Consequently, Middle-Eastern terrorism, military actions in the Middle East and political turmoil in Palestine and Israel only function as confirmations and signs that this battle will occur.

The Anti-Christ is a person who the world will follow as an answer to political and religious peace. He will integrate cultures and religions and will lead the world away from Christ, thus being in direct opposition to Christians and the nations that support them. Political leaders are often targeted as being the Anti-Christ in order to foment eschatological interpretations. In recent years, US Presidents Bill Clinton and Barack Obama have been labelled as such due to their push to quell military build-up and their predispositions toward answering human problems with human answers. As a result, binary systems are constructed: Clinton and Obama supporters being deceived and willing to fight against God while their opponents are aware of their true agendas and identities.

The 'Teleological Suspension of the Ethical' theory (TSE) is a concept conceived by Soren Kierkegaard in his drive to explore why God, the embodiment of righteousness and goodness, would ask Abraham to kill his son as a way of demonstrating loyalty. For Kierkegaard, this dilemma was an imperfection on the perfection of God. He pondered God's transcendence of man's ethical constructions and devised that God's Will would be incomprehensible and seem inconsistent to finite man. God's position as Creator of all things placed Him in the station of escaping man's conception of *good* and *bad*. For that reason, it is God's prerogative to direct His followers in pursuit of agendas that further His greater plans no matter how unethical they may seem to man. In recent years, a simplified interpretation has become popular with SBC leadership. The most important factor in this scenario is the ability of God to transcend human ethics in pursuit of His plan. It became fashionable to use this theory in the early 1990s as a way of explaining human actions in the context of God's will rather than as an attempt to contemplate the nature of God. Therefore, it has been linked to the post-9/11 belief that although war kills innocent people, if it is used to further God's plans, then all is justifiable. TSE has also been used in conjunction with Just War theory, which is explored later.

As one can see, these complex eschatological formulations, which dictate the cultural hegemony, binaries and discourse formation of religious perspectives, cannot be overlooked when developing an articulate analysis of SBC support for US foreign policy. However, the reader must also bear in mind how these eschatological viewpoints evolved in theological debates on foreign policy. For

Southern Baptists, their history on how to deal with the world has an interesting background that does more to confound than elucidate.

Deciphering Theo-political Context and Identity

Because the SBC was constructed to further legitimise the North/South-Free/Slave binary system that existed prior to the American Civil War, the evolutionary course in consolidating a comprehensive stance on issues such as foreign policy follows a predisposition for binaries. This is seen in their aggravated approach in dealing with exclusion: the Triennial Convention in the 1830s due to differing opinions on slavery and the federal government in the context of the Missouri Compromise of 1820. With these two perceived assaults on the south, Baptists in the south chose to create their own destiny in both religion and politics (Hester 1971).[4] The creation of the SBC in 1845 instilled a deep commitment to binaries and has shaped how the Convention has interpreted political support throughout its history.

When inaugurated in 1845, The Convention automatically admitted 350,000 members and instantly became the dominant denomination of the South. From that point, membership continued to grow to make it the leading Protestant denomination in the United States. During the nineteenth century, the SBC did a great deal to develop its infrastructure. Its only resolutions concerning events outside religious life came during the Civil War when it voiced its distrust for Lincoln and their abhorrence that he would wage a 'bloody and destructive war' against the 'peaceful inhabitants of the Confederate States' and stated objection to any possible reconciliation with the Union (SBC 1863). The Convention supported southern soldiers and the South's fight for independence, and clergy used biblical analogies to promote support for the war. Both political and religious leaders claimed that the South was Zion and that God had a special plan, but only if southerners had enough faith (Hester 1971). The discourse formed around the conflict placed the success or failure of the South squarely on the shoulders of southerners' faith. Consequently, when the South lost the war and was forced to endure the Reconstruction periods, religious leaders claimed defeat and Reconstruction to be punishment for lack of faith.

Eventually, the SBC moved into a long period of pacifism and pursuit of global peace, using the South's experiences of the Civil War and subsequent consequences as reasons for not supporting war endeavours. Therefore, Woodrow Wilson's move to enter World War I was condemned by the Convention; but his vision for a League of Nations was embraced. The possibility of creating an international body that could work to resolve issues by using negotiations rather than military action was something the SBC had envisaged for decades (Junker

4 This split was biblically justified by using the example of Paul's split with Barnabas over missionary disagreements (Acts 15:36–41).

1996). However, with the League of Nations defeated by American isolationism, the Convention moved forward in social arenas such as supporting suffrage, promoting prohibition, limiting the number of Catholics allowed to immigrate and eradicating evolutionary theory. The SBC worked continually to promote the identity of *southern-ness* in its construction of political interpretations. Discourse on issues such as suffrage, prohibition and evolution were framed in a way that fostered the belief that only southerners knew how God would interpret social issues.

After the attack on Pearl Harbor in 1941, the Convention issued a resolution of non-support for American retaliation on the Japanese and military intervention in the European war. Since the US chose to enter, the Convention did not mention the war or any other political issues until Franklin D. Roosevelt (FDR) began to announce his plans for a United Nations (UN) (SBC 1943). This was an endeavour the SBC wanted to be successful, so it offered help and support with its implementation. Church leaders believed the UN was the key to ensuring world peace as well as eradication of global poverty; therefore, discussions on inadequacies of America's foreign policies were encouraged. With the death of FDR and Truman taking up the Presidential post, the SBC again offered help; however, Truman, a Southern Baptist from Missouri, ignored their proffer (Polenberg 2000).

As war in Europe ended, the SBC believed it needed an organisation in Washington DC to be a political presence; this led to the establishment of the Baptist Joint Committee (BJC)[5] in 1946 which provided up to date information on legislation. As the BJC began its journey into the arena of American public and foreign policies, the SBC began developing its rhetoric on and dissemination of eschatology (Junker 1996). For years, eschatology had been the subject of fiery back-woods sermons, the reason for opposing the Vatican and for not endorsing ecumenicalism which was believed to be the foundation point of a 'one world government'. However, as the Cold War burgeoned, eschatological beliefs began to flourish throughout SBC discourse, media, publications, education and sermons (Torbet 1978). Consequently, seminary students began to be required to take courses such as Systematic Theology in which debates over the various views of *eschatology* worked toward a singular and consistent interpretation (Spain 2003).

Since Biblical prophecies seemed to abound with the advent of the nation-state of Israel, Dispensationalism became the foundation upon which Pre-millennial dialogue interpreted US actions abroad. Rather than looking at prophecies as historical indicators of events, prophecies took on new life and were viewed as progressive and immediate (Flynt 1998). The Anti-Christ was embedded in America's struggle against communist ideology, and Armageddon was sure to involve the USSR as Satan's agent.

As eschatological discourse developed, the Convention did not shy away from opposing other American military actions abroad. The Vietnam War caused the

---

5 Since the political shift of the SBC in the early 1990s, it is no longer a member of the BJC.

SBC to issue many resolutions based on its pacifist history concerning America's position and the role of individual citizens. Since the scars of the Civil War and Reconstruction periods were still present in the Southern culture, resolutions were issued in 1969, 1972, 1974 and 1977 condemning participation in the conflict and subsequent draft, advocating 'draft dodging' and protest initiatives and denouncing the use of any form of torture for any reason by US military. Members were encouraged to support protestors and seek refuge in Canada or Mexico as a means of avoiding the draft. Unlike World Wars I and II, the Vietnam conflict was viewed as a voluntary and aggressive assault on a sovereign foreign government and its citizens (SBC 1967).

Reframing Political Loyalty

It cannot be avoided that during this period of contentious political history, radical shifts began to take place in political alignment. Democrats began expanding FDR's social and economic commitments to broaden debates on equality which allowed Republicans a means of formulating a way out of the political decline they had been experiencing since the 1930s. Southerners were experiencing isolation from Democrats due to federal pursuits of desegregation policies, and this provided Republican elites with opportunities to reframe their battle against Democrats (Phillips 1970). RNC leadership was able to construct discourse in such a way that provided support for politically disaffected southerners; and one by one, southern states began electing federal Congressmen from the Republican Party for the first time since Reconstruction (Key 1984). Political realignment came to the south as a way, once again, of reinforcing the southern identity of opposition to the federal government; and as predicted by Kevin Phillips, Republicans were given a rare opportunity to provide ideological solace for southern discontent.

For their part, Republican hegemony assiduously worked to revive the party in the 1960s. Kevin Phillips, who coined the term 'Religious Right', was the strategist and campaign manager for Nixon's presidential victory in 1968 and re-election victory in 1972; he was the central strategist for the Republican move to the southern states with his research and insight on southern political de-alignment. He predicted that southern voters, mostly a religiously and familial oriented rural society characterised by contention and opposition, would forsake the Democratic Party in favour of another more sympathetic party. He believed the only way to revive the party was by constructing discourse on symbolic issues, such as abortion. He purported that symbolic political issues were imperative to the RNC's integration into southern political culture in order to propagate RNC policy agendas and provide southerners with an avenue to express political discontentment (Phillips 1970). Phillips also knew that cooperation with a reputable pre-existing cultural hegemonic force would be essential in assuaging the domination of the Democratic Party.

While Phillips predicted political shifts and developed innovative ways of manipulating media usage, other Republican leaders began to sort out resourceful ways of diminishing Democratic control. During the 1970s, an influx of conservative think tanks and interest groups began to flourish by way of the brewing magnate Joseph Coors (Bellent 1991). He wanted to influence a conservative shift in politics (FCF 2008; Diamond 1995); and after disseminating letters to Republican Congressmen, Mr Coors's representative, Jack Wilson, was able to contact Paul Weyrich, Press Secretary for Senator Gordon Alcott. The letter stated, 'I have been hired by Joe Coors to help him determine where he should put his money so it can further the conservative cause' (FCF 2008). Mr Weyrich later acknowledged that he had attempted to formulate a way of staving off the Democratic Party by creating outside interest groups that could provide information to Congress and voters. The proposed interest group could stimulate a loyal electorate and privately brief Congressmen (FCF 2008). Strategy meetings led to meetings with businessmen in order to gain financial funds, and Weyrich was able to utilise Phillips's 1968 socio-political research on the southern electorate as a vehicle for conservative agendas which were based on military expansion and dominance, maintaining the 'traditional' social and familial structures, abdicating American liberalism, prevention of impending equal rights legislation, decreasing taxation and regulation for corporations, unhindered capitalism and maintaining a dominant presence in the Middle East via Israel (Crawford 1980).

Thus, the design for malediction of the Democratic tide in American politics was pursued outside the typical political structure. Weyrich was able to create viable financial and political plans on how to generate and implement new interest groups that would revive the Republican Party. Joseph Coors approved his plans and later told Weyrich, 'We need an outside organization to counter the left and [you] fellows are the right people to make it happen' (FCF 2008).

In 1973, Paul Weyrich co-founded the Heritage Foundation with Joseph Coors. This new coalition led to a long list of think tanks and interest groups he helped form in the following years (Patricia 2008). In order to maintain a consistent conservative message over the years, Weyrich conducted weekly lunch meetings every Wednesday during Congressional sessions. This forum allowed leaders of various grassroots, religious and political interest groups the opportunity to mingle and discuss strategies and agendas with politicians; this meeting also ensured that everyone understood the legislative agenda (Braml 2005; Bruce 2008).

Shortly after the creation of the Heritage Foundation, Howard Phillips, who had worked in the Nixon Administration as Director of the US Office of Economic Opportunity in the Executive Office of the President, re-joined the conservative right initiative and eventually co-founded the Council for National Policy. He had focused his career on abolishing Johnson's Great Society Reforms, rolling back much of FDR's New Deal legislation, opposing corporate taxation and regulation and preventing Carter's plan to handover the Panama Canal. He was considered extremely radical in his belief that any attribute of American liberalism should be stricken from US legislation (Diamond 1995).

With Phillips on board, Weyrich approached Richard Viguerie, who was a mastermind in direct mailing and fundraising schemes. In his ambition to pioneer a new way of connecting with voters and supporters, Viguerie copied names and addresses of supporters of Goldwater and Wallace during their respective Presidential campaigns. This information was used to send out information directly from the candidate to supporters; this, in turn, provided larger donations to campaigns and the ability for campaigners to focus on single and symbolic issues (Diamond 1995). With Viguerie's acumen, Weyrich and Phillips attempted to overtake the American Independent Party [AIP]. In 1976, they approached the leadership of AIP with offers of financial support for party agendas for a trade in the deciding vote for the party's presidential candidate; however, party leaders rejected the offer. Consequently, Weyrich, Phillips and Viguerie moved on to focus their attention on religious factions in order to reach their political goals, particularly targeting Jerry Falwell (Diamond 1995).

Creating a Common Ground

The southern preacher Jerry Falwell proved to be a verbose asset. While he was considered to be a fundamentalist Baptist by the evangelical SBC, he nonetheless provided a forum for religious trepidation and political discontent to a large national audience via his weekly televised sermons on the Old Time Gospel Hour (Liebman 1982). Weyrich, Viguerie and Phillips approached Falwell in 1979 to convince him that he should start the Moral Majority. This was a venture much like their move toward the AIP in 1976, but this venture amalgamated the political agendas of Weyrich's team with theological rhetoric. In 1981, Frances Fitzgerald stated, 'The goal of the Moral Majority was to politicise and unify the frustrated and fragmented conservative, fundamentalist religious community and mould it into a political voting block' (Fitzgerald 1981).

Since southerners in the 1960s and 1970s saw what they believed to be a disintegration of the *Solid South* construct, they needed a way to reinforce southern identity in the midst of its dissolution (McAdam et al. 2001). An opportunity to reframe the fragmented southern cultural hegemony and empower it with validation, dignity and connection provided mobilisation material for the new conservative political movement. Hence, the political framework needed by Weyrich was contemporaneous, complete with a new binary construction of who were enemies and allies of the south. It became strategically possible to exploit the collective contention of the southern electorate.

The new discourse created by the Moral Majority in the 1980s labelled 'enemies' as those who were non-religious, against traditional familial structures and Democrat/liberal. Meanwhile, 'allies' were defined as the Republican minority that was numerically powerless to block liberal legislation and those who supported religion. This was particularly true in light of a Congressional move to re-examine the tax-exempt status of religious organisations and churches and its move to prevent federal funding of religious education. This directly threatened economic interests of mega-churches like Falwell's Thomas Road Baptist Church and Liberty University, several SBC universities and seminaries, Charles Stanley's First Baptist Church Atlanta and its affiliates and Pat Robertson's associated media and educational organisations. Since the SBC dominated the south and was the largest Protestant denomination in the US, it was imperative to reframe the experiences of the 1960s and 1970s within a religious context (Phillips 1970). The Moral Majority's two-fold agenda equated spirituality with political involvement and redefined theological discourse on what Christians did and did not politically and economically support.

Discourse on peace and military downsizing was replaced with promotion of military dominance and expansion. Eradication of poverty was replaced with a Christian's duty to allow unhindered capitalism around the world and support for non-taxation and deregulation of corporations. The vision of providing safety and peace for all was replaced with opposition to American liberalism, which was in the form of social welfare, social security, worker protections, etc. (Connolly 2005). A traditional stance of supporting minorities and women in their struggles (SBC 2009) was replaced with the need to preserve the traditional patriarchal family. Finally, the growing sentiment of detaching from Israel was replaced with an apocalyptical command to defend it for God.

Although symbolic domestic single issues mobilised voters, one can see that foreign policy issues truly began to evolve and take on new life. Timothy LaHaye was instrumental in distilling lurid Tribulation, Anti-Christ and Armageddon scenarios to the mass Christian population through his highly successful series of books, *Left Behind.* He provided volumes of written material on End Time prophecies and worked to propagate Dispensational interpretations of contemporary world situations to further support Pre-millennial dialogue. LaHaye's books opened the door for Christians to discuss their fears and beliefs about social and political situations and express wanton revenge on 'outsiders' without fear of being labelled fanatical. Shifting the focus of religious voters away from the social gospel and toward a vengeance oriented perception of the Godless world, proved to be one of the most powerful identity permutations that delivered frightened and vengeful support (Connolly 2005).

Hegemonic Battles

While ministers such as Falwell and LaHaye laboured to shift Christian theo-political foci, the SBC began going through a fierce ideological battle. For over 100 years, global peace and eradication of poverty were paramount to the Convention's mission statement. However, as a fundamentalist hegemony moved into Convention leadership, they began altering SBC basic beliefs in an attempt to cut out anyone who did not agree with the new fundamentalist direction. The Convention fought a ten year paradigmatic battle in which moderates and fundamentalists vied for control of the Convention, seminaries, bookstores and publishing companies, universities and seminaries, media, history and soul (Ammerman 2006). Fundamentalists' most powerful tool was the identity of opposition and contention that had been the core of southern, as well as Southern Baptist, identity for 150 years. It was important to redefine binary systems in order to identify who was on the side of God and who was not. This included attacking leaders and members of the Convention who were not on board with the new fundamentalist shift and dismissing church, university, seminary and Convention leaders who did not commit to the new conservative political focus and fundamentalist theology of the Convention (Ammerman 2006).

Leaders such as Paige Patterson and Paul Pressler were unrelenting in their pursuit to reframe the Convention's history and theology. Adrian Rogers (1979) was the first fundamentalist to be elected President of the evangelically oriented SBC. Meanwhile, Richard Land, who had long time ties to the Heritage Foundation, waged a campaign against Dr Foy Valentine, Director of the Christian Life Commission (CLC) (Ammerman 1995). Valentine was a supporter of secular society's right to create laws, including abortion; and he adamantly advocated a strict interpretation of separation of church and state. Richard Land eventually became the new Director of the CLC after Dr Valentine was exiled from his post, and Land transformed the SBC organisation into a political entity, now named the Ethics and Religious Liberties Commission (ERLC). Consequently, after 1987, fundamentalists and the overthrown moderates were shifted and reframed within new identities. Fundamentalists became known as conservatives whose duty was to uphold biblical truth and authority, while moderates were labelled liberals and betrayers of the faith. It was at this point that disagreement was equated with disloyalty, and those who disagreed were ostracised (Ammerman 1995).

SBC leadership began to stoke the fires of alienation and opposition that had long characterised southern identity. With a reframing of alienation, members of the Convention slowly began to see themselves as alone in their fight to protect their way of life, families, religion, identity, nation, culture and society from Godless liberals. This contention was reminiscent of the adversity that befell citizens of the South prior to, during and after the Civil War. The contentious structures were the same, but the language had changed. Framing Republican candidates as sympathetic to the plight of religious families and as being the only ones competent enough to wage war on communism was achieved through the rhetoric of Republican candidates as well as through the discourse of the SBC and other leading religious leaders. Therefore, political candidates could utilise religious language to indicate similitude with targeted constituencies.

A Brave New World

Southern Baptists were, for the first time, awakened to a world of political interactions that did not involve foreign missions for the sake of spreading the gospel. They began to see humanity on a path that had been predetermined thousands of years prior, which meant they needed to ensure Christ would be able to fulfil His destiny as the Earth's ruler. Support for Israel came as a bitter pill. On the one hand, support for America's role in protecting Israel was good news in fulfilling eschatological prophecies; while on the other hand, it meant possibly enduring a tribulation. Meanwhile, national leaders touted the importance of Israel and America's supportive role as SBC leaders steered congregations in the direction of eschatologically supporting Israel. Rather than being a strategic alliance in the Middle East, Israel became a strategic cog in God's prophecies.

According to the newly fashionable Pre-millennial Dispensationalism, Jerusalem played a central role in leading the world down an ominous and unavoidable path. One cannot forget that much of the focus of the Religious Right movement during the 1980s was on preventing the spread of communism and rolling back its influence in South America and Eastern Europe. Stories of the USSR producing the Anti-Christ and engaging the US, and its godly leader Reagan, in a war for souls became common fare in Baptist Press releases and LifeWay publications. Framing the spread of capitalism in discourse as the propagation of Protestant Christian ideals and *values* functioned to persuade SBC members that support of Republican economic agendas coincided with biblical mandates (Connolly 2005). With all of this, the stage is set to examine the evolution of foreign policy stances within the SBC.

Transformed by His Power …

For 146 years, the SBC opposed all military conflict in which the US was involved. It also opposed military build-up and spending during periods of conflict and non-conflict. The ultimate goal of the Convention was to assist in ushering global peace into the world. However, in 1991, the Convention produced its first resolution in support of military action, Operation Desert Storm (SBC 2008). The resolutions stated:

> … The liberation of Kuwait from the Iraqi Forces was carried out by the military forces of the United States … with precision, speed, and minimum casualties … The cause of freedom, democracy and peace was advanced by the diligent and courageous performance of duty throughout all segments of our armed services … we the messengers [of the SBC] commend and salute the President of the United States as Commander-in-Chief of the Armed Forces … [for] their overwhelming victory in Operation Desert Storm … we express reverent thanksgiving to Almighty God, the Judge of all nations, who is mightier than all armies and who alone is able to save, for His guidance, His mercy, and His blessing on our nation in Operation Desert Storm. (SBC 2008)

This drastic alteration to core beliefs came after the fundamentalist takeover of the Convention and reflected conservative political agendas. From this point forward, the SBC advocated a strong military, greater military spending within annual budgets and a show of force any time American power was assaulted or questioned. American presence in the Middle East, military or otherwise, became increasingly important to the SBC and was viewed as a way of following an eschatological path.

As support for military actions and build-up grew in the SBC, Ralph Reed, co-founder of the American Center for Law and Justice, began espousing economic and taxation issues because he believed Christians would need to have perceived personal or financial reasons to contend with targeted political leaders in order to guarantee mobilisation. The SBC eventually resolved that 'Capitalism is the only economic system compatible with Christianity' (SBC 2007). Leadership moved to advocate an unfettered global capitalist economic system, and the Convention abandoned its pursuit of eradicating global poverty. Dearth began to be discussed as though it were the result of sin. This also meant that discourse about global issues such as human rights, workers' rights or social welfare became framed as secular or humanist pursuits to alleviate social problems. Thus, it was the responsibility of the SBC to spread the Gospel rather than literally alleviating human problems with human answers. SBC hegemony began discussing free trade, zero-sum game and uninhibited foreign capital investment of corporations as being in the best interest of all and consistent with Christian beliefs (Baker 2008). It became important to non-business owners within the SBC to advocate blockage of governmental taxation and regulation on large corporations as a means of preserving Capitalism and Christianity. Therefore, foreign policy legislation that supported unhindered business expansion in the developing world fulfilled Christian principles (SBC 2009).

Convention hegemony guided members on how to interpret current issues which plagued America in a pursuit to create a cultural hegemony that would govern future questions and perceptions. With the advent of President George W Bush, SBC leaders such as Richard Land communicated to members that Bush was God's answer to the evil and Godless years of the Clinton administration. He ensured members that Bush was guided by God and only wanted what was best for families, religious voters and God's nation (ERLC 2001). Information on Bush's initiatives were spun to redirect what had not happened in the past, as an example: Bush touted the benefits of his tax cuts, SBC leadership backed up his claims with the lack of tax cuts implemented by Clinton rather than delving into the types of tax cuts proposed by the Bush administration and how this would affect middle to lower income families and future retirees (ERLC 2008).

During the first year of Bush's Presidency, America experienced 9/11. The Convention's reaction to this event was cloaked in revenge and hatred. Teleological Suspension of the Ethical began to make its way through the discourse of clergy, and Richard Land used its tenets to explain why America should go to war (Land 2007). The annual Convention passed several resolutions not simply supporting military action but requiring it (SBC 2002). During the 2003 national debate on whether the US should invade Iraq, one pastor in training told his congregation that 'if Jesus were alive today He would pick up an M-16 and kill those Muslims'.[6] This was common sentiment among clergy and stated in various ways to congregations. As one can see, the hostility apparent within the ranks of SBC leadership is in direct opposition to its history of dealing with conflict. For example, after Pearl Habor was attacked, SBC leadership responded to FDR's call for military action with vocal opposition to military action as well as through official resolutions in 1942 which states the organisation's stance against retaliation. This was also true for the American involvement in World War I with a resolution in 1917 stating the SBC's non-support for military action in Europe. This same resolve for peace was demonstrated throughout the Vietnam Conflict with several resolutions calling for the US military to withdraw as well as support for protests and 'draft-dodging'. As the conflicts in Afghanistan and Iraq progressed, information concerning torture used by American operatives and military interrogators came to light. For many in SBC leadership, torture became a necessary tool for extraction of information from America's enemies, thus resorting to utilitarianism as a means of its justification and negating its 1976 resolution condemning any form of torture for any reason (ERLC 2003). Consequently, there have been four resolutions since 2002 justifying any decision made by President Bush that might lead to US defeating terrorism (SBC 2002).

One of the primary reasons members of the SBC were on board with Bush's implementation of the wars in Afghanistan and Iraq was due to the infamous Land Letter (ERLC 2002). This was a letter written by Richard Land that expounded just war theory and was signed by other religious leaders and conservative organisers. He used this concept along with TSE to convince members of the Convention that God wanted America to go to war in Iraq. This took on various forms of interpretation such as fulfilling prophesies related to the tribulation or simply as a way of defending God's chosen western countries. This letter appeared at the 2003 Annual Convention and claimed that President Bush's reasons for war met all of the criteria laid out by this theory. He also claimed that the SBC based its foundational perspective of war support on the writings of Augustine and Aquinas rather than the historical position of pacifism stemming from experiences of the Civil War. However, Land did not create this letter on his own. The contents of the letter closely resembled two previous letters written by the neo-conservative think tank Project for a New American Century that was sent to Clinton in 1998 and Bush in 2001 one week after 9/11 (Lucas 2008). Thus, one can draw the conclusion that Richard Land's letter was not completely inspired by God as many SBC claimed.

6 New Orleans Baptist Theological Seminary. January 2002-December 2004. Group conversation/interview in 16 August 2003.

Conclusion

The path of US foreign policy is not always as clear cut as many researchers would like to believe. While most policies exist in order to protect and secure America and its interests, these policies must have support from citizens. Thus, mobilisation of support for policies the government wants to implement has to be disseminated into the population and normalised by its leaders. The Religious Right in the United States has become a reliable tool in this endeavour and has managed to transform theological beliefs to be congruent with neo-conservative Republican agendas. As has been shown in this chapter, the fathers of the Religious Right movement were incredible entrepreneurs who toiled for an emergence of the Republican Party and its agendas.

Republican leadership's ingenious use of reconstructed religious discourses to support conservative agendas shows the origins of the Religious Right movement and how SBC theology and beliefs transformed to fit into the Republican agenda. The emergence of a strong Republican Party was achieved by using Southern Baptist hegemony to propagate re-interpretations of historical binaries and discourses within the Convention and to foster foreign policies that were at the heart of RNC agendas. Thus, foreign policy in the United States can be viewed as being influenced by the Religious Right, but one must first look at how the Religious Right formulates its viewpoints on issues such as the war in Iraq or torture. As such, investigations of religion in the political arena need to be re-oriented in order to allow explorations beyond the obvious and to understand why theo-political actions are not solely based on religion. As such, reactions to political situations tend to transcend religious and national boundaries and lead to a discovery of ideological similitude between seemingly oppositional religious and political constructs.

Bibiography

Ammerman, N.T. 2006. *Baptist Battles: Social Change and Religious Conflict in the Southern Baptist Convention*. Piscataway, NJ: Rutgers University Press.

Baker, R. 2008. Southern Baptist Beginnings. *Baptist History*. Online. Available at: http://www.baptisthistory.org/sbaptistbeginnings.htm (accessed 6 July 2006).

Balmer, R. 2002. *Encyclopedia of Evangelism*. Louisville, KY: Westminster John Knox Press.

Balmer, R. 2006. *Thy Kingdom Come: An Evangelical's Lament*. New York: Basic Books.

Bellent, R. 1991. *The Coors Connection: How Coors Family Philanthropy Undermines Democratic Pluralism*. Boston, MA: South End Press/Political Research Associates Series.

Berlet, C. 2008. *Conceptualizing the US Political Right*. Boston, MA: Public Research Associates Series.

Braml, J. 2005. The Religious Right and US Middle East Policy. *The Emirates Occasional Papers* 59.

Bruns, R. 2004. *Billy Graham: A Biography*. Santa Barbara, CA: Greenwood Publishing Group.

Butler, J., Wacker, G. and Balmer, R. 2008. *Religion in American Life: A Short History.* Oxford: Oxford University Press.

Clements, K.A. 1982. *William Jennings Bryan: Missionary Isolationist*. Knoxville, TN: University of Tennessee Press.

Connolly, W.E. 2005. The Evangelical-Capitalist Resonance Machine. *Political Theory* 33.

Copley, E.H. 1836. *A History of Slavery, and its Abolition*. London: Sunday School Union.

Crawford, A. 1980. *Thunder on the Right: The 'New Right' and the Politics of Resentment*. New York: Pantheon Books.

Diamond, S. 1989. *Spiritual Warfare: The Politics of the Christian Right*. Boston, MA: South End Press.

Diamond, S. 1995. *Roads to Dominion: Right Wing Movements and Political Power in the United States*. New York: Guilford Press.

Elwell, W. (ed.) 2001. *Evangelical Dictionary of Theology*. Grand Rapids, MI: Baker Publishing.

ERLC for Faith and Family 2001. The Power of a Presidential Promise. *The Ethics and Religious Liberties Commission of the Southern Baptist Convention*. Online. Available at: http://faithandfamily.com/article/the-power-of-a-presidential-promise/ (accessed 1 November 2004).

ERLC 2002. The So-Called Land Letter. *The Ethics and Religious Liberties Commission of the Southern Baptist Convention*. Online. Available at: http://erlc.com/article/the-so-called-land-letter/ (accessed 17 May 2007).

ERLC 2003. This is not Vietnam. *The Ethics and Religious Liberties Commission of the Southern Baptist Convention.* Online. Available at: https://erlc.com/article/this-is-not-vietnam/article/legislative-agenda-for-2009/ (accessed 27 September 2007).

ERLC 2008a. Topics. *The Ethics and Religious Liberties Commission of the Southern Baptist Convention*. Online. Available at: http://erlc.com/topics/ (accessed 12 October 2008).

ERLC 2008b. War. *The Ethics and Religious Liberties Commission of the Southern Baptist Convention*. Online. Available at: http://erlc.com/topics/C35/links/ (accessed 27 September 2007).

FCF 2008. The Most Important Legacy of Joseph Coors. *The Free Congress Foundation*. Online. Available at: http://www.enterstageright.com/archive/articles/0303/0303coors.txt (accessed 10 May 2007).

Fitzgerald, F. 1981. A Disciplined, Charging Army. *The New Yorker*, 18 May.

Flynt, W. 1998. *Alabama Baptists: Southern Baptists in the Heart of Dixie*. Tuscaloosa, AL: The University of Alabama Press.

Frank, T. 2000. *One Market Under God: Extreme Capitalism, Market Populism, and the End of Economic Democracy*. New York: Doubleday Books.

Geisler, N.L. 2005. *Systematic Theology: Church/Last Things*. Grand Rapids, MI: Bethany House.

Golay, M. 1999. *A Ruined Land: The End of the Civil War*. New York: John Wiley and Sons, Inc.

Grudem, W. 1995. *Systematic Theology: An Introduction to Biblical Doctrine*. Grand Rapids, MI: Zondervan Publishing.

Hester, H.I. 1971. *Southern Baptists and their History*. New York: CSA Press.

Junker, W. 1996. *Contending for the Right to Know: A History of Southern Baptist Press 1895–1995*. Franklin, TN: Providence House Publishers.

Key, V.O. 1984. *Southern Politics in State and Nation*. Knoxville, TN: University of Tennessee Press.

Land, R. 2007. *The Divided States of America?* Nashville, TN: Thomas Nelson.

Liebman, R. 1982. Mobilizing the Moral Majority. Paper to the 1982 Annual Meetings of the American Sociological Association, San Francisco.

Liebman, R.C. and Wuthnow, R. 1983. *The New Christian Right: Mobilization and Legitimation*. New York: Aldine Publishing Company.

Lucas, S. 2008. Shifting the Gorilla: American Studies and the De-Centering of America. Paper to the Scottish Association for the Study of America: Ninth Annual SASA Conference, Glasgow, 8 February.

McAdam, D., Tarrow, S., and Tilley, C. 2001. *Dynamics of Contention*. New York: Cambridge University Press.

Phillips, K. 1969. *The Emerging Republican Majority*. New York: Arlington House.

Phillips, K. 1982. *Post Conservative America: People, Politics, and Ideology*. New York: Random House Inc.

Phillips, K. 2004 *American Dynasty: Aristocracy, Fortune, and the Politics of Deceit in the House of Bush*. New York: Viking Books.

Phillips, K. 2006. *American Theocracy: The Peril and Politics of Radical Religion, Oil, and Borrowed Money in the 21st Century*. New York: Viking Books.

Pierson, P. and Skocpol, T. 2007. *The Transformation of American Politics: Activist Government and the Rise of Conservatism*. Princeton, NJ: Princeton University Press.

Polenberg, R.D. 2000. *The Era of Franklin D. Roosevelt, 1933–1945: A Brief History with Documents*. New York: Bedford/St Martins.

SBC. 1863. Resolution on Peace. *Southern Baptist Convention*. Online. Available at: http://www.sbc.net/resolutions/amResolution.asp?ID=801 (accessed 16 April 2007).

SBC. 1943. Resolution on Peace. *Southern Baptist Convention*. Online. Available at: http://www.sbc.net/resolutions/amResolution.asp?ID=816 (accessed 14 February 2008.

SBC. 1946. Resolution Petitioning the Department of State of the United States. *Southern Baptist Convention*. Online. Available at: http://www.sbc.net/resolutions/amResolution.asp?ID=930 (accessed 20 October 2008).

SBC. 1967. Resolution on Peace. *Southern Baptist Convention*. Online. Available at: http://www.sbc.net/resolutions/amResolution.asp?ID=822 (accessed 10 June 2007).

SBC. 1991. Resolution on Operation Desert Storm. *Southern Baptist Convention*. Online. Available at: http://www.sbc.net/resolutions/amResolution.asp?ID=433 (accessed 1 May 2008).

SBC. 2002. On the War on Terrorism. *Southern Baptist Convention*. Online. Available at: http://www.sbc.net/resolutions/AMResSearchYear.asp?SearchBy=Year&frmData=2002&Search2=Search (accessed 9 January 2008).

SBC. 2009. Resolutions. *Southern Baptist Convention*. Online. Available at: http://www.sbc.net/resolutions/default.asp (accessed 1 May 2008).

SBC. 2009. The Baptist Faith and Message. *Southern Baptist Convention*. Online. Available at: http://www.sbc.net/bfm/bfm2000.asp#xv (accessed 1 October 2008).

Schapiro, M. 1994. *Who's Behind the Culture War: Contemporary Attacks on the Freedom of Expression*. New York: Nathan Cummings Foundation.

Spain, R. 1967. *At Ease in Zion: Social History of Southern Baptists*. Nashville, TN: Vanderbilt University Press.

Spain, R. 2003. *At Ease in Zion: Social History of Southern Baptists, 1865–1900*. Tuscaloosa, AL: University of Alabama Press.

Sullivan, P. 2008. A Father of the Modern Conservative Movement. *The Washington Post*, 19 December.

Torbet, R.G. 1978. *A History of Baptists*. Valley Forge, PA: Judson Press.

Weber, B. 2008. Paul Weyrich, 66, A Conservative Strategist Dies. *The New York Times*, 19 December.

PART 3
Disentangling Religion from Politics

Chapter 7

Coercing Solidarism: The Secular and Religious in US Exceptionalism

Nicholas Kerton-Johnson

No virtuous act is quite as virtuous from the standpoint of our friend or foe as it is from our standpoint.

Reinhold Niebuhr, *The Irony of American History* (1952)

Introduction

This chapter explores the idea of coercive solidarism through the lens of US freedom and more particularly through its promotion post-9/11. The chapter argues that US action post-9/11 can be interpreted in terms of coercive solidarism, an English School term that adds explanatory power to our understanding of US foreign policy.[1] This coercive solidarism must be seen to exist not as solidarism is normally viewed, as a result of strengthening norms of international society or as an emerging world society, but characterised by significant elements of hierarchy and an imposed political morality. This is illustrated by an analysis of US presidential justifications for war since 1990 as well as drawing on Martin Wight's revolutionism. The chapter will begin with a discussion of coercive solidarism, briefly discuss the idea of freedom and go on to examine post-1990 US military action in the Gulf War, Kosovo, Afghanistan and Iraq.

---

1 The ES rests on the three pillars of international system, international society and world society, all existing simultaneously both as objects of discussion and as aspects of international reality (Buzan 2004: 10; Little 1995: 21). A comprehensive understanding of IR must embrace all three traditions (Little 2000: 398). As Dunne argues, the English school tries to 'understand historical and normative change by engaging with 'texts' such as legal treaties, speeches, and diplomatic discourses' and includes 'the inescapability of ethical considerations and a realization that the study of world politics must engage with (and interpret) the dilemmas faced by practitioners' (2007: 332–3).

Solidarism and Coercive Solidarism

Solidarism is seen as having the following two characteristics. First, a solidarist international society is one in which states have a high level of cooperation and adherence to common norms involving a 'wider range of issues, whether in pursuit of joint gains or realisation of shared values' (Buzan 2004: xviii). Second, for solidarism, the individual is privileged above the state and as such in a solidarist international society a right and duty of intervention against humanitarian abuses exists. Solidarism includes the guardianship of human rights (Jackson and Sorensen 2007: 313; Dunne et al. 2007: 340; Wheeler 2000: 38). As Linklater and Suganami (2006: 65) argue: 'Pluralism and solidarism, as initially defined by Bull, are in essence differing empirical judgements about the extent of solidarity or potential solidarity present in the existing international society.'

For pluralists, the promotion of solidarist values can be problematic for international order, but what is not adequately considered within English School literature is the consequence of solidarist values being enmeshed in a superpower's search for security, affecting a coercive solidarism.[2] Rather than seeing this coercive solidarism as seeking the elimination of international society through the creation of a world society, it should be seen as the manifestation of a particular view of international society that seeks solidarity of membership but which is dominated by a particular state or group of states. In this sense coercive solidarism presents solidarist statements of human worth, the pluralist belief in the importance of states, systemic use of power and the revolutionist's imposition of values against contrary positions.

The solidarist–pluralist debate has largely centred on that between justice and order, with the latter being vulnerable to the promotion of the former. The challenge of coercive solidarism is not, however, in relation to order alone but rather in terms of the manner in which the 'solidarist' norms are advanced. Well before 9/11, Kai Alderson and Andrew Hurrell (2000: 67) asked in relation to norm implementation: 'Are we witnessing a concerted move towards more coercive patterns of enforcement … a move from consensual to coercive solidarism?' In this sense solidarist values no longer evolve through international practice, agreement and law, but are enforced.

The US's promotion of freedom is focussed on individual rights and emancipation and reflects the solidarist desire for human rights being pre-eminent in international society. The promotion of freedom and the liberal values that are espoused within this can be seen throughout US foreign policy in the twentieth century and particularly in the legacy of Wilsonianism. As Smith (2000) argues, US foreign policy has consistently promoted liberalism, not for liberal values alone but ultimately for securing the US. This liberal project was promoted more easily or less hypocritically in the post-Cold War period, but it was in the US's response

2 See Linklater and Suganami (2006) for an excellent discussion of the progression of the solidarist–pluralist debate within English School literature.

to 9/11 that this projection of values shifted significantly such that George W. Bush's foreign policy has been labelled 'Wilsonianism on steroids'. As Knock (2008: 31) argues, while Wilson saw the US model guiding other nations to peace and liberty, he would not condone unilateral military action unless there was an unprovoked attack.

Bush's policy differed markedly, as will be shown below, and it is this policy that can be illustrated through incorporating the idea of coercive rather than consensual solidarism. In this sense, the actions of the US can clearly be seen as coercive and solidarist. The coercion is seen in the use of military force and the contested failure to observe legal rules, and in the solidarism, not in explicit enforcement of international rules, but the enforcement of the values and morality underpinning the solidarist architecture which the US had done so much to establish in international society and over which it claimed status as ultimate protector. Indeed, it is hard to see within any of the US justifications for war in either Afghanistan and Iraq ideas or values different from any other Western liberal state; it was rather the placing of authority in the US which was problematic.

Hedley Bull wrote of a 'premature global solidarism' which is solidarism enforced by a hegemonic power or group of powers (Dunne et al. 2007: 138). This can be equated with Alderson and Hurrell's coercive solidarism (2000: 67). Solidarism is usually expressed in terms of shared values arising from 'normative integration', but it can also be seen in terms of the imposition of particular values by a hegemonic power or group of powers (Clark 2005: 156). Coercive solidarism 'shares the surface phenomenon of solidarism, but differs radically as to the conditions that have brought this about', according to Clark. Coercive solidarism is driven by powerful states, or, as in the case of the post-Cold War world, by a single state with hegemonic power, and as such the degree of solidarism and shared values became a function of hegemonic power, which shifted focus markedly across both 1990 and 9/11 (Hurrell 1999: 291).

We can of course question whether solidarism is, or has ever been, consensual. It is moot whether solidarism is always coercive for some part of the world, or whether the drivers of solidarism are consensual within their own border and coercive without, as can be seen in Jackson's view of the resurgence of spheres of influence to be discussed below. It is assumed, given solidarism's liberal basis, that solidarist international society and perhaps even a world society, must emerge out of international society norms, based as it is, principally, on human value; but human value can be driven equally by a hegemonic state, particularly if the hegemon identifies freedom as humanity's most aspired value, and itself as freedom's defender. Clark (2005: 156) quotes Hurrell, who argues that 'the paradox of universalism is that the successful promotion of "universal" or "global" values will often depend on the willingness of particularly powerful states to promote them'. Wight illustrates the tension between consensual and coercive solidarism:

> Either the society of states will become cooperative and homogeneous through the universal acceptance of some standard of legitimacy … or the principles

> of transformation will establish themselves first, in accordance with the law of uneven development, in a single country … This state becomes the bearer and exemplar of the new order, and its relations with the unregenerate society of states will reproduce the relations of the Church militant with the secular and infidel world. (Wight 1966: 94)

Freedom

Freedom is central to the US. When searching the American Presidency Project records, freedom is referenced by US presidents more often than 'democracy' or 'liberty', beaten substantially only by 'peace'. The nation was established on the idea of freedom and has fought to secure freedom. This is clearly testified to by President Abraham Lincoln's statement in his Gettysburg address:

> It is for us, the living, rather, to be dedicated to the great task remaining before us that from these honored dead we take increased devotion to that cause for which they gave the last full measure of devotion; that we here highly resolved these dead shall not have died in vain; that this nation, under God, shall have a new birth of freedom; and that government of the people by the people, for the people, shall not perish from the earth. (Lincoln 1863)

This echoed his earlier message to Congress:

> In giving freedom to the slave we assure freedom to the free – honorable alike in what we give and what we preserve. We shall nobly save or meanly lose the last best hope of earth. Other means may succeed; this could not fail. The way is plain, peaceful, generous, just – a way which if followed the world will forever applaud and God must forever bless. (Lincoln 1862)

As Richard Hyde (2007) argues, anyone 'articulating a vision of America has to contend with Lincoln', and it is his promise of a 'new birth of freedom and a just and lasting peace among ourselves, and with all nations', that has coloured America's history as a fight for freedom. 'Freedom is the very propulsion of America's greatness', says Hyde.[3] US expansion within the North American continent was itself seen as the 'extension of the area of freedom' (Weinberg 1963: 101).

The memorials to fallen US soldiers are a testament to this. All memorials point to the deaths of US soldiers in pursuit of freedom, the controversial Vietnam War memorial most pointedly so. 'America exerts world leadership on behalf of

---

3 Interestingly, the sixtieth anniversary edition of *Commentary* in November 2005 on US strategy in Iraq included the opinions of 36 key US foreign policy thinkers and was entitled 'Defending and Advancing Freedom'.

freedom … Freedom is not just absence of conflict or absence of foreign control, but the presence of well-being', says Hyde (2007), and his argument continues that it is this well-being that is clearly evident in the heavy references to peace, freedom and democracy in President Bush's post-9/11 justifications for war, references which accounted for over a third of all his justifications for the war in Iraq (Kerton-Johnson 2008: 1002). What occurs after 9/11 in particular is 'the unequivocal universalization of the idea of freedom and liberty … For Mr Bush, there is no other "model of human progress". It is the answer and it is final' (Lindberg 2002).

While this chapter does not have the scope to examine in great detail the extent to which Bush's foreign policy is an aberration or continuation of US foreign policy throughout its history, his position is surely reflected in Lincoln's words in 1861.

> I have often inquired of myself, what great principle or idea it was kept this confederacy so long together. It was not the mere matter of the separation of the colonies from the mother land; but something in that Declaration giving liberty, not alone to the people of this country, but hope to the world for all future time. It was that which gave promise that in due time the weights should be lifted from the shoulders of all men, and that all should have an equal chance. (Hyde 2007)

General George Marshall, later author of the Marshall Plan, declared during World War II: 'We are determined that before the sun sets on this terrible struggle, our flag will be recognized throughout the world as a symbol of freedom on the one hand and of overwhelming force on the other' (Lindberg 2002). President George W. Bush echoed these sentiments 60 years later (2002a):

> Wherever we carry it, the American flag will stand not only for our power but for freedom … We fight, as we always fight, for a just peace, a peace that favors human liberty. We will defend the peace against threats from terrorists and tyrants. We will preserve the peace by building good relations among the great powers. And we will extend the peace by encouraging free and open societies on every continent.

This is not the place to compare the post-WW2 period with the post-9/11 period, but the democracy-building, freedom-enhancing, liberty-creating parallel should not be missed. As Lindberg argued (2002), President Bush's speech can be seen as a 'founding document of a new international order with American power at its center and the spread of freedom as its aim'. He goes on to argue that Bush's 'liberty doctrine' is as consequential as the ideas of Manifest Destiny and the Monroe Doctrine.

For Niall Ferguson (2004: x), the American idea of freedom means 'the American model of democracy and capitalism … They may not aspire to rule, but they do aspire to have others rule themselves in the American way'. President Bush's view of US freedom needs to be quoted at length (2004).

> The story of America is the story of expanding liberty, an ever-widening circle, constantly growing to reach further and include more. Our Nation's founding commitment is still our deepest commitment: In our world and here at home, we will extend the frontiers of freedom … I believe in the transformational power of liberty. The wisest use of American strength is to advance freedom … And as freedom advances, heart by heart and nation by nation, America will be more secure and the world more peaceful … I believe that America is called to lead the cause of freedom in a new century. I believe that millions in the Middle East plead in silence for their liberty. I believe that, given the chance, they will embrace the most honorable form of government ever devised by man. I believe all these things because freedom is not America's gift to the world; it is the Almighty God's gift to every man and woman in this world. This moment in the life of our country will be remembered. Generations will know if we kept our faith and kept our word. Generations will know if we seized this moment and used it to build a future of safety and peace. The freedom of many and the future security of our Nation now depend on us.

Lincoln's legacy, the model provided by Marshall in both war and peace and Bush's promotion of freedom all point to a coercive solidarism founded on freedom, liberty and democracy.

Revolutionism

Before continuing it is necessary to explore Wight's revolutionism in order to locate coercive solidarism in Wightian terms. The revolutionist's goal is social change that 'involves bringing into existence an ideal world of some kind, whether the real world is based on a revolutionary religion … or a revolutionary ideology, such as republican liberalism or Marxism-Leninism' (Jackson and Sorensen 2007: 136).

Revolutionism can be left or right-wing and is a 'doctrine of overthrowing and eradicating existing regimes, if necessary by violence' (Jackson and Sorensen 2007: 138). Wight (1991: 228) noted that revolutionary leaders express 'very simply the revolutionist principle of Holy War: divide mankind into good and bad on a criterion provided by your doctrine, and then kill all the bad'. Hard revolutionists are 'close to the tough-minded position of extreme realists – except that hard revolutionists want to destroy the state system, whereas extreme realists want to preserve it'.

Bush's justifications for war lie between the two: knowing the international system needs to change, seeking this change, but still being rooted in the state system, in effect encapsulating a form of coercive solidarism (Jackson and

Sorensen 2007: 139). As in previous centuries, US revolutionism can be compared with European experiences of revolutionism which 'engulf[ed] the society of states in violent transnational conflict' (Linklater and Suganami 2006: 156).

If hard revolutionism is to be seen in terms of violent transformation then US foreign policy may well be more easily situated here than with the soft revolutionists. This is evident in the description of Bush's policy as being one of 'Wilsonianism on steroids' – hard rather than soft revolutionism. If Woodrow Wilson has typified US foreign policy and can be positioned as a post-war revolutionist, can Bush not be seen as a post-9/11 revolutionist (Wight 1991: 46, Linklater and Suganami 2006: 157–8)? This is not to say that Bush or US foreign policy is wholly revolutionist, but rather that 9/11 created the catalyst for revolutionism to come to the fore.[4] US foreign policy post-9/11 parallels Wight's revolutionism in that it is to be achieved by ideological or doctrinal imperialism, especially when linked to the US's idea of Manifest Destiny and Chosen Nation explicitly pointed out by Wight (1991: 43–4).

It seems that the majority of International Society literature takes for granted the liberal nature of solidarism but more problematically ignores the connect between realism and revolutionism – that one state, and a democratic state, could be the driving force behind revolutionary change. That revolutionism can be linked to coercive solidarism is clearly evident in President Bush's words:

> I believe that by doing what we need to do to secure the world from terrorist attack … by doing our job, that the world will be more peaceful, by standing strong for what we believe, by remembering that freedom is not America's gift to the world, but God's gift to each and every human being, that we can achieve peace … our drive and our vision is for a peaceful world in which everybody can realize their potential and live in peace. (2002b)

> This goal of a free and peaceful Iraq unites our coalition. And this goal comes from the deepest convictions of America. The freedom you defend is the right of every person and the future of every nation. The liberty we prize is not America's gift to the world; it is God's gift to humanity. (2003)

Regime change in Iraq on the basis of Saddam's brutality and values which ran counter to those represented by the US 'pointed towards the wholesale abandonment of the post-colonial settlement on institutions of sovereign equality and non-intervention, and their replacement by an explicitly imperial regime of inequality and an imposed "standard of civilization"', but this was not as remarkable as many proposed, given the legacy of Kosovo or Afghanistan (Buzan 2004: 177).

---

4 See Buzan (2004: 173–7) for a discussion of the impact of the 9/11 attacks in conjunction with US exceptionalism and unipolarity.

Justifying War

An analysis of the presidential justifications for war post-1990 reveals a shift in the promotion of pluralist to solidarist norms, but post-9/11, to a more problematic set of norms being advanced which can be interpreted as coercively solidarist. For more detail on the justifications see Kerton-Johnson (2008).

An analysis of the justificatory statements made by President George Bush senior for the US intervention in the Gulf War showed a clear dominance of pluralist statements relating to international peace and security and the sanctity of sovereignty. President Clinton's justifications for war in Kosovo focussed principally on human rights with surprisingly few references to international law when compared with national interest, and it is here that an indication of coercive solidarism became apparent, a coercion built on NATO's multinationalism, but coercive nonetheless. The Afghanistan intervention brought this coercive element to the fore, with over 90 per cent of all statements related to national interest/security, national morality or democracy promotion, and 85 per cent of justifications for the Iraq War falling into these categories (Kerton-Johnson 2008).

In the next chapter, Ivan Manokha's discussion of just war and humanitarian intervention to ensure fundamental rights and freedom and the ending of tyranny is reflected in Clinton's justifications for war in Kosovo, and far more profoundly in Bush's justifications for war in both Afghanistan and Iraq. Indeed, as Manokha shows, the justifications align with Grotius' view that war should only be fought for the assertion of individuals' rights.

Jackson (2000: 281) interpreted US actions in Kosovo as clearly implying that 'dictatorships and abusive governments had no place in Europe and were to be stamped out. Europe was defined as a region of democracies which respected human rights'. Jackson expanded on this theme, stating that land anywhere in Europe 'was characterized as the common property of all Europeans', that sovereignty in Europe 'was conditional on democracy and human rights' and that this war of democracy versus dictatorship was 'strongly suggestive of a geographical sphere of influence where Western norms and values shall prevail'.

Elements of coercive solidarism clearly emerged in this intervention, intermingled with consensual solidarism – coercive for Europe's and the US's spheres of influence, consensual elsewhere. Seeking to remove a government by force clearly points to a coercive solidarism in an expanding sphere of influence. What occurs with 9/11 is the expansion of the US's sphere of influence to include the whole world and the impulse to coercively spread its values for its own security, which ultimately would benefit all those coerced (Roberts 2003: 33).

As Smith (2000: 95) argues, the George Bush senior and Clinton administrations pursued a 'neo-Wilsonian framework for world order in the post-Cold War world' in which 'sovereign nation states, democratically based and economically open, might cooperate in a variety of already established international agreements and institutions that American power had provided for order in those parts of the world where such arrangements could be maintained'. Madeleine Albright also reflected this Wilsonian position, stating:

> … we must take advantage of the historic opportunity that now exists to bring the world together in an international system based on democracy, open markets, law and a commitment to peace. Today the greatest danger to America is not some foreign enemy; it is the possibility that we will fail to heed the example of [the post-war] generation; that we will allow the momentum toward democracy to stall, take for granted the institutions and principles upon which our own freedom is based, and forget what the history of this century reminds us: that problems, if left unattended, will all too often come home to America. A decade or two from now, we will be known as the neo-isolationists, who allowed tyranny and lawlessness to rise again, or as the generation that solidified the global triumph of democratic principles. (Smith 2000: 94)

US foreign policy in the 1990s was a clear Wilsonian moment focussed on the strengthening of international institutions and guided by human rights.

Post-9/11 intervention witnessed the promotion of an international order that reflected the US – that the US was the promoter of democracy, not through international law and institutions, but in its own right if need be. It is here that the effect of 9/11 on international society can be seen, in that the leading founding member of world order chose to step away from that which it had helped to create and laid out a new pre-emptive use of force and a hierarchical system, and warned the world to cooperate. As Robert Kagan (2004) argues, the Bush doctrine 'has naturally sprung out of the United States' liberal revolutionary tradition', the result being that if the US was willing in Kosovo to ignore international law, then an attack on its own soil would most likely elicit a response even more dismissive of constraints on its ability to protect itself.

Democracy Promotion: A Revolution Towards Freedom

Democracy promotion is clearly linked with US exceptionalism and national security. Its underlying tenet is that democracy is the political expression of the freedom and peace that the US feels called to export. No longer are freedom and democracy an option for international order but, after 9/11, in the US's eyes, they became compulsory, given that the US could not seek to balance power with terrorists, but had to spread those values, which it interpreted as being able to defeat the new enemy. President George W. Bush spoke intently not only of freedom, but of the fact that the post-9/11 world was one in which 'America's oceans' no longer protected her, arguing both for freedom and against isolationism.

The US has intervened in the hopes of seeing new liberal states created, but it is no longer a matter of reason or prosperity, nor even principally freedom for others, but rather the fact that freedom is so connected to national interest, eradicating the possibility or temptation to isolation which has been a historic tendency for the US. The US, particularly post-1945, embarked on a Wilsonian promotion of democracy and freedom. This was clearly aligned with the Cold War, and national security was implicit in this venture, but this liberalism was enshrined in international law and institutions. The US's expansionism under Bush is unilateral and is focussed on US exceptionalism and security, with the freedom of others part of, but subservient to, this, and must be seen to differ considerably from pre-9/11 cases. Liberal ideas are certainly contained within the neo-conservative-inspired foreign policy, but to define Bush foreign policy in these terms misses the impact and momentum of 9/11. The expansion of democracy and freedom, and the securing of the US contained liberal principles, but these were undertaken on the basis of US power and exceptionalism, not liberal theory alone. As Wight (1966: 95) argued, 'the revolutionary state opts out of the existing law of nations because it is defective and unjust, or observes it as a matter of expediency, not of legal obligation'.

Has the US found itself being viewed by some nations in the same way it previously viewed Russia? George Kennan's discussion is illustrative here:

> What attributes are we … entitled to look for in the personality of a foreign state, and of Russia in particular? … It would not take the ideological position that its own purposes cannot finally prosper unless all systems of government not under its control are subverted and eventually destroyed … and that she abandon, as ruinous and unworthy, the ancient game of imperialist expansion and oppression. (Wight 1966: 99)

The following quote from a senior Bush adviser, chosen to start Ferguson's *Colossus*, sums up the shift from soft to hard, or perhaps better defined, into a more virulent coercive solidarism (Ferguson 2004). Note that this comment was made towards the end of 2004, when it was already apparent Iraq was not going to progress towards democracy as had been expected.

> We're an empire now, and when we act, we create our own reality. And while you're studying that reality … we'll act again, creating other realities, which you can study too, and that's how things will sort out. We're history's actors … and you, all of you, will be left to just study what we do. (Suskind 2004)

Indeed the Bush doctrine can be seen to be not so much a theoretical departure from post-1914 or post-1945 US foreign policy but rather a practical departure as the promotion of freedom went from consensual to coercive. Put differently, with the security of the US now at stake, freedom and democratic liberty had to be advanced against those that posed a real or potential threat (Ferguson 2004: 152). This thinking might also explain the failure to heed the historical legacy that would have cautioned the idea that 'democracy was the default regime to which societies would revert once dictatorships were removed' (Fukuyama 2006: 31). Whereas with the Gulf War and Kosovo one could talk about norm innovation or norm elevation, the post-9/11 interventions indicate what can more usefully be seen as a 're-centring' of norms as the US shifted focus away from the UN, multilateralism and universal human rights and towards itself. The competing pressures between pluralist and solidarist positions within international society were all relocated and centred on the US, which placed itself as the provider of human rights, freedom and justice – competing norms and pressures now held to be in union in the US's post-9/11 world.

Importantly, President Bush (2002) stated: 'America has no empire to extend or utopia to establish. We wish for others only what we wish for ourselves: safety from violence, the rewards of liberty, and the hope for a better life … America cannot impose this vision – yet we can support and reward governments that make the right choices for their own people.' But the US did, of course, have every intention of helping the others become part of the new democratic order, led by itself (Lindberg 2002). As A.J.P. Taylor said of Bismarck, principles and beliefs can be very effective if 'translated to blood and iron and not simply into resolutions and majority votes' (quoted in Wight 1978: 27). In 2002 Bush stated: 'America stands for more than the absence of war. We have a great opportunity to extend a just peace by replacing poverty, repression and resentment around the world with hope of a better day.' He appeared to be implying that the means of war was worth the stated end.

Tom Donnelly believes that Americans find the idea of empire discomforting, preferring to use 'code phrases like "America is the sole superpower"', yet the positive aspect of empire should not be ignored in its ability to create a benign order or *pax Americana* (Ferguson 2004: 4–5). While neoconservative policy can be seen as heavily involved in post-9/11 US foreign policy, it would be a mistake to view this use of hard power as an anathema of the US state. It merely exposed the iron hand within the velvet glove that is US soft power (Ferguson 2004: 24). As Buzan argues, 'the US is moving sharply away from the practice of projecting its values by a logic of persuasion, and towards the persuasive end of the spectrum' (2004: 154), in many ways attacking the institutions of international society it was instrumental in creating.

With the election of Democrat Barack Obama as US President, it is not clear whether the shift from a multilateralist, liberal approach to imperial mode was a result of the Bush administration or represents a deeper shift in US politics, but Buzan (2004) identifies 'three prominent candidates for explaining this apparent turn under Bush: American exceptionalism, unipolarity and September 11'. That the first two were evident prior to Bush suggests a deeper underlying characteristic of US foreign policy.

The idea of the US as a 'city on a hill' or New Jerusalem, although rooted in Christian tradition, has a secular outworking, and this is visible in the Wilsonian enticement of on-looking nations by offering economic and political liberty (Nye 2002: 141). As Davidson (2005: 158–9) argues, the 'American political, economic and social culture was the God-ordained ideal version of the already glorified

Western culture', and the connection between God, Western civilisation and the US was 'more or less taken for granted'. Ikenberry (2000: 105) illustrates the religious in Wilson's position, arguing that he 'brought to his political thinking and principles of political action deeply held religious and ethical beliefs that unified and defined his orientation towards the outside world'. Democracy was central to US foreign policy and Wilson saw 'democracy as the highest form of government', leading him to the 'conclusion that democracy must some day be the universal rule of political life' (Ikenberry 2000: 105–6).

As Davidson (2005: 168) notes, Bush, like Wilson, was heavily influenced by his evangelical beliefs, but in Bush's case this was coupled with American nationalism. Exceptionalism melded with nationalism results in coercive solidarism intent on expanding freedom and liberty. This is a God-ordained mission for all men but also, post-9/11, for US security.

Max Boot (2002: 349) argues that the US's 'empire consists not of far-flung territorial possessions but of a family of democratic, capitalist nations that eagerly seek shelter under Uncle Sam's umbrella'. All three of Buzan's candidates are visible in the post-1990 interventions by the US: unipolarity implicated in the Gulf War, exceptionalism and unipolarity emergent in Kosovo and all three clearly visible post-9/11, indicating that it was 9/11 in particular that magnified the exceptionalism and unipolarity, which were already existent.

As Harries argues, using slightly different terms to Buzan: hegemony 'encouraged the belief that anything the United States willed was achievable', exceptionalism 'insisted that what should be willed was the remaking of the world in America's own image' and the American outrage at 9/11 'created an enormously powerful pressure for immediate and drastic action' (*Commentary* 2005: 34).

The security of states and international order has for centuries been 'maintained by ensuring an absence of overarching power in the international system', and the society of states, including traditional US allies, were concerned at the presentation of the US as 'a unipolar *fait accompli*' (Ikenberry 2005). Commonly held 'liberal democratic principles meant a good deal more in a world threatened by totalitarianism than they have in a world made safer for democracy' (Kagan 2004). The US post-9/11 is no longer seen as the leader of the free world, but more the leader of those states willing to ally with the US project, which excludes many former allies (Kagan 2004). This is why unipolarity is so important to understand. The discourse of President Bush held within itself the competing pressures of freedom, justice (solidarist) and national interest and security (pluralist), centring all of these in the US and pointing to a position of coercive solidarism in unity with revolutionism.

President Bush's National Security Strategy of 2002 saw the US arbitrating 'right and wrong' and enforcing a peace in which it becomes the 'order-creating Leviathan' in a new global hierarchy, instead of a situation involving the 'dangers of anarchy and balance of power politics' (Ikenberry 2005). The US could therefore be seen to be moving towards a two-tier system, with itself as the hegemon operating alongside, but apart from, the international community of states – a 'hegemonic strategy with imperial characteristics' (Ikenberry 2005, Wheeler 2003: 212). The Iraq War can be seen as the 'definitive expression of th[e] strategic reorientation' of the Bush administration post-9/11 which was committed to the War on Terror, confronting threats before they emerged, and thereby spoke out for a two-tier system in which the US would deny states certain key rights, dependent on a new standard of membership apart from the UN and separate to the normative pressure of humanitarianism prevalent through the 1990s (Ikenberry 2005, Bush 2002a). The threat posed by US unilateralism must also be seen in the light of the weakening norm of sovereignty. Seen throughout the 1990s but increasingly evident in the War on Terror, the Bush doctrine threatened the pluralist norms designed to ensure order and security – sovereignty and non-intervention – based on principles of pre-emption and contingent sovereignty (Ikenberry 2005). Ikenberry (2005) furthers this argument:

> There is an additional attraction of this unipolar grand strategy – it gives full sway to American exceptionalism. This self-perception, as old as the nation's founding, sees America as a unique world experiment; a polity more noble and enlightened that any other on earth. If in the past, American exceptionalism was possible only through isolation or withdrawal from the outside world, now American exceptionalism is made possible by global dominance.

US exceptionalism believes that 'liberal values are universal, and that the intrinsic moral and practical superiority of liberal values gives them the right to claim the future of humankind', combined with a morality that tends to cast its foreign policy in terms of crusades and the destruction of the evil opponent (Buzan 2004: 156–7).

The US claimed to be supporting all freedom-loving states – this was therefore different from the international system of all against all but was rather closer to empire or coercive solidarism, and interestingly coercive of states as well as individuals. The US was the defender of those who sought freedom, and even if the political elites of traditional allies did not value this, the US did. It claimed the right to free those who were oppressed and defeat all who threatened it – an exceptionalist/systemic synthesis. While liberals have never liked the balance of power and would gladly see it replaced, the option of a hegemonic order where the hegemon stands aloof from the institutions it protects presents a 'conservative Leviathan' – an order where the US rules but does not live by the rules – in effect creating empire, but a justified empire in so far as the US will protect what it sees every person ultimately wanting – freedom and democracy. In this way it moves ever closer to Wight, Butterfield and Niebuhr's warnings of the dangers of any dominant power (Ikenberry 2005, Wight 1991: 99).

However, the US's justifications for war and resultant use of force were an attempt to create a world reflective of many of the solidarist claims. Theirs was not a solidarism built on consensual norms integrated over time, but rather an imposition, as Alderson and Hurrell argue, over which the US and its allies would stand guard. Paradoxically, the degree of solidarism and shared values in international society can be seen as a function of the US's willingness to promote them, given its hegemonic power as a result of the Cold War victory (Hurrell 1999: 291). Between 1990 and 2001, the US can be seen promoting pluralist norms of international society in the Gulf War and more solidarist claims in Somalia and Kosovo, albeit that these interventions – particularly in Kosovo – contained the seeds of coercion. The post-9/11 period, however, brought about the pursuit of a solidarist society forged not through consensual normative development but rather through the hegemonic power's violent promotion of these norms. Therein lies the danger inherent in solidarism: that it is always the expression of a particular moral and political view represented by the hegemon, but not universally.

What did 9/11 do to the US? It created a catalyst for US exceptionalism and unipolarity. The US was instrumental in creating the institutions of international society but ultimately is beholden to no organisation. It remained multilateral, but now in terms of a coalition of the willing. US action post-9/11 is clearly coercive. It also promotes many solidarist values, not least of which is individual freedom. It is still too early to determine the future of US foreign policy, despite a Democrat President. The difficulties experienced in Afghanistan and Iraq should push the US towards multilateralism.

What is most important to understand is the impact of 9/11 – that the US can no longer rely on isolation but must engage internationally. Whether this will be in terms of a hierarchy or an attempt to create a parallel society or indeed to return to building the liberal institutions it created remains to be seen. As Wight (1978: 30) argued, the 'most conscious theme in international history is not the growth of internationalism. It is the series of efforts by one power after another to gain mastery of the states system'. Indeed, could we not ask whether US foreign policy post/9-11 is the fourth conflagration of a recurrent historical trend of a 'blaze of conviction and fanaticism' (Wight 1978: 82)? The US has found itself challenged in Iraq, but this should not distract us from the reality of what led to the war, an attempt at enforcing revolutionary change on international society.

What is the essential difference in US foreign policy after 9/11? It is certainly more confrontational, but it is here that the justifications for war are pertinent, showing a clear reference to the installation of peace and freedom. Yet is there any real, essential difference between this and the rhetoric of human rights? Has solidarism ever been anything other than coercive in some form? Surely it is the method of promotion. Essential solidarist values do not change, but the method of their advance and, as importantly, their source, can. It is in both of these that solidarism can be seen to be advanced by a hegemonic US state as much as it can in terms of widening circles of Western values and political organisation.

We need to move away from the realist idea that 'we are much beholden to Machiavelli and others, that write what men do and not what they ought to do', but rather understand that coercive solidarists firmly believe in the project they are advancing in both word and deed (Francis Bacon, in Wight 1978: 26). Solidarism attempts to prioritise human life, yet the slow consensual solidarism evident in international relations has ensured the creation of regional solidarist societies, while the majority of humanity suffers in societies far too resemblant of systemic anarchy. Solidarism needs to critically engage with its 'darker' potential, but it may very well be that for many living in insecurity, coercive solidarism carries both great threat and great promise.

Perhaps it is best to finish with a question posed by Paul Johnson, who wondered, 'How much more fearful and violent would our world be if America did not exist?' He answers himself by saying: 'We must thank God that there is a nation strong enough to accept the role of Leviathan, and to protect us from the evil forces that roam the world, seeking to destroy' (Boot 2005: 42). Of course, many would argue that it is US action that has caused the most harm and violence, yet their exporting of freedom and coercive pursuit of solidarist values is no different from the often found historical precedent of freedom being found in the peace after war – indeed, this *is* the American experience.

Bibliography

Alderson, K. and Hurrell, A. (eds) 2000. *Hedley Bull on International Society*. London: Macmillan.

Boot, M. 2005. Defending and advancing freedom. *Commentary*. Council on Foreign Relations.

Boot, M. 2002. *The Savage Wars of Peace: Small Wars and the Rise of American Power*. New York: Basic Books.

Bush, G.W. 2002a. Commencement Address at the United States Military Academy in West Point, New York. 1 June. Available at: http://www.presidency.ucsb.edu/ws/index.php?pid=62730&st=freedom&st1 (accessed 19 September 2007).

Bush, G.W. 2002b. Remarks in Shreveport, Louisiana. 3 December. Available at: http://www.presidency.ucsb.edu/ws/?pid=73189 (accessed 21 September 2007).

Bush, G.W. 2003. Remarks at MacDill air force base in Tampa, Florida. Available at: http://www.presidency.ucsb.edu/ws/index.php?pid=64980&st=saddam&st1=iraq (accessed 19 September 2007).

Bush, G.W. 2004. Remarks made when accepting the Presidential nomination at the Republican National Convention in New York City. 2 September. Available at: http://www.presidency.ucsb.edu/ws/index.php?pid=72727&st=&st1 (accessed 23 September 2007).

Butterfield, H. and Wight, M. (eds) 1966. *Diplomatic Investigations: Essays in the Theory of International Politics*. London: Allen and Unwin.

Buzan, B. 2004. *The United States and the Great Powers: World Politics in the Twenty-first Century*. Cambridge: Polity Press.

Clark, I. 2005. *Legitimacy in International Society*. Oxford: Oxford University Press.

Cox, M., Ikenberry, J. and Inoguchi, T. 2000. *American Democracy Promotion – Impulses, Strategies and Impacts*. Oxford: Oxford University Press.

Davidson, L. 2005. Christian Zionism as a representation of American manifest destiny. *Critique: Critical Middle Eastern Studies* 14 (2), 157–69.

Dunne, T. 1998. *Inventing International Society: A History of the English School*. London: Macmillan.

Dunne, T., Kurki, M., Smith, S. (eds) 2007. *International Relations: Theories, Discipline and Diversity*. Oxford: Oxford University Press.

Ferguson, N. 2004. *Colossus: The Rise and Fall of the American Empire*. London: Penguin Books.

Fukuyama, F. 2006. *After the Neocons: America at the Crossroads*. London: Profile Books.

Hurrell, A. and Woods, N. 1999. *Inequality, Globalization and World Politics*. New York: Oxford University Press.

Hyde, R. 2007. *Altar of World Leadership*, Christians in Political Science series. Wheaton College: Wheaton.

Ikenberry, G.J. 2000. America's liberal grand strategy: democracy and national security in the post-war era. In M. Cox et al. (eds) *American Democracy Promotion: Impulses, Strategies and Impacts*. Oxford: Oxford University Press, 103–150.

Ikenberry, G.J. 2005. Review of legitimacy in international relations. *Foreign Affairs*. September/October. Available at: http://www.foreignaffairs.org/20050901 fabook84517/ian-clark/legitimacy-in-international-society.html (accessed 17 April 2009).

Jackson, R.H. 2000. *The Global Covenant: Human Conduct in a World of States*. Oxford: Oxford University Press.

Jackson, R.H. and Sorensen, G. 2007. *Introduction to International Relations: Theories and Approaches*. New York: Oxford University Press.

Kagan, R. 2004. America's Crisis of Legitimacy. *Foreign Affairs* (82), March/ April.

Kerton-Johnson, N. 2008. Justifying the use of force in a post-9/11 world: striving for hierarchy in international society. *International Affairs* 84(5), 991–1007.

Knock, T.J. 2008. Woodrow Wilson's internationalism. In G.J. Ikenberry et al. (eds) *The Crisis of American Foreign Policy: Wilsonianism in the Twenty-First Century*. Princeton: Princeton University Press, 25–52.

Linklater, A. and Suganami, H. 2006. *The English School of International Relations: A Contemporary Reassessment*. Cambridge: Cambridge University Press.

Lincoln, A. 1862. Second annual message. Available at: http://www.presidency.ucsb.edu/ws/index.php?pid=29503&st=&st1 (accessed 15 November 2008).

Lincoln, A. 1863. Gettysburg address. Available at: http://www.lincolnstudies.com/documents/11191863.html (accessed 15 November 2008).

Lindberg, T. 2002. The War on Terror: the Bush doctrine. *Hoover Digest* 4. Available at: http://www.hoover.org/publications/digest/4495996.html (accessed 10 November 2008).

Niebuhr, R. 1952. *The Irony of American History*. New York: Charles Scribner's Sons.

Nye, J.S. 2002. *The Paradox of American Power: Why the World's Only Superpower Can't Go It Alone*. New York: Oxford University Press.

Roberts, A. 2003. Law and the use of force after Iraq. *Survival* 45(2), 31–56.

Smith, T. 2000. National security liberalism and American foreign policy. In M. Cox et al. (eds) *American Democracy Promotion: Impulses, Strategies and Impacts*. Oxford: Oxford University Press, 85–102.

Suskind, R. 2004. Without a doubt. *New York Times Magazine*, 17 October.

Weinberg, A.K. 1963. *Manifest Destiny: A Study of Nationalist Expansionism in American History.* Chicago: Quadrangle Books.

Wheeler, N.J. 1992. Pluralist or solidarist conceptions of international society: Bull and Vincent on humanitarian intervention. *Millennium* 21(3), 463–87.

Wheeler, N.J. 1996. Guardian angel or global gangster: a review of the ethical claims of international society. *Political Studies* XLIV.

Wheeler, N.J. 2000. *Saving Strangers: Humanitarian Intervention in International Society*. Oxford: Oxford University Press.

Wheeler, N.J. 2003. The Bush doctrine: the dangers of American exceptionalism in a revolutionary Age. *Asian Perspective* 27 (4), 183–216.

Wight, M. 1978. *Power Politics*, ed. H. Bull and H. Carsten. London: Leicester University Press.

Wight, M. 1991. *International Theory. The Three Traditions/Martin Wight*, ed. G. Wight and B. Porter. London: Leicester University Press.

Wight, M. 1966. Western values in international relations. In H. Butterfield and M. Wight (eds) *Diplomatic Investigations: Essays in the Theory of International Politics*. London: Allen and Unwin.

Chapter 8

The History of Modern Military Humanitarianism Revisited

Ivan Manokha

Introduction

The history of modern military humanitarianism has been constructed as an evolution from just war theory of the Middle Ages, through to early modern humanitarianism as an exception to the rule of state sovereignty codified by the Treaty of Westphalia, through to modern human rights-based humanitarianism as an exception to the UN Charter (e.g., Fonteyne 1974; Bull 1977; Brownlie 1981; Vincent 1990; Abiew 1999). Such a view conceives of the modern doctrine of humanitarian intervention as a continuation of practices whose origins go back to the early Medieval period. This chapter seeks to demonstrate the deficiencies of such a construction of the history of modern military humanitarianism, and to show that apparently similar actions, such as the use of force by Medieval monarchs to protect Christians outside their kingdoms and contemporary instances of humanitarian intervention to enforce human rights, are in fact fundamentally different phenomena in terms of their causal relations with their respective socio-economic contexts. The argument focuses on the historical relationship of dialectical causality between social structures of production on the one hand, and forms of military humanitarianism on the other. The nature of this relationship is analysed with the help of the concept of 'ideology' used as a critical concept, or ideology in the negative sense (Larrain 1983; Maclean 1981, 1988; Allman 2001; Žižek 1994; Laclau and Mouffe 1985; Therborn 1980).

The term 'ideology' has generally been used to refer to political programmes of social classes or political parties, and this is a meaning which Jorg Larrain designates as 'positive' (1983: 4). However, there is another usage of the term, namely what Larrain calls 'ideology in the negative sense', which Marx, particularly in *The German Ideology*, uses as a critical concept to refer to 'ideas which express practice inadequately' (Larrain 1983: 23). For Marx 'ideology is conceived of as a distorted form of knowledge' (Maclean 1988: 309) or as 'a defective way of thinking' (Allman 2001: 47). Such a 'distorted form of knowledge' is not reducible to a deliberate project of a class; ideological ideas are 'encouraged to a great extent' (Lukacs 1971) by a social reality which is 'inverted', that is, which appears different from what it really is and favours the development of ideas that express it inadequately, and may be shared by all social classes. However, ideology necessarily serves the interests of those social forces that benefit from the existing order, for the role it plays in the negation or concealment of contradictions inevitably contributes to the reproduction of those contradictions (Larrain 1983: 28).

This chapter demonstrates that religious humanitarianism of the Middle Ages advanced a view of justice which was an integral part of the feudal order, characterised by surplus extraction based on relations of personal and juridical dependence, carried out by means of political and military coercion. The unequal relations between feudal lords and serfs were cemented by their belief in divine will. Religious representation and understanding of social relations, shared by all classes, was an ideology in the negative sense, which necessarily reproduced the feudal relations of power and inequality and helped sustain the dominant position of feudal lords and the continuous subordination of serfs. What has been overlooked in the existing analyses of the history of just war is that the early Christian humanitarianism of Augustine, and the Medieval humanitarianism of Aquinas, Vitoria, Suarez and others of their era was part of this ideology, as it was wholly premised on arguments that expressed the meaning and purpose of just wars as being an outcome of God's will. In this way, one of the causal roles of the doctrine of just war was a contribution to the perpetuation of a divine interpretation of feudal social relations and their reproduction. With the development of capitalism a totally different social setting emerges and with it the nature of just war just wary is fundamentally transformed.

Feudalism, the Ideology of Divine Right and Just War

Feudal relations of production were characterised by various forms of personal and juridical dependence of producers on those appropriating the surplus of their labour, and the function of surplus extraction was carried out by means of political coercion. It was a mode of production dominated by the land and a natural economy, in which neither labour nor the products of labour were commodities. The peasants who occupied and tilled the land were not its owners, with agrarian property being privately controlled by feudal lords, who extracted surplus from the peasants by politico-legal relations of compulsion in the form of labour-service, in kind or in the form of money (Hindness and Hirst 1975: 223). The feudal society was thereby characterised by a juridical amalgamation of economic exploitation with political authority and property was 'politically constituted' (Brenner 1993). The feudal lord, in his turn, would often be the vassal of a feudal superior, and the chain of such dependent tenures (linked to military service) would extend upwards to the peak of the system – a monarch. Political sovereignty was not focused in a single centre but was divided into particularist zones with overlapping boundaries, and no universal centre of competence (Anderson 1996: 148). There were no secular sovereign states in Medieval Europe but diverse ill-defined Christian political communities which were seen as comprising a greater family of a Christian Commonwealth and which owed allegiance to the Pope (Boucher 1998: 204).

The direct political exploitation of producers and unequal class relations of the feudal order had an ideology which helped to sustain them. This ideology involved interpreting social relations as having a divine origin and purpose with each individual performing a specific function ascribed by God: every member of society must receive the means suited to his or her function, and must claim no more. This ideology spiritualised the material by incorporating it in a divine universe (Tawney 1990: 35–6), or as Larrain puts it, in feudalism 'ideology assumes a religious form; the justification of personal dependence is found in a sacred order which is revealed by God and which consequently cannot be altered by man. Personal dependence upon, and loyalty to, the landlord is spontaneously expressed in the ideological submission to God, from which all subordination is modeled' (Larrain 1983: 38). As one Medieval English hymn verse had it, 'The rich man in his castle, The poor man at his gate, God made them, high or lowly, And ordered their estate' (Barrett 1994: 253).

In this social setting, with Christianity providing the basis and meaning for all social relations and institutions, the question of waging a war was not an easy one, for killing was prohibited by the Commandment, 'Thou shall not kill'. The reconciliation of war and Christian values emerged in the notion of just war as a God-ordained war that served to punish those who violated God's laws: although killing is prohibited by God, in some cases God not only permits the use of violence, but in fact orders its use to punish those who sinned. As Saint Augustine (354–430) states, just wars are those 'which avenge injuries' and 'punish wrongs', 'wars which *God Himself ordains*' (Eppstein 1935: 74, emphasis added). The wrongs to be punished include 'the desire for harming, the cruelty of avenging, an unruly and implacable animosity, the rage of rebellion, the lust of domination and the like … justly wars are waged by the good by God's will and at some legitimate command' (Eppstein 1935: 69). We may note in passing the inclusion by Augustine of 'the rage of rebellion' as an example of wrongdoing; in the humanitarianism that would develop with the rise of capitalism it is the violent *suppression* of rebellion that would be seen as a just cause for war. Augustine, however, believed in the divine origin of rulers and saw rebellion of subjects as unjust. This is apparent when he talks of the dilemma a soldier faces when his king gives him an order, which he thinks is unjust: 'A righteous man … may do the duty belonging to his position in the state in fighting at the command of his sovereign: in some cases it is plainly the Will of God that he should fight, and in others where it is not so plain, the command on the part of the king may be unrighteous … [but the soldier is innocent] because his position makes obedience a duty' (Scott 1934: 184). Thus, the arguments of Augustine confirm the view of religion as being the ultimate authority, and they are based on a divine interpretation of social relations. To put it differently, they were clearly part of that ideology which helped consolidate the relations of personal and political dependence by seeing them as God-given.

The foundations laid by Saint Augustine constituted the reference point for subsequent writings on war by medieval theologians and theorists, such as Saint Isidore (560–636), who added to Augustine's criteria of just war a requirement of formal declaration (Brière 1938: 27); Saint Yves of Chartres (1040–1116) who propagated Augustine's teachings, including his ideas about just war (Regout 1935: 47–8); and Gratian, a twelfth-century canon lawyer from Bologna, whose attempt to systematise Augustine's views on just war was the most elaborate one before Saint Thomas Aquinas. In his *Decretals*, and particularly in *Causa XXIII*, Gratian states that 'it is not a sin to serve as a soldier' and that 'soldiers can please God with warlike arms', for they can wage a just war willed by God (Eppstein 1935: 81). He further maintains that a just war must be formally declared, and must be waged for a Just Cause, which may include the following motives: to regain what has been stolen, to repel an attack of enemies and to defend the fatherland from barbarians. 'With the true servants of God', he says, 'even wars are pacific as they are entered upon not through cruelty or greed and have as their object peace, the repression of the wicked and the deliverance of the good (Eppstein 1935: 89).

Saint Thomas Aquinas (1226–1274) develops the doctrine further with repeated references to Augustine and is explicit about a divine view of just war, as well as about the divine meaning of political authority. He identifies three conditions for a war to be considered as just: the legitimate authority of the sovereign that is God-ordained, 'for he is God's minister, an avenger to execute wrath upon him that doth evil' (Scott 1934: 192); a just cause and a rightful intention. For Aquinas, 'a just cause is required … a just war … avenges wrongs, when a nation or state has to be punished, for refusing to make amends for the wrongs inflicted by its subjects, or to restore what it has seized unjustly … Thirdly, it is necessary that the belligerents should have a rightful intention, so that they intend the advancement of good, or the avoidance of evil … The passion for inflicting harm, the cruel thirst for vengeance, an unpacific and relentless spirit, the fever of revolt, the lust of power, and suchlike things, all these are rightly condemned in war' (Scott 1934: 192–3). Here we may note once again how 'revolt' or rebellion is classified among such other wrongdoings as the lust of power and cruelty.

Another Medieval thinker to speak about just war is Francisco de Vitoria (1480–1546) in his discussion of the Spanish war against American Indians. His beliefs are also grounded in religion and the just cause consists in the conversion of barbarians to Christianity. Vitoria states that the Indians engaged in acts that 'prevented the Spaniards from freely preaching the Gospel' and this justified the use of force by the Spaniards 'until they succeed in obtaining facilities and safety for preaching the Gospel' (Muldoon 1979: 155). Furthermore, the Spanish wars against princes who force the converts to return to idolatry were just 'not only on religion, but on human friendship and alliance, inasmuch as the native converts to Christianity have become friends and allies of Christians' (Muldoon 1979: 156). Here Vitoria is in agreement with another thinker, Suarez, who argued that a just war may be waged if a native prince 'forcibly compelled his subjects to return to idolatry' (Abiew 1999: 34). For Vitoria, when 'a large part of the Indians' had been converted to Christianity, the Pope 'might give them a Christian sovereign and depose their unbelieving rulers' (Muldoon 1979: 156). Thus, once again we find in statements on just war the ideological assumptions of the religiously grounded just cause and of divine origins of social relations and political authority.

Capitalism, the Ideology of Individual Rights and Humanitarianism in the Pre-Charter Period

Beginning with the late-sixteenth and early-seventeenth century profound transformations of social relations take place in Europe, starting in England and later spreading to the rest of Europe[1] (Wood and Wood 1997: 5–26, Wood 2002; Brenner 1993; Hill 1978). What is characteristic of the emerging order is the central role of the market: capitalism is a system in which goods and services are produced for profitable exchange and all economic actors are dependent on the market. This is true not only of workers, who must sell their labour power for a wage, but also of capitalists, who depend on the market to buy their inputs and to sell their outputs (Wood 2002: 2). The function of surplus extraction is gradually transformed from being based on politico-juridical means into one carried out in the market by economic means. It is now performed through a wage-labour relation as the producer is completely separated from the conditions of labour and the appropriator has absolute private property in the means of production. Once producers lose free access to the means of production, labour becomes a commodity, 'that very special commodity that makes capitalism possible' (Marx 1976: 270). As labour-power becomes a commodity, feudal politico-juridical inequality and coercion become unnecessary for surplus extraction since it is now the economic need that supplies the immediate compulsion forcing the worker to transfer surplus labour to the capitalist in order to gain access to the means of production. In other words, the social allocation of resources and labour no longer takes place by means of political direction or religious obligation, but through the mechanisms of commodity exchange (Wood 1995: 28–9).

Such a method of surplus extraction gradually makes possible political emancipation and political equality, as political coercion is no longer necessary for surplus to be extracted from the direct producers (Marx 1976: 270–71). This allows for the development of new political structures breaking with the tradition of divine right and emphasising the equality of individuals, their natural rights and their power to establish and change political authority. However, what is crucial is that political and civil liberty and equality are increasingly seen as *the* liberty

1 The discussion of the origins of capitalism, particularly the development of merchant capital in the fifteenth and sixteenth century, the impact of trade (especially in spices) and of the gradual accumulation of capital on medieval societies (the role of money and particularly the permissibility of lending money at an interest) and their role in the Reformation, are beyond the scope of this chapter.

and *the* equality, while the fact that there exist exploitation and inequality in the market is taken for granted and objectified. In other words, there develops a new form of ideology constituted in the view that in capitalism individuals are free and equal, freedom and equality being in fact confined to the realm of the political. Such an ideology first appears in the writings of social contract theorists such as Hobbes and Locke, while the foundations of its internationalisation are laid by Kant (Manokha 2008a: 86–93).

The development of capitalism and the transformation of the relationship between people and political authority was accompanied by the emergence of the notion of state sovereignty and modern conceptions of international relations and international law. Beginning with the late sixteenth century, well-organised political units, monarchic and national in form and secular in government, started replacing ill-defined feudal entities and principalities, owing allegiance to Pope and Emperor (Brownlie 1981: 11). Different institutions evolved to maintain order and stability in a system of sovereign states such as international law, treaties, international conferences and diplomacy (Watson 1984: 23–5). With the development of the rule of sovereignty a question emerged as to whether it was absolute or whether there could be exceptions to it. A number of theorists, beginning with Grotius, started asserting that the rule of sovereignty ought to have an exception, namely, the use of force for just ends. Although arguments of these thinkers resembled those of Medieval just war theory, there was a crucial difference in terms of social assumptions that permeated their theories, namely, the notion of individual natural rights and freedom from political oppression which were seen as just causes, and the absence of the divine interpretation of political authority. The question of the permissibility of interventions 'became secularized in the principle of lending lawful assistance to peoples struggling against tyranny' (Abiew 1999: 34) and such publicists as Grotius, Vattel and others 'formulated the rules of international law in terms of the recognition of natural rights' (Abiew 1999: 36). In other words, a *new* doctrine of just war emerged as part of the new ideology peculiar to capitalism.

It is in the following statement by Grotius, regarded by Lauterpacht as 'the first authoritative statement of the principle of humanitarian intervention' (Lauterpacht 1946: 46), that we may discern the beginning of a new view of humanitarianism: 'there is a question, whether a war for the subjects of another be just, for the purpose of defending them from injuries by their ruler … If a tyrant … practices atrocities towards his subjects, which no just man can approve, the right of human social connexion is not cut off in such a case … It would not follow that others may not take up arms for them' (Abiew 1999: 35). Thus, in Grotius we begin to see implicitly a different view of relations between political authority and its subjects. It is the atrocities by a tyrannical ruler that 'no man can approve', and not rebellion of subjects as Augustine or Aquinas would have it that are seen as a just cause for war. Grotius, as noted by Lauterpacht (1944: 24–5), endorsed the fundamental rights and freedoms of the individual in a way similar to Locke. Similar views on just war may be found in the writings of another thinker of the period, Vattel.

Vattel embraces the new relationship between political authority and the subjects as no longer based on divine right but on the will of the people, and argues that a foreign intervention to end tyranny is just: 'the Sovereign is one to whom the Nation has entrusted the empire and the care of the government; it has endowed him with his rights … [But] if the Prince, attacking the fundamental laws, gives his people a legitimate reason to resist him, if tyranny becomes so unbearable as to cause the Nation to rise, any foreign power is entitled to help an oppressed people that has requested assistance' (Fonteyne 1974: 214–15).

Such a view of what constitutes a just cause for the use of force since then becomes explicit in the doctrine of humanitarian use of force. A body of international law that develops, particularly in the nineteenth century, discusses humanitarian intervention in these terms, that is, in terms of individual legal rights and political freedom, or in ideological terms. For example, Bluntschli, argues that 'one is authorized to intervene to ensure respect for the individual rights … whenever they happen to be violated in the struggles between citizens of a single state' (Bluntschli 1874: 73). Another publicist, Woolsey, asserts that an intervention is justified if 'some extraordinary state of things is brought about by the crime of a government against its subjects' (Woolsey 1875: 73). The same can be seen in Fiore's statement a few years later: 'if a prince, in order to put down a revolution, violates all the generally accepted laws of war, has prisoners executed, authorizes destruction, looting, arson … inaction and indifference of other states would constitute an egocentric policy contrary to the rights of all' (Fiore 1885: 521–2). Similar views were later expressed by such prominent jurists as Rougier (1910: 489), Fauchille (1921: 570), Borchard, (1922: 14), Graham (1924: 327) and other prominent authorities in international law who saw protection of 'the rights of man' such as the right to life, liberty, freedom from oppression and illegal persecution as a legitimate reason for the violation of the rule of sovereignty and non-intervention.

As regards state practice, the instances of intervention seen by a number of scholars as examples of humanitarian war in the pre-Charter period include a series of actions of European Powers against the Ottoman Empire following the massacres of Christians (Mandelstam 1923; Stowell 1932; Fonteyne 1974; Abiew 1999; Kolb 2003). Although waged for the purpose of religious freedom, they were not justified on religious grounds in the manner of Vitoria or Innocent IV, but on the grounds of rights and humanity. As Abiew observes, the doctrine as practiced in the nineteenth century 'was mainly concerned with the rights of Christians, although secularisation of religious belief led to basing such intervention on behalf of the dignity of man' (Abiew 1999: 47). Thus, there was an intervention of France, Great Britain and Russia in Greece in 1829 to stop massacres by the Sublime Porte, justified by the Major Powers on the grounds of the 'sentiments of humanity' (Ganji 1962: 22). As Moskowitz observed, this intervention was an occasion 'on which the doctrine of 'humanitarian intervention' has been invoked on behalf of nationals or inhabitants of foreign countries felt to have been subjected to practices which shock the conscience of mankind' (Moskowitz 1958: 16,

Lillich 1967: 332; Reisman and McDougal 1969: 180). Another case is the 1860 intervention of France in Syria following the massacre of thousands of Maronite Christians by the local population with the complicity of Turkey (Stowell 1921). Rougier observed at the time that 'the Syrian intervention was a humanitarian intervention' (Rougier 1910: 474).This view is also shared by Brownlie (1981: 340). The European Powers also acted in Bosnia, Herzegovina and Bulgaria in 1876–1878 following Turkish oppression of the Christian populations which was described by Morley, an observer as 'the most heinous crimes that had stained the history of the century' (Stowell 1921: 127). After Turkey's refusal to improve the position of Christians, Russia declared war on Porte with the consent of Austria, Prussia France and Italy.

It is important to note that the ideological interpretation of social relations in capitalist societies was not confined to taking partial (political and civil) emancipation and equality of individuals as *the* freedom and *the* equality. It also involved the equation of these individual rights with 'civilised behaviour'. In this respect, the doctrine of just war had as one of its causal powers, in particular in the nineteenth century, a contribution to the international expansion of capital through colonisation. Colonisation was constructed and justified as a civilising mission, and part of what distinguished 'civilised' nations from 'barbarians' involved respect for individual liberties. For example, one of the fathers of Western liberalism John Stuart Mill argued that some uncivilised nations had no right to sovereignty and 'to suppose that the same international customs, and the same rules of international morality, can obtain between one civilized nation and another, and between civilized nations and barbarians, is a grave error' (Mill 1859: 167). Part of what he describes as 'uncivilised' is related to a denial of individual liberties to subjects by tyrannical rulers and Mill thereby, even if implicitly, invokes the new doctrine of a just war (Mill 1859: 169–70). Similar arguments that restricted the applicability of norms of international law to the civilised states were made by some jurists. For example, Martens argued that 'vis-à-vis non-civilized nations … intervention by the civilized powers is legitimate, when the population of those countries is exposed to persecutions or massacres. In those circumstances, it is justified by humanitarian considerations [which] are not applicable to the relations between civilized powers' (Fonteyne 1974: 219). Stated at the time of colonial expansion of the 'civilised' states into the 'non-civilised world', such a doctrine may be said to have contributed to its legitimation. Similar arguments may be found in other nineteenth century writings, most notably in Lorimer who distinguished between civilised, barbarian and savage societies, the latter two categories being excluded from the rule of sovereignty (Elonge Osako 2002). Again, part of what made them barbaric and uncivilised was absence of individual liberties and colonial wars were therefore just wars (Bula-Bula 1999).

Let us now look at the relationship between capitalism and human rights enforcement in the period following the adoption of the UN Charter when the 'rights of man' are proclaimed as universal human rights.

Global Capitalism, Human Rights and Human Rights Enforcement in the Post-Charter Period

With the creation of the United Nations and the adoption of the Universal Declaration of Human Rights, humanitarian use of force or humanitarian intervention become defined as the use of force in cases where governments abuse (fundamental) human rights of their citizens, meaning political and civil rights. For example, Lauterpacht observed in 1955 that 'there is a substantial body of opinion and of practice in support of the view … that when a State renders itself guilty of cruelties against and persecution of its nationals in such a way as to deny their fundamental human rights and to shock the conscience of mankind, intervention is legally permissible' (Lauterpacht 1955: 312). This view was shared by numerous other jurists and publicists (Lillich 1967: 210; Reisman and McDougal 1969: 444; Fonteyne 1974: 257–8; Moore 1969: 264; Perez-Vera 1969: 418; Brownlie 1974; Scheffer 1992). Thus, the ideological arguments of the likes of Grotius and Vattel when the modern doctrine of just war emerged with the rise of capitalism, remained at the core of the doctrine of humanitarian intervention in the post-Charter period.

During the Cold War, however, the development of humanitarian intervention was constrained by considerations of international stability which were privileged over other values. There were three cases of intervention that had humanitarian outcomes and although they were predominantly justified on other than humanitarian grounds, a number of scholars argue that the Indian intervention in East Pakistan in 1971, the Tanzanian intervention in Uganda in 1979, and Vietnam's intervention in Cambodia in 1978, were nevertheless examples of humanitarian intervention (Abiew 1999: 113; Teson 1988: 179–88; International Commission of Jurists 1972: 24–7). However, with the disappearance of the Cold War 'straightjacket' there has been a veritable explosion in the development of the notion of human rights and in the practice of their enforcement. In the rest of the chapter it is argued that today, in the context of what neo-Gramscian scholars refer to as a global hegemony of capital, this global concern with (fundamental) human rights on the part of (Western) states, international organisations, business firms and NGOs, and the practice of their enforcement, have an unintended consequence of constituting *moral leadership* that any hegemonic formation, according to Gramsci, requires. There is no place here to analyse all the various pledges and practices aimed at global human rights promotion and protection and we will deal only with humanitarian intervention, which is their strongest expression.[2]

Gramsci distinguishes between a rule based on coercion and a rule based on consent and 'intellectual and moral leadership' or hegemony (Gramsci 1971: 57). He argues that consent is secured by dominant social forces by means of

2 For more detailed argument concerning the development of a form of Gramscian moral *and* intellectual leadership in the late modern global political economy see Manokha 2006, 2008a and 2008b.

education of subordinate groups to ensure that they share a particular world outlook and a particular set of beliefs (intellectual leadership) on the one hand, and the universalisation of certain moral values and norms (moral leadership), on the other. For Gramsci, the task of hegemonic forces is to 'educate' the masses, to '*produce*' subordinate groups' [emphasis added] understanding of their role in society and of society itself, to make sure that they accept the existing society 'without criticism' (Gramsci 1957: 66). Such a 'production' of consent must be complemented by a system of moral values which, once established, influences the subordinate group's 'moral behaviour and the direction of [their] will' (Gramsci 1957: 67). In short, the establishment of a hegemony consists in 'building a new intellectual and moral order, and hence the need to elaborate the most universal concepts' (Gramsci 1957: 5).

Gramsci's concept of hegemony has been applied to the realm of the international by a number of scholars who are referred to as the 'neo-Gramscians'. They share the view that the last three decades have constituted a phase of transition from a post-war US hegemony to a new form of hegemonic formation centred around transnational capital (Manokha 2008a, 2008b). The hegemonic position of highly mobile capital is institutionalised in a variety of multilateral organisations and treaties under pressure from not only transnational corporations, but also 'organic' intellectuals such as corporate allies in governments, inter-state organisations, and different policy-making and advisory networks, which develop neoliberal policy guidelines and reduce the role of states to ensuring the working of the market mechanism. Gill argues that at the core of the emerging hegemonic formation is a nucleus which comprises the following elements: G-8 state apparatuses, transnational capital, associated privileged workers and smaller firms (businesses linked as contractors or suppliers, import-export firms, and service companies, such as stockbrokers, accountants, consultancies and lobbyists) (Gill 1995: 400–401).

Competitiveness in the world market has become the ultimate criterion of state policy which justifies the gradual removal of the measures of social protection built up in the era of Keynesianism and welfare state (Cox 1999: 12), and there has developed a form of 'new constitutionalism' or the institutionalisation of neoliberalism at the macro-level of power in the quasi-legal restructuring of the state and international political forms' (Gill 1995: 412). The element of consent in the developing global order, despite international civil society protests, is underlined by a relative decline of class and radical politics, and a noticeable decline in the power and activity of trade unions as enterprises increasingly locate their plants in different countries which makes trade union organisation and bargaining more difficult (Cox 1999; Beck 1997).

The role of moral leadership in the development of consent has so far been neglected in neo-Gramscian analyses, and yet it is repeatedly emphasised by Gramsci. In addition to the arguments quoted above with respect to the need to create 'a new moral order', that is 'to elaborate the most universal concepts', Gramsci maintains that even coercion or punishment should play a role in moral leadership and should be carried out 'with moral import' (Gramsci 1957: 187–8), an argument which is of particular importance for the present analysis of the use of humanitarian force. For Gramsci the role of moral leadership consists in contributing to the development of consent through providing the existing order with moral qualities which, at the same time, would contribute to the reproduction and objectification of the existing relations of production, for 'although hegemony is ethical-political, it must also be economic, must necessarily be based on the decisive function exercised by the leading group in the decisive nucleus of economic activity' (Gramsci 1971: 161). From these observations by Gramsci we may infer that moral leadership has two principal characteristics: on the one hand, it involves universalisable moral values, and on the other it naturalises, via these values, the existing order and its *material* foundations so that they are taken for granted or attain the status of 'common sense' (Gramsci 1957: 67). Below it is argued that modern military humanitarianism satisfies both of these criteria. That is to say, although humanitarian use of force is a noble practice which may save people from slaughter or genocide, in the late-modern world it has an *unintended* consequence of contributing to the development of a global hegemony of capital, which has condemned millions of people to a miserable existence, poverty, malnutrition and death. We begin with its 'moral import' or appeal, and then examine its compatibility with capital's interests.

The Cold War was followed by a number of military humanitarian operations: the UN Security Council-authorised actions in Northern Iraq, carried out mainly by the US, Britain and France; in Bosnia-Herzegovina, by a multinational UN contingent UNPROFOR; in Somalia, by the US-led UNITAF force and later by the UNOSOM II contingent; in East Timor, mainly by Australian forces and a series of interventions in Sierra Leone by the Economic Community of West African States (ECOWAS), Britain and the UN. There was also the case of humanitarian intervention in Kosovo, which was undertaken by the North Atlantic Treaty Organisation (NATO) without UN authorisation.

The most recent US operations in Afghanistan and Iraq were not humanitarian operations *per se* (officially, they were to combat terrorism and destroy weapons of mass destruction), but they involved numerous references to human rights and individual freedom and were accompanied by moral rhetoric. In the case of Afghanistan, George W. Bush stated that the tragedies of 11 September were an 'attack on individual human rights' and 'against civilization itself', and the war on terrorism must 'defend human dignity and individual freedoms which constitute a core tenet of civilized people everywhere' (Bush 2001). The Italian Prime Minister Berlusconi stated that 'the superiority of Western civilisation which guarantees respect for human rights and religion' justifies the war because 'this respect certainly does not exist in Afghanistan' (Bush 2001: 3). Tony Blair stated that the war in Afghanistan was 'a fight for freedom and justice … to bring those same values of democracy and freedom to people round the world' (Bush 2001). In the case of Iraq, George W. Bush, presenting the case for war, stated that 'Iraq continues to commit extremely grave violations of human rights', and that 'these horrors concealed from the world by the apparatus of a totalitarian state' (Bush 2002). The US Department of State explicitly placed the war in Iraq in the same category with other humanitarian interventions when it stated that 'those who supported the Clinton administration's armed interventions in Bosnia, Haiti and Kosovo have even more reason to support a US-led war with Iraq' for 'Saddam Hussein is one of the worst tyrants of the past 50 years' (USDOS 2003).

In all these declarations we can see a sense of a moral mission, an ever growing commitment to liberate peoples living far away, a sense of moral leadership. Here we are not concerned with sincerity of these declarations, nor their relationship with national interests of states undertaking interventions. What we may note is that all these pledges taken together, along with policies aimed at human rights promotion and protection of other actors such as international organisations, increasingly provide the existing order with moral qualities. That is to say, it is an order in which it is claimed that freedom of people all over the world will be ensured, where dictators will be combated, and where practices of severe human rights abuses will be punished by force. In short, we can clearly see here a certain degree of Gramsci's 'moral import' and the post-Cold War 'decade of humanitarian intervention' (Kaldor 2001: 109) inevitably plays a crucial role in this.

But Gramsci's moral leadership, in addition to universalising moral values, is also supposed to contribute to consent, to normalisation and taking for granted of the existing economic relations. As we have already seen, the modern doctrine of humanitarian intervention embeds ideological assumptions concerning freedom, that is, freedom and emancipation are equated with political and civil individual rights. Economic exploitation and inequality not only continue to exist alongside these rights, but are objectified and taken for granted. This is not to say that they are rendered invisible – there is a lot of official statistical information about the growing gap between the rich and the poor, about millions of people living below any imaginable standard and about misery that affects the majority of the world's population. However, global poverty and massive inequality are treated as an outcome of objective forces of the market in which free agents come to trade voluntarily and freely with each other, or at worst as 'market failures' or 'market imperfections'. The most fundamental institutions of capitalism such as private property, wage labour, capital accumulation, production of commodities for their exchange value and not their use value, which necessarily involve the relations of exclusion (absolute private property means exclusion of non-owners from access to the owned item), of power (wage labour necessarily means that those who have to seek employment will be in a weaker position with respect to capital and its representatives) and inequality (capital accumulation, especially today, has led to flagrant inequalities), are thereby naturalised and objectified. The ideology of individual freedom, of the equality of individual rights, and of political emancipation inevitably contributes to their further naturalisation and objectification.

In addition to this, in the late-modern period there have developed certain global standards or what we may call a 'matrix' of the state form. Today the state is expected to be an efficient market economy with a reasonable economic growth, which is achieved through neoliberal structural reforms such as deregulation, the reduction of public spending and the privatisation of various state functions, and the liberalisation of trade. All these standards clearly serve the interests of transnational capital and ideological assumptions at the core of modern military humanitarianism are not only compatible with these standards, but contribute to their further normalisation. An indication of this is provided by post-intervention economic reforms in two countries, Haiti and Bosnia and Herzegovina. In both cases, the post-intervention reforms involved the implementation of standard neoliberal reforms (*Guardian* 1994: 9; IMF 1995a; *Washington Post* 2000: 1; Paris 1997: 55; Pugh 2002: 467–8; OHR 1995; IMF 1995b, 1998; World Bank 2000: iv). The results of these structural adjustment programmes in Haiti, referred to by Haitians as a 'Death Plan' (*Guardian* 1996: 4) were disastrous: they effectively destroyed Haiti's peasant economy by flooding it with cheap US imports, particularly rice, which forced Haitian farmers off their land to seek work in sweatshops and impoverished the population (per capita income dropped from around $600 in 1980 to $369 in 2001) (*Guardian* 2002: 9; McGowan 1997: 24–5; *Washington Post* 2000: 1).

In the case of Bosnia and Herzegovina, the outcome of neoliberal economic reforms had less dramatic outcome: they simply failed to lead to any substantial improvement in the quality of life. These two examples are conjunctural and do not illustrate the internal relationship between global capital and individual rights; their ontological status is comparable to the discussion of just war and Western colonial expansion above. However, they point to the way the ideological view of freedom as the respect of civil and political rights of individuals which is at the heart of modern military humanitarianism contributes to the further development of consent as regards the policies of deregulation, liberalisation of trade and capital flows and exploitation of labour, their further normalisation and objectification. In other words, they help us see how the practice of human rights enforcement contributes to the continuous reproduction of the conditions of the hegemonic position of capital in relation to the state/society complex.

Conclusion

This chapter has examined the historical development of modern military humanitarianism in relation to social context. With the help of the concept of ideology in the negative sense it has been argued that changes in the social context, in particular in the relations of production, have produced transformations in the causal powers of the use of humanitarian force. We have seen that just war theory of Medieval thinkers was part of the feudal ideology which consisted in interpreting social relations as God-ordained. The feudal relations of power, inequality and personal dependence were understood as having a divine origin and purpose, and religion-based Medieval just war theory played a causal role in reproducing such an interpretation of social relations, and thereby contributed to their continuous sustenance.

With the rise of capitalism and the transformations in the mode of surplus extraction, there developed a new ideology and the notion of just war gradually embodied its core assumptions. Political coercion and personal dependence of producers on those appropriating surplus became unnecessary as surplus extraction began to be carried in the realm of the market through the wage labour relationship. This made possible the political emancipation of individuals and the eventual equality of their political and civil rights, with the relations of exploitation and inequality now being located in the market. At the heart of the new ideology lay treating political equality and freedom as *the* freedom, with the inequality of property and the relations of exploitation being naturalised as objective outcomes of the functioning of the market.

The new humanitarianism, beginning with Grotius gradually embedded these assumptions and became part of the new ideology playing a causal role in its reproduction. Humanitarian intervention continued to have a causal relationship with capital and its international expansion after World War II when it became defined as the protection of (fundamental) human rights. With the disappearance of the Cold War 'straightjacket' and the unprecedented development of the practice of humanitarian intervention, its relationship with global capital has become significant once again. It has been argued that today the practice of human rights enforcement constitutes a crucial part of Gramsci's moral leadership in the context of the developing global hegemony of capital.

Here it is necessary to emphasise that modern military humanitarianism and the notion of human rights are in themselves noble ideas, which allow us to expose and hinder various forms of political oppression. In the late-modern world there exist numerous regimes which flagrantly violate political and civil rights of individuals, and there are many states marked by prolonged civil and ethnic wars accompanied by horrible crimes. Humanitarian use of force in such extreme situations is often an imperative. However, the implication of the argument developed in this chapter is that in the context of the late-modern world marked by incomparably larger forms of human suffering resulting from the functioning of global capitalism, the practice of human rights enforcement through humanitarian intervention has this paradoxical *unintended* consequence of contributing to the perpetuation of poverty and misery in the world. It deals with political crimes, while massive human suffering related to economic causes does not receive comparable attention, remains underprivileged, and the mechanisms responsible for this state of affairs are continuously objectified. To repeat, in cases of massive human rights violations humanitarian intervention is a necessity; however, a more long-term goal lies in the reform or transcendence of global capitalism, in particular its neoliberal version.

Bibliography

Abiew, F.K. 1999. *The Evolution of the Doctrine and Practice of Humanitarian Intervention*. London: Kluwer.

Allman, P. 2001. *Critical Education against Global Capitalism: Karl Marx and Revolutionary Critical Education*. London: Bergin and Garvey.

Anderson, P. 1996. *Passages from Antiquity to Feudalism*. London: Verso.

Barrett, M. 1994. Ideology, politics, hegemony: from Gramsci to Laclau and Mouffe. In S. Žižek (ed.) *Mapping Ideology*. London: Verso.

Beck, U. 1997. *The Reinvention of Politics: Rethinking Modernity in the Global Social Order*. Cambridge: Polity Press.

Bluntschli, M. 1874. *Le Droit International Codifié*, 2nd edn. Paris: Lardy.

Borchard, E. 1922. *The Diplomatic Protection of Citizens Abroad*. New York: The Banks Law Publishers.

Boucher, D. 1998. *Political Theories of International Relations: From Thucydides to the Present*. Oxford: Oxford University Press.

Brenner, R. 1993. *Merchants and Revolution: Commercial Change, Political Conflict and London's Overseas Traders, 1550–1653*. Princeton: Princeton University Press.

Brière, Y. de la 1938. *Le Droit de Juste Guerre: Tradition Théologique, Adaptations Contemporaines*. Paris: A. Pedone.

Brownlie, I. 1974. Humanitarian intervention. In J. Moore (ed.) *Law and Civil War in the Modern World*. Baltimore, MD: Johns Hopkins University Press.

Brownlie, I. 1981. *International Law and the Use of Force by States*. Oxford: Clarendon Press.

Bula-Bula, S. 1999 *L'ambiguité de l'humanité en droit international*. Kinshasa: PUK.

Bull, H. 1977. *The Anarchical Society: A Study of Order in World Politics*. London: Macmillan.

Bush, G.W. 2001. Proclamation of Human Rights Day and Bill of Rights Office Week. Online. Office of the Press Secretary. 9 December. Available at: http://www.whitehouse.gov/news/releases/2001/12/20011209.html (accessed: 2 November 2002).

Bush, G.W. 2002. Address to the United Nations General Assembly New York. Online. 12 September. Available at: http://www.whitehouse.gov/news/releases/2002/09/20020912-1.html (accessed: 1 August 2003).

Cox, R. 1999. Civil society at the turn of the millennium: prospects for an alternative world order. *Review of International Studies* 25 (1), 3–28.

Elonge Osako, M. 2002. L'ambiguïté de la mondialisation face à la tragédie des Grands Lacs Nécessité d'une 'pax democratica' au cœur de l'Afrique.Online. Ethno-Net Africa Publications. Available at: http://www.ethnonet-africa.org/pubs/meochap2.htm#4.

Eppstein, J. 1935. *The Catholic Tradition of the Law of Nations*. London: Oates and Washbourne.

Fauchille, V. 1921. *Traité De Droit International Public*, 8th edn. Paris: H. Bonfils.
Fiore, P. 1885. *Nouveau Droit International*, 2nd edn. Paris : Charles Antoine.
Fonteyne, J-P. 1974. The customary international law doctrine of humanitarian intervention: its current validity under the UN Charter. *California Western International Law Journal* 4 (2), 203–70.
Ganji, M. 1962. *International Protection of Human Rights*. Geneva: E. Droz.
Gill, S. 1995. Globalization, market civilization, and disciplinary neoliberalism, *Millennium* 24 (3), 399–423.
Gramsci, A. 1957. *The Modern Prince and Other_Writings.* New York: Lawrence and Wishart.
Gramsci, A. 1971. *Antonio Gramsci: Selections from Prison Notebooks*, ed. Q. Hoare, and G. Nowell Smith. London: Lawrence and Wishart.
Guardian, The 1994. Clinton prepares financial cushion for Aristide. 26 September.
Guardian, The 1996. First person: picking a fight with Uncle Sam. 3 December, 4.
Guardian, The 2002. Greed in action: US farming subsidies will hit world's poor. 5 June, 9.
Hill, C. 1978. *Reformation to Industrial Revolution*. Harmondsworth: Penguin.
Hindness, B and Hirst, P. 1975. *Pre-Capitalist Modes of Production*. London: Routledge.
International Commission of Jurists 1972. *The Events in East Pakistan*. Geneva: International Commission of Jurists.
International Monetary Fund 1995a. IMF approves stand-by credit for Haiti. Online. Press Release No. 95/14. 8 March. Available at: http://www.imf.org/external/np/sec/pr/1995/pr9514.htm (accessed: 12 February 2004).
International Monetary Fund 1995b. Bosnia and Herzegovina becomes a member of the IMF; receives IMF credit from emergency window. Online. Press Release No. 95/70. 20 December. Available at: http://www.imf.org/external/np/sec/pr/1995/pr9570.htm (accessed: 12 February 2004).
International Monetary Fund 1998. IMF approves stand-by for Bosnia and Herzegovina. Online. Press Release No. 98/19. 29 May. Available at: http://www.imf.org/external/np/sec/pr/1998/pr9819.htm (accessed: 12 February 2004).
Kaldor, M. 2001. A decade of humanitarian intervention: the role of global civil society. In H. Anheier, M. Glasius and M. Kaldor (eds) *Global Civil Society 2001*. Oxford: Oxford University Press.
Kolb, R. 2003. Note on humanitarian intervention. *International Review of the Red Cross* 85 (849), 119–34.
Laclau, E. 1977. *Politics and Ideology in Marxist Theory*. London: New Left Books.
Laclau, E. and Mouffe, C. 1985. *Hegemony and Socialist Strategy*. London: Verso.
Larrain, J. 1983. *Marxism and Ideology*. London: Macmillan.
Lauterpacht, H. 1944. The law of nations, the law of nature and the rights of man. *Transactions of the Grotius Society* 29, 1–33.
Lauterpacht, H. 1946. The Grotian tradition in international law. *British Year Book of International Law*, 1–53.

Lauterpacht, H. 1955. *International Law: A Treatise, Vol. 1*. London: Longmans, Green and Co.
Lillich, R. 1967. Forcible self-help by states to protect human rights. *Iowa Law Review* 53, 325–51.
Lukacs, G. 1971. *History and Class Consciousness*. London: Merlin Press.
Maclean, J. 1981. Political theory, international theory, and problems of ideology. *Millennium* 10 (2), 102–25.
Maclean, J. 1988. Marxism and international relations: a strange case of mutual neglect. *Millennium* 17 (2), 295–319.
Mandelstam, A. 1923. La protection des minorités. *Recueil des cours de l'Académie de Droit International* 1, 367–401.
Manokha, I. 2006. Business ethics and the spirit of global capitalism: moral leadership in the context of global hegemony. *Journal of Global Ethics* 2 (1), June, 27–41.
Manokha, I. 2008a. *The Political Economy of Human Rights Enforcement*. London/New York: Palgrave.
Manokha, I. 2008b. Al-Qaeda terrorism and global poverty: new social banditry. *Journal of Global Ethics* 4 (2), August, 95–105.
Marx, K. 1976. *Capital: A Critique of Political Economy Vol. 1*. Harmondsworth: Penguin Books.
McGowan, L. 1997. Democracy undermined, economic justice denied: structural adjustment and the aid juggernaut in Haiti. *Development GAP*, January.
Mill, J.S. 1859. A few words on non-intervention. In *Dissertations and Discussions: Political, Philosophical and Historical*. London: Longmans, Green, Reader and Dyer.
Moore, J. 1969. The control of foreign intervention in internal conflict. *Virginia Journal of International Law* 9, 205.
Moskowitz, C. 1958. *Human Rights and World Order*. New York: Oceana Publications.
Muldoon, J. 1979. *Popes, Lawyers, and Infidels: The Church and the Non-Christian World 1250–1550*. Philadelphia: University of Pennsylvania Press.
OHR 1995. Peace Implementation Conference, London, 8-9 December 1995. PIC Statements on Economic Matters. Online. Available at: http://www.ohr.int/ohr-dept/econ/picstmt/default.asp?content_id=5870#1 (accessed: 12 February 2004).
Paris, R. 1997. Peacebuilding and the limits of liberal internationalism. *International Security* 22 (2), 54–89.
Perez-Vera, E. 1969. La protection d'humanité en droit international. *Revue Belge de Droit International* 5, 401–24.
Pugh, M. 2002. Postwar political economy in Bosnia and Herzegovina: the spoils of peace. *Global Governance* 8 (4), 467–82.
Regout, R. 1935. *La doctrine de la guerre juste: de saint Augustin à nos jours: d'après les théologiens et les canonistes catholiques*. Paris: A. Pedone.

Reisman, M. and McDougal, M. 1969. Response by Professors McDougal and Reisman. *International Lawyer* 3, 437–50.
Rougier, A. 1910. The theory of humanitarian intervention. *Revue Generale De Droit International Publique* 17, 497–525.
Scheffer, D. 1992. Toward a modern doctrine of humanitarian intervention. *University of Toledo Law Review* 23, 253–93.
Scott, J. 1934. *The Spanish Origin of International Law*. Oxford: Clarendon Press.
Stowell, E. 1921. *Intervention in International Law*. Washington: John Byrne.
Stowell, E. 1932. La théorie et la pratique de l'intervention. *Recueil des Cours* 40, 91.
Tawney, R. 1990. *Religion and the Rise of Capitalism*. London: Penguin.
Teson, F. 1988. *Humanitarian Intervention: An Inquiry into Law and Morality*. Dobbs Ferry: Transnational Publishers.
Therborn, G. 1980. *The Ideology of Power and the Power of Ideology*. London: Verso.
Vincent, J. 1986. *Human Rights and International Relations*. New York: Cambridge University Press.
Washington Post, The 2000. In Haiti. 13 April, 1.
Watson, A. 1984. European international society and its expansion. In H. Bull and A. Watson (eds) *The Expansion of International Society*. New York: Clarendon Press.
Wood, E.M. 1995. *Democracy against Capitalism: Renewing Historical Materialism*. Cambridge: Cambridge University Press.
Wood, E.M. 2002. *The Origins of Capitalism: A Longer View*. London: Verso.
Wood, E.M. and Wood, N. 1997. *A Trumpet of Sedition: Political Theory and the Rise of Capitalism, 1509–1688*. London: Pluto Press.
Woolsey, T. 1875. *Introduction to the Study of International Law, Designed as an Aid in Teaching, and in Historical Studies*. New York: Armstrong and Co.
World Bank 2000. *Memorandum of the President of the International Development Association to the Executive Directors on a Country Assistance Strategy of the World Bank Group for Bosnia and Herzegovina*, Report No. 20592 BIH, 14 June.

PART 4
Conflict Resolution

Chapter 9

Pakistan's Tribal Areas: A Battle for Jihad

Shazadi Beg

It has been eight long years since the US-led coalition ousted the Taliban from Afghanistan and pushed the leadership of both the Taliban and Al Qaeda into the tribal areas of Pakistan, known as the Federally Administered Tribal Areas (FATA). If the objective of military action in Afghanistan was to capture Bin Laden and prevent Afghanistan from becoming a safe haven for Al Qaeda, then the coalition has failed spectacularly. Bin Laden remains free, there is a raging insurgency in Afghanistan and the conflict has spread into neighbouring Pakistan. The attack on the Sri Lankan cricket team in Lahore at the beginning of 2009 demonstrated the relative ease with which terrorists can now strike at the heart of Pakistan's largest and arguably most important Province.

The 2,250 km border between Pakistan and Afghanistan is increasingly becoming the decisive battleground in the fight against global terrorism. Yet the US recognises that it cannot wage an indefinite war with American ground troops just to deny Al Qaeda safe havens. The US Administration in its 'Af/Pak' strategy[1] proposes a troop 'surge' in Afghanistan and parachuting in of civil aid experts. This is to be undertaken against the backdrop of a strengthened Taliban, political instability, corruption and narcotics. Afghanistan now provides 90 per cent of the world's heroin which equates to half of the Afghan economy. The surge also risks acting as a magnet for global jihadis resulting in unintended consequences.

The Federally Administered Tribal Areas (FATA)

Pakistan's cooperation is vital to any success in Afghanistan. Cross border attacks by militants in FATA are seen as providing significant support to the insurgency in Afghanistan. Targeted missile attacks by Central Intelligence Agency operated drones until now have been limited to the tribal areas. However, as part of the review of US policy in Afghanistan and Pakistan, the Obama administration is considering extending the attacks into Baluchistan, where the Taliban leader, Mullah Omar is considered to be hiding. This may further fuel anti-Americanism and impose a significant strategic price.

---

1 Bruce Reidel, Ambassador Richard Holbrooke and Michelle Flournoy: 27 March 2009. The White House Press briefing on the new strategy for Afghanistan and Pakistan.

The porous border traffic on the Pakistan/Afghanistan border consists not only of Pashtuns exercising easement rights granted to them decades ago across the Durand line but also internally displaced persons fleeing violence on both sides of the border. FATA has long been regarded as a 'playground' for imperialists and jihadists alike. The seven tribal agencies which make up FATA are still administered by the British introduced Frontier Crimes Regulation Act of 1901. The Act provides for customary laws though its purpose was to exercise control over the tribes. A council of elders or *jirga* was allowed to settle disputes as long as it was not against the interests of the rulers. These *jirgas*, which in recent times negotiated peace agreements between militants and the government in parts of the tribal areas, have been the subject of vocal criticism by the West for appeasing terrorists.

Although FATA has a representative in Parliament, no mainstream political parties are allowed to operate there. The disenfranchisement has allowed militancy to flourish. In the political void, religious factions have peddled politics and wielded disproportionate power. The new generation of militants have learnt from this and through the medium of religion they are able to exercise power and influence out of all proportion to their numbers. These externally funded non State actors attempt to convince others that their version of Islam is the only right one and that all others are perversions or heresies. Assisted by the gun, they have silenced voices of dissent and reason in deeply conservative communities. They have burnt down schools in parts of the North West Frontier Province (NWFP) to ensure that education can never be a threat.

The political and administrative system in FATA has been so vulnerable to corruption that contracts have been openly awarded for loyalty or to reward favourites. The smuggling of drugs and arms remain rampant. Despite government promises of reconstruction and job creation most tribesmen live in poverty in a region of deep neglect. FATA's political and administrative isolation from mainstream Pakistan must end if there is to be economic progress. Only then can theological and societal reconciliation take place in any meaningful way.

Despite Pakistan's capture of prominent Al Qaeda members and with the Army having suffered heavy losses there remain allegations of 'safe havens' in parts of the tribal belt. Members of Pakistan's intelligence agencies have repeatedly been accused by the West of retaining links with former Kashmiri militants. The US on the one hand considers Pakistan an ally and on the other makes direct verbal attacks on its premier intelligence agency, the ISI for its obsession with India. Yet, the international community has repeatedly failed to address the Kashmir issue and thereby address Pakistan's legitimate security concerns in any meaningful way. A leading Pakistan daily has asked: 'Can the US expect effective cooperation by totalling disregarding Pakistan's legitimate concerns, glossing over its geo-strategic interests and playing up themes that originate in India?' (Gul 2009).

The perception in Pakistan is that India is exercising undue influence in Afghanistan through it contacts with former members of the Northern Alliance and its cooperation in infrastructure projects. There is increasing international concern that India is actively involved in operations to de-stabilise Pakistan through its missions in Afghanistan and in Zahedan, Iran (Fair 2009). The rise of Hindu fundamentalism in India, Hindu-Muslim riots in recent years, attacks such as that on the Samjota Express have all resulted in thousands of Muslim deaths, further deteriorating relations between the two countries. Moreover many Pakistanis perceive that the Israeli-Indian-Afghan alliance extends beyond cooperation on counter terrorism training and is not only aimed at reducing Pakistan's influence in the region, but also aimed at countering China, securing the energy resources of Central Asia and ultimately controlling Pakistan's nuclear weapons.

The Road to Political Militant Islam

Although prior to the invasion of Iraq by the US, Pakistan had few suicide bombers, it had a history of 'holy war'. The Afghan resistance movement against Soviet occupation conducted by the mujahadeen, or jihadi fighters from across the Muslim world, were assisted by Pakistan in partnership with the US and Saudi Arabia. Collectively they funded, armed and trained the mujahadeen to fight the *kufr* or unbelieving 'Godless' Communists. Millions of dollars were spent in indoctrinating fighters with Wahabbi ideology glorifying jihad through literature and militant seminaries. This movement of 'holy warriors' evolved into modern political militant Islam in Pakistan.

After the Soviet Army withdrew from Afghanistan, Pakistan was left with thousands of battle hardened mujahadeen who had no homes or families to return to. Many settled into refugee camps in Peshawar and Quetta (Marwat 2005). Some were encouraged to take the holy war to Kashmir. In the years before 9/11 Pakistan's madrassas mushroomed. A small percentage of these were used as vehicles of choice to indoctrinate young men towards violent extremism. These young men primed for jihad found their vocation after the invasion of Iraq and Afghanistan. Many more have done so since the massacres in Gaza at the start of 2009.

The madrassa system in Pakistan has continued to grow. It provides religious education, free board and lodging to poor children who would otherwise receive no education at all. Pakistan has a low literacy rate and less than two per cent of GDP is spent on government schools. Religious seminaries provide an alternative to a deficient schooling system in the public sector. Unfortunately the government has been unable to enforce madrassa registration, order full disclosure of all sources of funding or monitor the type of Islam being taught, e.g. Salafi, Deobandi, etc. Nor is there credible monitoring of the qualifications or radical views of teachers, many of whom have strong links with seminaries in Afghanistan.

A stark weakness of the madrassa system is that students are not provided with the education or skills that will enable them to take up employment in civil society upon graduating. Unsurprisingly those not wanting to be madrassa teachers, often opt to go to war. Qari Hussein and his group of hundreds of fighters who kidnapped more than 260 soldiers in a Mehsud dominated tribal area in August 2007,[2] received his religious education at Jamia Farooqia in Karachi and graduated in 2003. He had little known employment until he opted to become a 'holy warrior'. He is associated with the sectarian banned terrorist group Sipah-e-Sahaba, wanted for hundreds of sectarian killings.

Since the government's storming of the Lal Masjid (Red Mosque) in July 2007, Pakistan has experienced a ten fold increase in the use of suicide bombings and improvised explosive devices (IEDs) in increasingly sophisticated asymmetric warfare. Large scale bombings have been seen in major cities such as Lahore and in the capital Islamabad including at the Marriott hotel in September 2008. The assault on the Red Mosque arguably led to the creation of the Taliban (TTP) when all loose militant groups merged under one umbrella organisation. Fierce battles have been fought in the tribal areas particularly Khyber, North and South Waziristan and Bajaur. Pakistan's political leadership has been viewed by a substantial section of the population since 9/11 as a proxy for the US. The rise of corruption and the steady erosion of state institutions have provided space to militant and sectarian organisations to operate with impunity.

Whilst it has long been considered by the Federal Investigation Agency that the tribal belt has provided the largest percentage of suicide bombers, Southern and central Punjab is considered to be the 'factory' that churns out improvised explosive devices (IEDs) and suicide jackets. Increasingly the 'Punjabi Taliban' with leadership in Harkatul mujahadeen, Jaish-i-Mohammad and Lashar-i-Jhangvi has linked up with other militant groups to take in the length and breadth of the country.

The link between Sunni sectarian groups, such as Sipah e Sahaba, the Taliban and Al Qaeda in Pakistan is close. After the revival of the Shia in Iraq following the US invasion, Sunni sectarian groups formed an affinity with wahabbi/deobandi ideology of the Taliban. Sectarian groups now cover most major cities in Pakistan. The sectarian conflict has been brought into the tribal belt most notably in Khurram Agency where Afghan refugees outnumber the local Shia population. Seeds of the sectarian conflict in Pakistan were planted during the proxy war fought on its soil in the 1980's between Iran and Saudi Arabia.

Fighting in the Way of God

Islam is often portrayed as a military religion with a history of fighting in conflicts across the Arabian Peninsula since its inception. Reza Aslan argues 'this deep-rooted stereotype of Islam as a warrior religion has its origins in the papal propaganda of the Crusades, when Muslims were depicted as the soldiers of the Antichrist in blasphemous occupation of the Holy Lands (and, far more importantly, of the silk route to China)' (Aslan 2006: 79).

2 *The Dawn* 29 August 2007.

Although it was Christianity through the crusades which gave theological legitimacy to 'holy war', it was not a term used by Muslim conquerors. The concept of 'Jihad' was not fully developed as an ideological expression until after the Byzantine era. *Jihad al Akbar* or the greater jihad means 'the struggle of the soul to overcome the sinful obstacles that keep a person away from God. This is why the word *jihad* is nearly always followed in the Qur'an by the phrase 'in the way of God' (Aslan 2006).

Jihad al Asghar, the lesser jihad is the struggle against oppression and tyranny. It is this jihad which has come to be known as 'Jihad of the sword'. Just war has been manipulated by extremists to give religious sanction to acts of terrorism and criminality against Muslim and non-Muslim people and governments. Social and political agendas often remain hidden from the individuals groomed and directed to carry out *Jihad of the sword.*

The Pakistani Islamist writer, Mawdudi defined jihad as expanding Islamic political dominance to establish a just rule by all possible means (Mawdudi 1939). Muslim revolutionaries Hasan al Banna and Sayyid Qutb further legitimised jihad to establish a truly Islamic government, even if that meant overthrowing a Muslim government because it failed to enforce Sharia. This argument continues to be used by Al Qaeda.

It has long been argued in mainstream Islam that the doctrine of jihad only sanctions defensive wars and that God does not like aggressors. Reza Aslan argues that although some verses of the Qu'ran speak of slaying the polytheists wherever they are confronted, this in fact was specifically directed at the *Quraysh* and the clandestine partisans in Yathrib (Medina) with whom the *Ummah* or community of Muslims were engaged in a terrible war during the life of the Prophet Muhammad (Mawdudi 1939: 84–5). Indeed jihad makes a distinction between combatants and non combatants, so that the killing of unarmed civilians is strictly prohibited. Muslim law eventually developed to outlaw torture and the indiscriminate destruction of property. These principles are now a part of the Geneva Conventions on the conduct of war and the treatment of prisoners.

Teenage Recruits and Martyrdom Cults

The youth bulge in the tribal areas where unemployment is running at 50 per cent works in favour of militant groups which are known to pay recruits more than the Afghan national Army pays its regular soldiers. The 15–30 year old age group accounts for 75 per cent of the population. They have easy access to weapons. Unemployed teenagers are easier to indoctrinate because they are often illiterate and make a commitment to religion without the ability to make rational or informed choices. It follows that they are in most cases unable to read or understand the text of the Qur'an which is often written in Arabic. This creates a dependency on teachers who teach their interpretation of Islam. The process of radicalisation and indoctrination takes place over a protracted period.

The motivation for suicide bombers is first and foremost a deep seated belief in martyrdom and its posthumous rewards. They view martyrdom as serving God by being a part of the liberation of Islam. In a *gharat* or honour based society, the notion of 'badla' or revenge in Pastunwali code of conduct is highly relevant. The US drone attack in Bajaur in November 2006, which killed 82 young students in their beds in a madrassa was a turning point in the conflict. It resulted in hundreds of boys offering themselves for martyrdom operations inside Afghanistan and against the Pakistan Army which was deemed complicit in the attack.[3] The probative value of drone attacks is questionable since they not only create more terrorists but they alienate the very tribesmen needed to win an insurgency.

As drone attacks by the US have continued, the concept of 'badla' has taken on a renewed significance to avenge the deaths of so many innocent people killed in the air strikes. Baitullah Mehsud, the Taliban commander in Waziristan has boasted of having hundreds of teenage boys willing to be suicide bombers. In 2008 in a gathering in Aurakzai Tribal Agency thousands of armed militants pledged to Maulana Hakimullah, deputy leader to Baituallah Mehsud, that they were ready become *shaheeds* or martyrs to fight in the way of God against the enemies of Islam.[4] Although jihadists from central Asia and the Arab world are fewer in number they are increasingly seen as seasoned warriors ready to teach recruits, to fight and travel anywhere categorised as a 'holy war' as long as someone is willing to fund them.

An insurgency based in no small part on religious belief can never be defeated unless the basis of that religious belief is understood and the narrative challenged to stem the flow of recruitment into militancy that feeds the insurgency. Jihadis recruited in tribal belt tend to be under the age of 30, and in many cases just teenagers belonging to poor families. They are indoctrinated on Wahabbi/Salafi ideology which refers to early Muslims i.e. those who died within the first 400 years after the Prophet Muhammad. Salafis believe in the annihilation of local variants of Islam and advocate a 'pure' version of Islam, with the aim of establishing a pan-Islamic Caliphate. Salafi-Takfiris are an extremist minority even within the Salafi movement and advocate the killing of opponent Muslims as *kufrs* or infidels.

The discovery of a 'suicide nursery' in 2008 in the Mehsud area of Spinkai in South Waziristan tribal agency followed a military operation known as operation 'Zalzala'[5] Computers, videos and literature seized from a house showed boys aged between 9 and 12 years wearing white headbands with verses of the Qur'an written on their foreheads being indoctrinated, some reciting verse, others carrying out an execution and training on how to detonate IEDs. No one was seen to debate sacred texts. They were told that they were in a privileged position and had to commit to jihad from the heart.

---

3 Author's interview with NWFP Governor, Gen. Aurakzai in Peshawar, November 2007.

4 An eye witness account relayed to interviewee on 12 May 2008.

5 *The Dawn* 19 May 2008.

Letters and videos left behind by suicide bombers indicate that they have been made to believe that the killing of fellow Muslims is acceptable as jihad if they have been deemed *kufrs* (unbelievers). Abid Hunzala, a former student of Lal Masjid, who bombed a Pakistan Air Force bus in Sargodha in November 2007, wrote to his wife Fatima on 8 September 2007.[6] The letter was recovered during a raid on his house in Rahimyar Khan following intelligence reports that he was part of the militant group Laskhar-e-Jahangvi. The letter reads as follows:

> Dear Fatima,
> Almighty Allah has given us life and I am sacrificing my life for the promotion of Allah's religion. The world of kufr is trying to wipe out Islam. One million Muslims have been killed in Iraq. The Islamic government of Afghanistan has been ousted. Muslims are being killed in every part of the world. And in Pakistan which was created in the name of Islam, true Muslims are being killed, detained or being handed over to infidel America. What did the people of Lal Masjid do to deserve being brutally killed and bathed in blood? In this situation Islam is seeking sacrifice … I know this will grieve you as God has blessed us with a child after 10 years of marriage … I advise you to make my son a hafiz-e-Qur'an and send him on jihad when he grows up. This is the path of sahabah and is the only way of salvation and promotion of Islam. I advise you to be patient and if you desire, you can marry either of my brothers, Mustaq, Asif or Junaid. I have been selected for a fidai mission, which is why I came to last week to see you and my son for the last time.

The letter demonstrates that motivations for martyrdom can be both revenge for the killing of other Muslims or family members and to be part of a global cause that perceives Islam to be under threat. The central theme is the defence of Islam and Muslims.

The mind of a suicide bomber is captured through the power of religious conviction which places cause before life. *Jihad Al Asghar* comes from the core of this conviction.

The Takfiri imprint is at the centre of the Salafi definition of jihad of the sword. Salafi recruitment methods rely on an aura of Islamic pride and history. There is often face to face contact over time between the recruiter and his 'soldier' as part of the process of trust. An Islamic identification based on faith crosses national and cultural boundaries. A suicide bomber perceives himself to be a soldier of God. The reward of heaven is in sharp contrast to his impoverished life on earth. As a *shaheed* he is allowed to intercede on behalf of 70 family members. His sense of worth is heightened.

---

6 Author's interview with a senior FIA official in Islamabad, 11 May 2008.

Rehabilitation

Pakistan's slide into violent extremism cannot be stemmed until religious ideology that is at the heart of recruitment is challenged directly and credibly. Well structured interventions striking at the core of the militants' ideology will impact significantly on the supply and demand of suicide bombers.

Disengagement from terrorism cannot be viewed in isolation. Even talking to 'reconcilable' elements of the Taliban cannot be achieved with reference to religious ideology. To understand how and why people leave terrorism behind, there must be recognition of how and why they joined terrorism in the first place. Martyrdom videos and farewell letters give an insight into the motivating factors.

The conflicts in Iraq and Afghanistan are seen as the occupation of Muslim lands by non-Muslim forces. Occupation continues to act as a magnet to attract militants from Pakistan into neighbouring Afghanistan to perform jihad. Human rights abuses against Muslims in places such as Abu Ghraib and Guantanamo have also provided motivating factors in the past.[7] There are also other more complex factors. These include the exploitation of the sons of the poor who have no other means of earning a livelihood other than to join a local terrorist movement which provides him with food, respect and a wage. There is also the sexual abuse of boys by powerful religious clerics who deem them to be expendable and therefore recruit them for suicide missions.

In more recent times there is increasing evidence that some teenagers coerced into jihad are seeking help to prevent themselves from being 'stranded' in jihad. It is not uncommon for suicide jackets to be found abandoned by desperate teenagers who had second thoughts before a mission.[8] Tragically this cry for help is being mostly ignored by the authorities who continue to be sidetracked by Peace Agreements, pressure from the US to do more and a debilitating turf war between intelligence agencies.[9]

Disengagement from Terrorism

A number of countries including Yemen, Saudi Arabia and Indonesia have embarked upon disengagement programmes for jihadis. These come through recognition that Wahabbi/Salafi ideology uses the concept of jihad to recruit into violent extremism to promote their perceived war against Western crusaders. Leading Salafi scholars are known to have powerful oratory skills that can inspire listeners to be part of a global jihad rather than local power politics. Global jihadis are aware that 'the battle of ideas' will be their key battleground.

7 Author's interview with Maliks of the Khyber Agency, November 2006.

8 Author's interview with NWFP Governor Owais Ghani, 14 May 2008.

9 Author's interview with a senior official of the Frontier Constabulary, 12 May 2008.

Judge Hamoud Al Hitar, President of Yemen's Dialogue Committee has argued that the dialogue has a special importance in counter terrorism because each terror act is based on a belief.[10] It is this belief which must be challenged through religious and intellectual discussion. In Yemen's rehabilitation programme credibility and competence were recognised as fundamental with the ability to derive Sharia rules from its sources. The subjects of the dialogue included jihad – when, how and who has the right to announce it, the concept of state, government, succession and rights of the ruler, laws of the land, the rights of non-Muslims, state security, violence, extremism, moral issues, migration and rights of individuals including those in detention. Central to the debate was the legitimacy of the head of state or 'wali al amir'.

Indonesia has taken the risky step of employing former fighters to wean radicalised youths away from terror. The former fighters who had street credibility were able to show that terror actually alienates people from their religion. They conveyed the message that the police and the Army are not un-Islamic but are performing their duty as protectors of their people and their country.

The religious re-education programme in Saudi Arabia includes 6–10 weeks of de-brainwashing. Scores of clerics and psychologists are involved so that religious re-education is coupled with psychological counselling. There is also direct financial and social support to help the former militants re-settle back into family life in a society where there is great focus on family and social networks.

Critics of all the programmes argue that jihadist violence is not just a product of religious ideology but also geopolitical grievances. Whilst this may be true in one sense, violent extremism in the jihadi context is very much rooted in religious indoctrination. Whilst some programmes have been more successful than others, all have significantly opened up the jihadi debate at a critical juncture.

A Debate on Jihad

Sayed Imam Abdulaziz al Sharif, also known as Dr Fadl, founder of Egyptian jihad released a 10-part document called 'Tarshid al amal al jihad wa al alam' ('Rationalising the jihadi action in Egypt and the world'), challenging Salafi jihadi ideology (Wright 2008). One of his previous publications was 'Al omda al edda' ('The master in making preparation in jihad'), considered compulsive reading for jihadis. This appeared in 1988 as the Afghan jihad was nearing its end.

Sayed Imam now argues that the duty to perform jihad is dependent upon comprehension and ability. There are a number of prerequisites before a person can embark upon jihad. These include providing for dependents whilst performing jihad, parental permission for minors to embark upon jihad. Indiscriminate bombings are not permitted. The lives and property of Muslims must be preserved. Jihad against the leaders of Muslim countries is not acceptable. Furthermore, it

10 Author's interview with Judge Hamoud Al Hitar, Sanaa, 25 October 2007.

is prohibited to kill foreigners and tourists in Muslim countries and treacherous to kill non-Muslims after entering a western country with its government's permission in the form of a visa, as some of the 9/11 hijackers did. He states that single individuals cannot conduct jihad on their own, nor use fraudulent means to fund jihad. There is no such thing in Islam as the end justifying the means.

Despite the fierce criticism of Sayed Imam by Al Qaeda, he has further has split wide open the debate on global jihad. His defection poses a monumental threat to Al Qaeda. This would account for a lengthy 200-page online rebuttal of Sayed Imam's views by Ayman Al Zawahiri entitled 'The Exoneration'. The central theme of the rebuttal is 'We bomb them as they bomb us, even if we kill someone who is not permitted to be killed'. Tragically in Pakistan's tribal belt where Sayed Imam is almost unheard of, a new and more lethal type of insurgency is gaining strength. An insurgency that is bigger than Mullah Omar and Osama Bin Laden, which is attracting criminals, adventurers and those living in grinding poverty and injustice all in the garb of committed Islamists.

Pakistan's Peace Agreements

Pakistan has no formal or known disengagement programme. The jihad debate has surfaced in the media but not taken off in the way that it has in the Middle East and South East Asia. Pakistan's attempts at peace building have come in the form of peace agreements with tribesmen. Peace Agreements must be understood not only in the political context but also in the religious context. The Qu'ran requires Muslims to make peace if their adversaries wish them to do so. This is known as the concept of *Dar al Sulh* (abode of peace).

In March 2004, an offensive by the military resulted in the death of 600 soldiers while many militants escaped. This led to the signing of the first peace agreement. Military operations were seen as short term. Pakistan has long recognised that a political solution is the only solution that can bring lasting peace. The peace agreements must be viewed against the backdrop of a heavily armed tribal society that is an honour (*gharat*) based society, where revenge plays an important part. The tribal system of administration is based upon the principles of merited tribesmen who intercede on behalf of their tribes through *jirgas*.

Central to the Peace Agreements have been a pledge by the tribes to expel foreign fighters. Those providing assistance to them risk collective punishment for the whole tribe including demolition of homes and the payment of substantial fines. The tribes have consistently requested a cessation of military operations and the withdrawal of Army check posts. The government from their perspective want the militants to lay down their arms. Little trust exists on either side.

The US fear that peace agreements solidify Al Qaeda safe havens, providing breathing space for Al Qaeda and the Taliban to re-group and train fighters is not without foundation. The Waziristan peace agreements have broken down several times and then reinstated after intense negotiations on both sides.

The peace agreements in Swat negotiated by Maulana Sufi Mohammad of the TNSM who fought with the Taliban in Afghanistan after 9/11 have been more vocally condemned both inside Pakistan and by the international community as capitulating to the militants. They have often been negotiated by the government from a position of weakness. The ANP, the provincial government in the NWFP, abandoned its secular values to support the Nizam-e-Adl Regulation which gives effect to Sharia law because it believed it has no support from the State to take on the Taliban (Hayat 2009).

The Nizam-e-Adl Regulation was cleared by the National Assembly and signed by the President after Tehrik-e-Nifaz Shariat-e-Muhammadi (TNSM) and the Swat Taliban warned Parliament against opposing the regulation. TNSM in a statement said 'If members of the National Assembly opposed the judicial system of Shariat-e-Muhammadi, they will enter the category of non-Muslims and Pakistan will become *Darul Harb* (land of war) … this will make jihad mandatory on the rulers' (Hayat 2009). The Regulation gives power to Qazis or religious 'judges' to declare any law un-Islamic and impose their version of Sharia. They will in effect be law making and setting up a parallel judicial system.

Maulana Sufi Mohammad's firebrand son-in-law, Maulana Fazullah who has been responsible for terrorising the valley, issuing Islamic injunctions on illegal radio stations and recruiting young boys for suicide missions, had de-facto control and therefore influence in Swat. On Friday 3 April 2009, he led prayers in his home village of Mamdirai and gave a threatening speech full of religious zeal. The congregation included military and district administration officials (Taj 2009). In this environment the dangerous delegation of legal authority to Qazis who enjoy wide discretionary powers, risks sectarian interpretations of Islamic law by passing the rights enshrined in the Constitution of Pakistan for all its citizens.

The central demand of the militants has always been the implementation of Sharia law. While there is a history of Qazi Courts and Sharia law, the dynamics in Swat changed by the infiltration of militants from Bajaur, Waziristan and other tribal agencies. The real prize for the militants was power and a defined role in Pashtun society. The Swat deal emboldened the Taliban to openly display arms in Buner (Hayat 2009) and they gained strength in Dera Ghazi Khan, the gateway to the heart of Punjab. In April 2009, the Army supported by the government and an increasing vocal middle class launched an assault on the militants in Swat angered by their increasing appetite for more power and territory. The Army has moved on to target the leadership of the TTP in Waziristan the base of all militant activity. A number of factors led to this change in strategy; the public mood turned against the Taliban creating an enabling environment to launch military operations. People were appalled by the public flogging of a teenage girl and evidence of unspeakable atrocities committed by the Taliban in beheading village elders and several members of the Special Forces.

Those who spoke out against the religious ideology of the militants were murdered such as the highly respected spiritual leader Dr Sarfraz Naeemi. Dr Naeemi through the Barelvi sect which is associated with the Sufi sect of Islam for the first time openly mobilised public support against the Taliban. People have been empowered through the use of cell phones, the internet and the electronic media. A rift in the Taliban leadership emerged after Baitullah Mehsud killed one of his own senior commanders Zainuddin Mehsud who publicly questioned the strategy of killing fellow Muslims in Pakistan. These developments have changed the direction and pace of the war. However substantial risks remain in fighting militants in their own inhospitable territory in Waziristan which could overstretch the army and add millions more to the two million or more internally displaced persons who have left their homes because of military operations .The looming humanitarian catastrophe risks undoing the gains made by the Army and fracturing public support for its operations.

Qisas, Diyat and Restorative Justice

Prosecution of those arrested on suspicion of committing terrorist offences is rarely heard of in Pakistan. Part of the problem lies in a deficient legal and judicial system. This has arguably contributed to the perception that militants who have committed atrocities remain safe in the knowledge that once a peace agreement with the government is sealed they will not be prosecuted for crimes committed under the criminal law because an amnesty is implied within the terms of the peace agreement.

Islamic law distinguishes between three kinds of punishment; Hadd, Qisas and Tazir. Hadd is punishment fixed by the Qur'an and Sunnah, for example theft. The Hadd is a right or claim of Allah therefore no pardon or settlement is possible. Qisas and Diyat involve homicide or physical injury to the person. Only premeditated homicide involves a penalty under the law of Qisas. The punishment is either a just retributive penalty though the infliction of harm cannot be greater than that inflicted, or Diyat, pecuniary compensation to the victim or his heirs.

Qisas in the Qur'anic system is repairing and regenerating life. The law of Qisas is an important concept of *Sulh* or compromise by which the victim and the offender is brought together to agree upon a way in which the offence is compounded and the offender forgiven. It has deep roots in Pakistani society and is often deliberated upon in jirgas. Diyat is imposed only if just retribution cannot be executed or the victim or his relatives waive their right to demand it. Tazir is a punishment inflicted for offences for which Sharia has not enacted written penalties. It consists of discretionary punishment under the criminal law.

The Pakistan Penal Code incorporates Qisas, Diyat and Tazir. Under Islamic law, the theory of punishment is seen through deterrence, reformation, prevention and rehabilitation. The Qur'an indicates a preference for Diyat and forgiveness; especially forgiving when the victim has the power to take revenge.[11] The words

11 'Those have the highest reward who, even when they are justifiably angry, can forgive' (Al Qur'an 42:37).

Al Ghafoor (the most forgiving) appear more than 70 times in the Qur'an. The process of forgiving is to promote individual and social healing.

The provincial authorities of the NWFP have debated over the last several years the need to provide a structural and societal basis to promote 'Restorative Justice'.[12] Restorative justice has been described as 'a process whereby all the parties with a stake in a particular offence come together to resolve collectively how to deal with the aftermath of the offence and its implication for the future' (Marshall 1996: 5). Arguably in Pakistan's current security climate where serious criminal offences have repeatedly been committed in the name of Islam, it has become increasingly difficult to make a case for restorative justice not only because offenders consider that they have God on their side but victims no longer have faith in the authorities to provide an enabling environment for any justice, either restorative or within the criminal justice system.

Strategies for Peace – Prevention vs Cure

Government strategies for peace risk being short term in the absence of functioning institutions that give a voice to the people. Meanwhile the militants continue to exploit a weak political system both at the national and provincial level and play on the government's neglect of the poor. The Taliban have intimidated both the police and the population providing space to hard-line Mullahs, many of whom have patrons amongst local landowners and politicians.

Amidst the chaos a dangerous new threat is posed by a 'Greater Pashtunistan' involving the presence of Al Qaeda, the Taliban and sectarian groups along the Afghan/Pakistan border. The narcotics corridor and the inevitable competition over natural resources in the region are further benchmarks for instability. The new US supply routes through the Central Asian Republics risk spreading the conflict still further. Concerns over repeated terrorist incidents in Lahore and Islamabad thereby penetrating the heart of the country close to the seat of power, lends credence to the view that Pakistan is now in free fall. Easy access to weapons and the power of the Mullah in politicising every religious issue through illegal radio stations and madrassas add to an already volatile situation.

Afghan refugees in camps in Peshawar are outside the tribal network and have in many cases been receptive to radical Islamic ideology. The growth of Deobandi madrassas have enabled the refugees to mix with Pashtuns, Baluchis, even Sindhis and Punjabis. Most speak both pashtu and urdu and have built a collective Islamic personality. UNHCR are aware of this and the allegations that some Afghan refugees harbour militants but consider that forced repatriation to Afghanistan of unemployed, powerless and alienated young men with Islamist sympathises will

---

12 Author's interview with Police Chief of NWFP, Malik Naveed Khan, 14 May 2008.

almost certainly ensure that they fall into the clutches of insurgents.[13] The Taliban have partly enforced sharia in North and South Waziristan, Bajaur, Khyber and Mohmand agencies. Music shops have been attacked. So too have barbers shaving off beards and tailors making western clothes. Militants have also expanded their sphere of activity to settled districts such as Bannu, Tank, Kohat and DI Khan.

The military failure of the Soviets in Afghanistan has empowered the militants that they can defeat the West. Training camps to train 'western' militants to attack the enemy on their own home ground in vulnerable open societies is seen as relatively easy revenge. Popular anger about the massacres of the Palestinian people in Gaza by the Israelis has emerged as demonstration of western hypocrisy which at best supported attacks on unarmed civilians and at worst stood on the sidelines and did nothing to stop the attacks or out rightly condemn them.

Strategies for peace must include addressing legitimate grievances including gaping sores like Palestine and Kashmir. The 24/7 media has contributed significantly to raising awareness of conflicts and foreign policy issues. This impacts on recruitment into militancy. Strategies for peace must then actively promote disengagement from terrorism. A long term strategy must not be sacrificed by short term gains. Intelligence agencies must work within the parameters of the rule of law. Although President Obama has announced an end to practises such as extraordinary rendition and the use of torture, his announcement not to criminally charge those who ordered and carried out these practises leaves an uncomfortable precedent of 'only following orders' mentality in complete contempt of the rule of law.

Although the flow of terrorist financing must be disrupted without unfairly targeting Islamic charities, the central focus must be the credible re-evaluating of Salafi–Jihadi ideology. This will strike at the heart of the process of recruitment into violent extremism. Ideology that permits and inspires violence must be understood and challenged. Illegal radio broadcasts promoting a false reading of religion must be countered with truth directly from Sharia sources, if necessary through Imams from Al Azhar in Egypt and Saudi Arabia; two recognised seats of Islamic jurisprudence. It is equally important to disseminate literature to discredit the militants and stem the flow of extremism through mosques, madrassas, *jirgas* and *taleemi jalsas*.

Pakistan urgently requires a formal programme for disengagement or rehabilitation for jihadis in detention, possibly along the lines of Yemen's Committee For Dialogue or the Saudi programme for disengagement. In the first quarter of 2009, the government announced a framework for a de-radicalisation working group though it has not given it the priority it deserves and adequate funds have yet to be allocated.[14] Central to any debate on rehabilitation, will be the concept of jihad and the legitimacy of the State by reference to the Qur'an and

13 Author's interview with representatives of UNHCR in Islamabad, 13 March 2008.

14 Author's interview with the Chairman Tariq Pervez, 1 April 2009.

Sunnah. In a country of high unemployment detainees must be provided skills training and the confidence to re-settle back into family and community life.

The programmes themselves need to be carefully and sensitively structured around religion, culture and the psychology of indoctrination. Trust and respect are important factors. Detainees can only be 'turned around' if there is some perception of equality. In Yemen the detainees and the cleric both sides took an oath on the Qur'an to respect each others views and to speak the truth. This established not only the ground rules but the necessary credibility to continue with the programme. The involvement of families in all rehabilitation programmes may be highly relevant to provide appropriate psychological support, forgiveness and to remove feelings of isolation. Aftercare including, where relevant, State protection and the ability to earn a living are essential. Poor aftercare could potentially do irreversible damage to future disengagement programmes and question the motives of the authorities.

Militants must not be allowed to continue to become the elite in FATA by further weakening the authority of the Maliks, hundreds of whom have been murdered. Rehabilitation programmes do not mean that those committing terrorist offences cannot be prosecuted for criminal offences under the law. There have been no high profile convictions leading to the perception that the authorities are unable to enforce the rule of law and hold terrorists accountable for serious criminal offences. Militants are aware of the possibility of negotiating amnesties as part of any peace agreement with the government. This impacts on the incentive to be part of a government sponsored rehabilitation programme.

Conclusion

Pakistan today suffers from weak political leadership, unable to institute meaningful reforms to build institutions so necessary to give meaning to democracy and the rule of law. Daniel Byman argues: 'civilian control over the military is non existent and, in addition to the jihadist problem, bitter ethnic sectarian and political divisions threaten Pakistan's unity' (Byman 2009). The bulk of the terrorists in Pakistan are made up of four distinct groups. Firstly the 'nationalists' in Baluchistan who want their grievances on allocation of resources to the Province politically addressed. They have for long allowed themselves to be used by foreign state and non-state agents through supply of funds and weapons to cause instability to their own country.

The second group are the sectarian organisations which have a bloody history of killings and kidnappings across the country and who have mutated into even more deadly groups which have found a new lucrative partnership with the third group, the Taliban. The Taliban are the most dangerous threat of all. They recognise that State machinery is corrupt and ineffective. They know that the Army has opened too many fronts. They are aware that their pool of recruits comes from the poor and dispossessed. Many are willing to send their sons on suicide missions for martyrdom and to receive financial support. The fourth group, Al Qaeda together with the Taliban are aware of the inability of the state to effectively challenge their narrative. They are aware of their unparalleled access to the poor and are able to nurture 'sleeper' cells within madrassas. They recognise the need to have back up safe havens outside Pakistan in countries such as Yemen, Somalia and the horn of Africa if military operations are intensified. Each group has different motives and agendas which may or may not come together at any given time.

Killing terrorists only produces more lethal terrorists. Richard Holbrooke, the US special envoy to Afghanistan and Pakistan recently said: 'You cannot deal with militants by giving away territory. They are now getting closer and closer to Islamabad and Punjab. However hitting them hard will not help.'[15] The conflict in Afghanistan and Pakistan cannot be won unless and until the false reading of religion which breeds so much hate and intolerance is socially and legally challenged. Though the 'occupation' of Afghanistan is seen as invasion of the territory of Islam (*Dar el Islam*), the religious parameters of the doctrine of jihad must be open to debate.

Dialogue has a special significance in Islamic history. It can break the wahabbi/salafi chain. It can prevent radical minds from being isolated and indoctrinated behind closed doors. The anger and uncomfortable responses to the publication of Sayed Imam's Revision by Al Qaeda aptly demonstrates this. Radical Islam must be opened to public debate, inside and outside prison. People need to understand what the militants represent and the risk of supporting militancy.

Peace agreements if they are to exist in any meaningful way must be between the government and tribesmen, not criminal armed militants, and they should be part of a wider disengagement and de-mobilisation process. Terrorist organisations and their justification for violence need to be discredited. This can be done by displaying posters across the tribal belt with verses from the Qur'an prohibiting terrorism and gratuitous acts of violence. Illegal FM radio stations churning out hate need to be jammed. Radio is a very effective method of communicating with rural communities. It should be used to promote the true spirit of Islam. Part of a national media debate could include a programme along the lines of an Iraqi programme where jihadis were confronted by the mothers of those whom they had killed.[16]

Terrorist organisations can be deprived of human capital by job creation, to provide an alternative means of livelihood to those on the cusp. Promised development in the tribal belt must be accelerated so that locals believe they have a stake in the future. There is also an urgent need to reform the public system of education. This must include the training of teachers and overhauling the curricula. There must also be monitoring of religious instructions in madrassas. The inclusion of mainstream subjects in the syllabus will assist graduates to find employment in civil society.

15 *The Dawn* 20 April 2009.

16 'Terrorism in the grip of Justice', January 2005, produced by Al Iraqiya Television.

Pakistan as a pivotal state in the global fight against terrorism must break the indoctrination of vulnerable young men. Terrorist organisations including Al Qaeda and the Taliban must not be allowed to recruit unabated. Collective and individual disengagement from terrorism has a chance to succeed since there is now more vocal societal support for opening up the jihadi debate and challenging the militants' false reading of religion. There also needs to be a well structured system of rehabilitation for those in detention and a de-radicalisation programme for those on the cusp. The first signs of rifts within militant groups must be exploited. Although these are cloaked in ideological disagreements they are not unconnected with territorial control. Pakistan must not squander public support and an enabling political environment to reassert the rule of law. Indiscriminate violence that kills and maims, traumatising entire communities must be shown for what it is. Pakistan is in the grip of psychological warfare. Militancy in Pakistan is now viewed as an existential threat. It is also increasingly spoken of as a global threat. US Secretary of State, Hillary Clinton called it 'a mortal threat to the security and safety of our country and the world'.[17] In a world turning increasingly towards religious justification for conflict, only challenging the false reading of religion including the sacred concept of Jihad will provide Pakistan with hope for the future and retard the slide into violent extremism that poses a grave threat to it and the world.

Bibliography

Aslan, R. 2006. *Fight in the Way of God, The Origins, Evolution and Future of Islam, No God but God*. London: Arrow Books.

Byman, D. 2009. Taliban vs Predator. *Foreign Affairs Magazine*, 18 March.

Fair, C. 2009. What's the problem with Pakistan? Foreign Affairs Roundtable discussion, 31 March.

Gul, I. 2009. Bulldozer diplomacy. *The Dawn*, 20 April. Online. Available at: http://www.dawn.com (accessed 21 April 2009).

Hayat, K. 2009. Can the state now make any difference? *The News*, 14 August.

Marshall, T. 1996. *Restorative Justice: An Overview*. London: Home Office.

Marwat, F. 2005. From Muhajir to Mujahid: the politics of war through aid: A case study of the Afghan refugees. In P.K. Toru (ed.) *The NWFP*. Peshawar: Pakistan Study Centre, University of Peshawar.

Mawdudi, S. 1939. Jihad in Islam. Address. 13 April 1939. Lahore. Online. Available at: http://www.Muhammadanism.org (accessed 29 April 2009).

Taj, F. 2009. Life in Swat after the peace deal. *The Dawn*, 16 April. Online. Available at http://www.dawn.com (accessed 17 April 2009).

Wright, L. 2008. The rebellion within. *The New Yorker*, 7 June.

17 House of Representatives Foreign Affairs Committee, 22 April 2009, available at www.Earth2Obama.org.

Chapter 10
'Just Peace' or Peace Postponed: *Jus Post Bellum* and the Aftermath of Iraq

Serena K. Sharma

Several years after the declared end of major combat operations peace continues to elude Iraq. While the recovery from any conflict is certainly arduous, it would be wrong to assume that the difficulties that plague Iraq today are somehow endemic to the regular processes of post-conflict reconstruction. Far from being inevitable, the situation in Iraq today is very much a product of the lack of foresight in post-war planning. Remarkably, this oversight was also mirrored within moral debates in the run up to war. Whereas earlier just war thinkers had viewed the end of peace as a precondition in any justified resort to war, the concept of peace has received significantly less attention in modern articulations of the just war tradition.

The neglect of peace in modern accounts of just war thought derives, in large part, from the prevailing structure of the tradition. Contemporary just war thought is organised around the categories of *jus ad bellum* (resort to war) and *jus in bello* (conduct in war). While certain thinkers have gestured towards the incorporation of a so-called *jus post bellum* to stand alongside the conventional just war categories, it is not without reason that commentators have referred to this category as 'the least developed part of just war theory' (Walzer 2006). Although just war scholars have emphasised the need to elaborate this aspect of the tradition, particularly in the aftermath of Iraq, current efforts to develop a *jus post bellum* have fallen short. In their attempts to restore the role of peace in the tradition, just war scholars have simply appended the *jus post bellum* on as a third just war category, completely autonomous from both *jus ad bellum* and *jus in bello*. As this chapter will argue, planning for peace should feature prior to the initiation of hostilities, and in this sense be part and parcel of the *jus ad bellum* calculation. Through their inattention to this factor, just war scholars are at risk of propagating future situations like post-war Iraq.

The first part of this chapter will survey the post-conflict situation in Iraq, with a view to determining the key factors responsible for the turmoil of today. The next section will examine the way in which just war scholars have responded to the aftermath of Iraq with the proposed development of a *jus post bellum*. The limits of this approach will be explored in the third section. As will be noted, of particular concern is the manner in which current approaches perpetuate the view of peace as a mere afterthought of war. With such limitations in mind, the fourth and final section will turn towards Christian just war thought, with an emphasis on St Augustine's rendering of peace. Augustine's writings contain a number of interesting insights on this subject, which could arguably serve as the basis for a much-needed reconceptualisation of peace.

Planning for the Wrong Peace

Although the formal cessation of hostilities was declared on 1 May 2003, one would hardly think of describing Iraq as a 'post-war' situation. Six years after the end of major combat operations – not to mention the transfer of sovereignty from the Coalition Provisional Authority (CPA) to the Iraqi governing Council and subsequent national elections – prevailing conditions in Iraq denote a country in the midst of ongoing warfare. How is it that the world's most powerful country continues to find itself struggling in Iraq several years after the fall of Saddam Hussein's regime? Richard Haass, president of the Council on Foreign Relations, ventured what is perhaps the best answer to this question: 'sometimes people plan for the wrong war … One can say in some ways that the Administration planned for the wrong peace' (Slevin and Priest 2003).

The scars of the Administration's shoddily approached plan for peace came to light only days after the declared end of major combat operations. The ill-contrived occupation commenced with the coalition forces' initial reluctance to assume their status as occupying powers. According to the report of the Third Infantry Division (2003): 'Because of the refusal to acknowledge occupier status, commanders did not initially take measures available to occupying powers, such as imposing curfews, directing civilians to return to work, and controlling the local governments and populace', all of which would have been extremely advantageous in the wake of the regime's collapse. The report goes on to note how the neglect to take this step: 'created a power vacuum, which others immediately tried to fill.' Apart from the issue of the coalition's legal status, there were a number of other decisions made by the CPA, which in retrospect appear to have abetted the country's descent into chaos. The two orders that have come under particularly intense scrutiny are the de-baathification order and the dissolution of the Iraqi army. According to Fred Ikle (2005), such orders were indicative of an unnecessary spirit of vengeance in US post-war efforts: 'During the critical weeks following the collapse of Saddam Hussein's rule in Baghdad, the emphasis on punishment and revenge clearly harmed America's long-term objectives.' The CPA orders have also been scrutinised in terms of aggravating sectarian violence, as Thomas Ricks (2006) has observed, 'in a country riven by sectarian and ethnic fault lines – Sunni versus Shiite versus Kurd – and possessing few unifying national institutions, Bremer had done away with two of the most important ones'.

In light of the errors of the CPA, Toby Dodge (2003) has drawn a rather stark parallel between the ongoing post-war efforts in Iraq and Britain's own experiences in Iraq during the 1920s. In his book, *Inventing Iraq: The Failure of Nation Building and a History Denied*, Dodge traces the major mistakes of the

British during their 18-year tenure in Iraq, while noting the uncanny duplication of some of these errors in the present US-led occupation: 'The United States in Iraq today must understand that it is both living with the consequences of that failure and is in danger of repeating it.'

As is quite evident, there is certainly no shortage of material focusing on the blunders and omissions of the Bush Administration with respect to post-war policy in Iraq. While this is clearly an issue warranting attention, emphasis on policy blunders does not get to the heart of what went wrong in the aftermath of the 2003 invasion. As the remainder of this section will demonstrate, the underlying difficulty with respect to post-war planning – which arguably fed into every major policy decision – was the very stark intellectual gap surrounding the actual conceptualisation of post-war peace. As will be noted, this intellectual gap first became evident in the context of the initial justification for the resort to force.

One of the most frequently criticised aspects of the war in Iraq has been the varying justifications offered for the invasion. The most oft-cited include: weapons of mass destruction, the need to liberate the Iraqi people, and the regime's prospective link to terrorist organisations. In spite of the apparent diversity of these legitimating factors, there remains a substantial degree of consistency between them: endemic to each was a common goal of ousting the Iraqi leader. Consequently, while the justifications may have not always been clearly presented by the Administration, the goal of the invasion certainly was. Having regime-change as the ultimate goal of the operation would tend to imply some forethought into the post-war environment; however, this did not come across in COBRA II, the classified US Army War Plan: 'The purpose of this operation is to force the collapse of the Iraqi regime and deny it the use of WMD to threaten its neighbours and US interests in the region … The end state for this operation is regime change' (Ricks 2006). Commenting on the War plan, Army Reserve Major Michael Eisenstadt has observed the following: 'We designed success in negative terms – getting rid of the regime, instead of establishing a democratic regime …' (Ricks 2006). In this respect, as Eisenstadt notes: 'When President Bush landed on that carrier with the "Mission Accomplished" banner, he was right: The mission, as defined for the military as getting rid of the regime, had indeed been accomplished' (Ricks 2006). Accordingly, among the US military establishment, post-war peace was viewed as synonymous with the end of major combat operations.

The notion of peace as the mere absence of fighting led to a determined emphasis on the tactical goal of 'winning the war', at the expense of the broader, strategic goal of winning the peace. For instance, on 27 February 2003, Paul Wolfowitz made the following statement to the House Budget Committee: 'It's hard to conceive that it would take more forces to provide stability in post-Saddam Iraq than it would take to conduct the war itself and to secure the surrender of Saddam's security forces and his army' (Ricks 2006) – a statement which now appears haunting considering that the coalition forces have incurred more casualties in the post-war phase than the actual combat phase. This fact alone is a testament to just how complicated the post-war phase of combat really is. Such complexities could not, however, be easily accommodated within the Administration's exceedingly simplistic conceptualisation of peace.

The Administration's emphasis on 'winning the war' also fed into its rather hubristic approach towards the UN. Viewed as a severe impediment to victory, certain think tanks and key officials had minimal time for engaging in a supposed detour of UN diplomacy.

Some even went so far as to argue for a minimal UN role in post-war Iraq (Gardiner and Rivkin 2003). While it is certainly true, as Simon Chesterman (2004) notes, 'President Bush didn't need the United Nations going into Iraq', it remains the case that 'he needs the UN's help to get out'. Indeed, one of the major impediments to bringing countries on board in the post-conflict reconstruction process has been the doubt cast on the legitimacy of the invasion, in terms of both the flouting of UN channels, and the inchoate justifications offered for the resort to force. In this respect, there are crucial connections between the resort to force – in terms of legitimacy and authority – and the prospects for post-war rebuilding efforts. Such connections were largely neglected by the Administration in the run up to war. The incapacity to see the connections between fighting the war and winning the peace constitutes a second key reason – along with the failure to adequately conceptualise post-war peace – as to why Iraq is in turmoil today.

Rather ironically, despite the emphasis placed on the legitimating factors for resorting to war, such justifications have completely faltered in the post-war context. No weapons of mass destruction have ever been found, and the suggestion of a war on behalf of human rights was put to shame in the wake of the Abu Ghraib scandal – something else, which commentators have attributed to a lack of proper planning. In terms of the alleged Iraq-terrorism nexus, there is clearly more international terrorist activity in Iraq today, than there was in the spring of 2003. Indeed, according to the National Intelligence Council (2005), Iraq has replaced Afghanistan as the main fulcrum of international terrorism. Therefore, in spite of the excessive focus on the actual resort to force – or perhaps because of it – the most significant legacy of the 2003 invasion of Iraq will remain its unfortunate aftermath. By no means was this outcome inevitable, nor can it be solely attributed to specific policy gaps. As this section has argued, the Iraq we see today is a direct consequence of the failure to properly envisage the complex nature of peace and the crucial connections between the resort to war and the war's aftermath.

Jus Post Bellum: Towards a More Complete Just War Theory

When it comes to deliberating on a prospective use of force in the international system, the just war tradition remains a powerful tool for appraising war. Given the divisive character of the debates surrounding the invasion of Iraq, the just war framework was put to good use in the run up to war. At times engagement with the tradition was explicit; other times it was more implicit. What was particularly noticeable in the pre-war debate, however, was the manner in which deliberations over the use of force seemed to take their cue from the Bush Administration's focus on the *jus ad bellum* component of the operation. In particular, the subject of the operation's legality received a significant amount of attention in the public arena. Apart from the impasse over resorting to force in the absence of explicit UN approval, there were the various debates surrounding the concept of pre-emption (Kaufman 2005; Luban 2004; Freedman 2003; Litwak 2002). Iraq constituted the first test case of the Administration's doctrine of pre-emption, which had been previously outlined in the National Security Strategy (Bush 2002). Questions surrounding the extent to which the 'Caroline' standard of imminence had been met seemed to capture the imagination of countless commentators in the run up to war. A rather unfortunate consequence of this emphasis on the *jus ad bellum* component of the operation was the rather blatant neglect of the war's aftermath within the moral debate.

While certainly troubling, the neglect of the post-war situation in the run up to war should come as no surprise. The main principles of the just war tradition are typically divided into two categories: the *jus ad bellum*, which concerns the resort to force, and *jus in bello*, concerned with the conduct of war. The component of just war theorising most concerned with the establishment of peace in the aftermath of war – *jus post bellum* – has been regarded as 'the least developed part of just war theory' (Walzer 2006). This is not to suggest that peace has always been given short shrift in the tradition; it is rather, the contemporary adaptation of the tradition, which insists on this strict bipartite structure. This categorisation has been wholeheartedly accepted by virtually every just war theorist of the modern period (Litchenberg 2006; Guthrie and Quinlan 2007; Atack 2005; Christopher 1994; Bellamy 2006; Elshtain 2003; Johnson 1975; Walzer 2000). Nevertheless, the extremely turbulent post-war situation in Iraq has brought home for just war scholars the considerable gap in our moral framework for evaluating the aftermath of war. Accordingly, just war scholars have been forced to confront the neglect of post-war issues within the just war tradition.

The first instance in which an explicit call was made for incorporating a *jus post bellum* actually pre-dates the recent invasion of Iraq. Writing in the aftermath of the first Gulf War in an article entitled: 'When the Shooting Stops: Missing Elements in Just War Theory', Michael Schuck (1994) noted a deficiency in just war categories on account of the absence of a *jus post bellum*: 'If Christians are called upon to probe the moral superiority of entering and conducting war by using the seven *jus ad bellum* principles … and two *jus in bello* principles, should they not also be called upon to monitor the moral propriety of concluding a war through some set of *jus post bellum* principles?' Accordingly, Schuck proposed the incorporation of a *jus post bellum* 'for the sake of a more complete just war theory', which for him could be embodied through an adherence to three specific principles: (1) the principle of repentance; (2) honourable surrender; (3) restoration.

Given that the *jus post bellum* has not been explicitly developed, some may wonder why such an addition is necessary. Robert Williams and Dan Caldwell (2006) explore the claim that the *jus post bellum* may already be sufficiently captured within other just war criteria, such as the principle of right intention, which has historically served as a restraint against the pursuit of unjust ends. Not only is the principle of right intention subject to diverse interpretations, and in that sense, highly unreliable for ensuring a just peace, but as Williams and Caldwell argue, the course of a war and its outcome are not entirely predictable, hence it is not unreasonable to look to different criteria to guide policy in the aftermath of war. In this respect, the development of a *jus post bellum* 'simply acknowledges the fact that we know different things and are confronted with different challenges before, during, and after a war'. Therefore, while Williams and Caldwell are sympathetic to the scepticism surrounding the development of *jus post bellum*, they remain strongly in favour it:

> We can concede that there is an important link between why and how a war is fought and how it concludes, but this no more eliminates the need for principles to ensure a just peace than the existence of *jus ad bellum* principles eliminates the need for principles to ensure that war is fought justly. (Williams and Caldwell 2006)

In recent years, the main expositor of the *jus post bellum* has been the philosopher, Brian Orend (2000). Of particular concern to Orend is the rather glaring absence of any substantive law governing war termination. The exception is of course Articles 32–41 of the Hague Convention, however, as Orend points out: 'These articles were ratified in 1907, and sound like it. Their quaint references to white flags and buglers, their vague commitments to military honour, their pedantic distinctions between general and local armistices, and the overwhelming emptiness of their nature renders these articles all but irrelevant in the current context.' Further to that, Orend draws a comparison between the state of the law governing war termination, and the substantially codified law pertaining to *jus ad bellum* and the *jus in bello*: 'One does not have to point to the incredible detail and sophistication of the Hague and Geneva Conventions on the Treatment of Prisoners of War to realise that there is a gross imbalance in the international laws of armed conflict. And it is war termination that gets the short end of the stick.' One might counter this argument by pointing to the law of occupation; yet even here, the law falls short in serving as a guide to post-war situations (Zwanenburg 2004). According to Orend, the failure to regulate war termination may not only prolong fighting, the absence of such normative constraints in this area leads to inconsistency and confusion. In building his case for the development of *jus post bellum*, Orend invokes the surgery metaphor: *jus ad bellum* constitutes the preparation phase, *jus in bello* is the actual surgery and *jus post bellum* the post-operative rehabilitation phase. Orend highlights five principles which are essential to the 'post-operative' phase: (1) just cause for war termination; (2) right intention; (3) public declaration and legitimate authority; (4) discrimination; and (5) proportionality.

Discussions over incorporating a *jus post bellum* have not been confined to the moral realm. In recognition of the blatant omissions in international law with respect to war termination, certain international lawyers (Stahn 2006) have begun to put forward a case for moving towards a tripartite conception of the laws of war in order to accommodate post war situations. There have also been attempts by NGOs to implement *jus post bellum* in practice, one example being the activities of the Campaign for Innocent Victims in Conflict. While there are certainly differing interpretations over how and in what specific context the *jus post bellum* should be developed, there seems to be a general consensus on the fact that *jus post bellum* is a positive development, as Mark Evans (2005) has argued:

> It is worth noting that *jus post bellum* is detachable from the other two parts of the theory in the following sense: one could believe that there was no just cause for war, nor any just way of fighting a war and yet, given that wars nevertheless occur, embrace *jus post bellum* as non-ideal theory's moral criteria to govern the post-war situation given that (immoral) wars have been fought.

In this respect, the *jus post bellum* is somewhat different than other just war principles in that it can boast support from unlikely sympathisers, as Evans notes: 'It is one part of just war theory that a pacifist can – and perhaps should – embrace.'

Although the endeavour to incorporate post-war concerns within the just war framework is certainly a noble undertaking, there are significant problems with the manner in which this is being done. For one, those seeking to develop this aspect of the tradition are not being critical enough in their task. That is, instead of asking why, or how it is that the *jus post bellum* was neglected within the tradition, their approach has been to simply append a set of *post bellum* norms to stand alongside the *jus ad bellum* and *jus in bello* categories. As the following section will argue, the neglect of *jus post bellum* within the tradition was not just a simple oversight – it stems directly from the tradition's inherited structure and the underlying assumptions implicit within this structure. Rather than working to correct this, just war scholars are consciously developing the *jus post bellum* within this framework. Yet, if the neglect of *jus post bellum* owes to structural, rather than mechanical reasons, various attempts to revise just war theory by incorporating a *jus post bellum* in this manner will remain largely insufficient.

Jus Post Bellum: 'Just Peace' or Peace Postponed?

If we simply look at the *jus ad bellum* and *jus in bello* categories, and refrain from asking what lies behind the categories or how they developed, the neglect of *jus post bellum* in just war thought does not appear to be that pressing. It might as well be considered a cosmetic problem: *jus post bellum* was neglected and now it's simply a matter of adding it. While for the most part this is how just war theorists have dealt with the development of *jus post bellum*, this simple approach will not do. It is important to question how it is that just war theorists, charged with the moral evaluation of war, have ended up neglecting a concept which is concerned with the establishment of peace. It is certainly the case that throughout the history of the tradition, its most prominent theorists have commented on the importance of peace in the broader just war framework, so why would it not feature more prominently? For the answer to this, we must take a closer look at the categories, which constitute the tradition as we know it today.

The *jus ad bellum/jus in bello* categorisation – though consistently accepted by virtually every major just war theorist of the modern period – was not made explicit in classical just war thought. The categories are in fact, rather new, imported from legal thought during the revival of just war theorising in the twentieth century (Kolb 1997). Behind these juristic categories is something quite fundamental, as Carsten Stahn (2006) has noted: 'The *jus ad bellum/jus in bello* narrative reflects, to some extent, the traditional dichotomy between war and peace.' Indeed, with respect to the field of international law there is certainly a sharp contrast between the two: *jus ad bellum* refers to the condition of peace, whereas *jus in bello* refers to a state of war. In this respect, these categories are seen as representing distinct legal regimes, each governing different aspects of the use of force. The notion of a dichotomy referred to by Stahn is instructive, for it sets up war and peace as antonyms, which can only be understood in relation to one another. The impact of this structure on conceptions of peace is rather significant, for if peace and war are taken to be opposites, peace is simply put, the absence of war, or in legal terms, a return to the *status quo ante-bellum*. With the just war tradition's inheritance of this schema came an acceptance of the one-dimensional understanding of peace implicit in these categories. In this sense, the *jus ad bellum/jus in bello* categorisation seriously stifled the development of a more expansive approach to peace within the tradition. Indeed, with a particular conception of peace –albeit, an excessively narrow one – already captured in this model, the need to elaborate principles pertaining to *jus post bellum* was not deemed a matter of great urgency.

It is interesting to observe how this rather simplistic rendering of peace embodied within the *ad bellum/in bello* framework has filtered into popular conceptions of peace. Earlier in this chapter, it was noted how peace was defined in largely negative terms among those responsible for post-war planning in Iraq. A similar approach to peace is echoed more generally in the discipline of International Relations (IR). For instance, Oliver Richmond (2007) has drawn attention to the neglect of peace within IR and the concomitant treatment of war as the disciplines' central pre-occupation. Since peace is taken to be the opposite of war, it is deemed inherently good, entirely unproblematic, and therefore, undeserving of further study. Unfortunately, just war scholars working on the development of a *jus post bellum* have not taken the occasion to critically assess conventional understandings of peace, but have accepted this rather simplistic rendering of peace and its relation to war. This is evident in the manner in which just war scholars have been unable to overcome the assumption, echoed in IR, of peace as something unproblematic. This sentiment is best captured in Mark Evans's (2005) approach wherein he refers to the *jus post bellum* as something 'detachable' from the other components of just war, to the extent that even a pacifist can embrace it.

The limitations referred to above cannot be rectified by simply expanding our definition of peace, for it is not just the assumptions of the *ad bellum/in bello* categories which present problems, but also the particular manner in which the categories are structured. For instance, the *jus ad bellum/jus in bello* categories are accompanied by the notion of a firm distinction between them. This is evident in Michael Walzer's (1977) work, wherein he refers to the 'logical independence' of the two. There are two key reasons for maintaining this separation: the first stems from legal pragmatism: those in political office are responsible for crimes of peace (*jus ad bellum*), while military personnel are responsible for crimes of war (*jus in bello*). The second reason for the separation is more humanitarian in scope in that it seeks to have the principles of *jus in bello* apply equally to all belligerents, irrespective of the causes of war (*jus ad bellum*). So ingrained is the notion of a separation within moral and legal thought, it now appears natural to advocate this approach on behalf of the *jus post bellum*, as Kristin Boon (2005) has argued: 'The rationale for separating *jus ad bellum* from *jus in bello* should similarly apply to *jus post bellum*.' Nevertheless, it is not entirely clear that a separate *jus post bellum* makes sense. Indeed, there are rather important connections between the *jus ad bellum* and *jus post bellum* that ought to be preserved. Thomas Ricks (2006) has pointed to the manner in which Abu Ghraib – though a crime on the part of individuals – was facilitated by decisions made at the upper levels of the Administration. Accordingly, while different people may be responsible for different aspects of war (a soldier responsible for crimes of war), and (someone in political office responsible for crimes of peace), there should be an overarching sense of moral culpability that filters through the resort to war, its conduct, and aftermath. It is this overarching sense of culpability/responsibility, which is lost when we begin speaking of an entirely separate *jus post bellum*.

A further reason why it might be unwise to insist on an entirely separate *jus post bellum* stems from the fact that the impetus for articulating a set of post-war principles derives in large part from developments on the *ad bellum* level. As Carsten Stahn (2006) has noted:

> The case in favour of the regulation of peacemaking is in part supported by a change of discourse about the justification of intervention. Traditionally, the use of military force was justified by the purpose of thwarting security threats or conquering foreign territories … Today interventions are often justified by a bundle of post-conflict oriented purposes, including, most notably, the defense of universal and communitarian values such as human rights, democracy and self-determination.

In support of this conclusion of a 'growing link between the use of force and the restoration of peace' Stahn refers to the International Commission on Intervention and State Sovereignty's (2001) espousal of a 'responsibility to rebuild'. The

Independent Commission on Kosovo (2000) has also acknowledged this link between pre-and post conflict stages in its proposal for an Additional Protocol III in cases of humanitarian intervention. According to Gary Bass (2004), so strong are these linkages, that a failure to abide by *jus post bellum* requirements might serve to 'negate the previous *jus ad bellum* rationale'. By this account, a clearly disjointed *jus post bellum* becomes untenable.

Rather than building on the connections between the various phases of war, those seeking to develop the *jus post bellum* have elected to regard peace as a stand-alone issue. We have already noted Evans' idea that the *jus post bellum* is detachable from the other components of just war. Noah Feldman (2004) has advanced a similar approach in his discussion of the rebuilding of Iraq. Yet, to make matters worse, just war scholars have started to explicitly take on board the idea of *jus post bellum* as a 'third' just war category. Elaborating on Michael Walzer's (2000) idea of war being judged twice, some have gone so far as to say that war should be judged three times (Williams and Caldwell 2006). Not only does this approach neglect the crucial linkages between the *ad bellum* and *post bellum*, it simply postpones planning for peace. Moreover, the delineation of rules for a specifically 'post conflict phase' rests on the assumptions that we can easily demarcate the end of a conflict. As the war in Iraq has demonstrated, the cessation of hostilities does not always coincide with the end of war. When it comes to contemporary warfare: 'We may have to deal with historical grey zones which will not permit historians of the future to engage in the periodisation of history into neat themes, phases, eras, and epochs …' (Coker 1997).

In short, while just war scholars are certainly right to be concerned by the absence of *jus post bellum* within the tradition, the manner in which they are developing this area has been largely inadequate. As this section has argued, the main problem is the *ad bellum/in bello* structure on two different counts. First, this structure accommodates a limited conception of peace as the absence of war; secondly, it insists on a stark separation between just war categories, which undermines the crucial linkages between the different phases of war, effectively prioritising the *ad bellum* phase and postponing the *post-bellum* phase. Nevertheless, those at the forefront in developing a *jus post bellum* have, by and large, continued to work within the conventional just war model. The issues at stake here are not purely of academic interest. As we saw earlier, the main drawbacks of the US plan for post-war Iraq were the inability to properly conceptualise peace, and the failure to appreciate the connections between the resort to war and the post-war phase. The replication of these issues signals a need to reconsider current approaches to peace. The next section attempts to draw lessons from St Augustine's rendering of peace. Although frequently dismissed by contemporary thinkers, Augustine's writings contain a number of insights, which could inform a more comprehensive understanding of peace today.

St Augustine's Rendering of Peace

If the structure of the tradition has stifled the development of *jus post bellum*, it is to a probing of that structure that just war scholars should turn. Admittedly, this would tend to go against the intuition of modern just war thinking. In many respects, the *ad bellum*/*in bello* structure constitutes the foundation of contemporary articulations of just war. So central have these categories become, they also tend to cloud historical commentary on the tradition. For instance, with the *ad bellum*/*in bello* structure firmly in mind, several just war theorists have gone back to evaluate earlier thinkers according to today's starkly separated categories. Perhaps the most common critique in this regard relates to the manner in which the norms of *jus in bello* were apparently neglected by early Christian just war thinkers. The tendency to read back into the history of just war thought has led to a particular emphasis on St Augustine given his designated role as the first major just war thinker:

> The elaboration of just war doctrine at the hands of Augustine of Hippo set the framework of discussion for the ensuing millennium. What was unmistakable about Augustine's treatment, an aspect that was to be characteristic of most just war theorizing throughout the medieval period, was its preoccupation with the *jus ad bellum* to the almost total exclusion of any explicit consideration of the conduct of war itself. (Clark 1988)

A similar historical reading has been echoed in Colm McKeogh's (2002) work: 'This book starts the search for the roots of the PNCI [Principle of Non-Combatant Immunity] in what might seem an unlikely place: the *ad bellum* thought of a "just war" thinker, Augustine, who had little to say about *jus in bello*'. Some even go so far as to charge Augustine with an outright indifference towards the fate of civilians: 'the subjective *culpa* or guilt of the enemy merited punishment of the enemy population without regard to the distinction between soldiers and civilians … the just warriors could kill with impunity even those who were morally innocent' (Russell 1975).

How are we to evaluate this supposed neglect of the *jus in bello* in Augustine's thought? While the Latin presentation of the terms, *jus ad bellum* and *jus in bello,* gives the appearance that this categorisation is of ancient heritage, as was noted in the previous section, this terminology is actually rather recent. In this respect, evaluating the historical treatment of restraint from the perspective of today's categories is a case of holding early just war thinkers up to an unsuitable standard. However, there is something more to this critique, for in much the same way that the *jus in bello* was apparently neglected within Augustine's thought, early Christian thinkers are now being reproached for overlooking the *jus post bellum*, as Williams and Caldwell (2006) argue:

> The effort to develop *jus post bellum* principles is necessary precisely because the theologians, philosophers, and lawyers who developed and refined the just

> war tradition gave insufficient attention to the aftermath of war. Consequently, the needed principles are not to be found merely by digging more deeply into the work of Augustine, Aquinas, Suarez, or Grotius …

What we find here is a tendency to view the three phases of war as developing sequentially: *jus ad bellum* was always present, then the *jus in bello* emerged, and now we are in the final phase of developing the *jus post bellum*. Ultimately, this will lead to a 'complete just war theory'. This understanding of the tradition resonates with the phased approach to war inherent in the structure of contemporary just war thought.

While it is certainly the case that the first just war thinkers did not structure their deliberations on war into neatly defined categories, to suggest that matters of restraint and the end of peace did not feature in their articulations of the tradition is simply untrue. If we revisit the writings of Augustine, it becomes apparent how contemporary understandings of just war, informed by today's clearly delineated categories, have erroneously filtered into our assessment of early just war thinkers. First of all, while it is true that there was no explicit mention of a *jus in bello* and *jus post bellum* in Augustine's thought, to suggest that the two were wholly neglected is incorrect. If we begin with the latter, even a cursory glance at Augustine's body of work will reveal a rather striking preoccupation with peace: 'no word ever falls more gratefully upon the ear, nothing is desired with greater longing, in fact, nothing better can be found. Peace is 'delightful' and 'dear to the heart of all mankind' (Dyson 1998). Hence, peace was certainly of interest to him, and not the one-dimensional peace we are typically confronted with today, but a much more multifarious brand of peace. This is evident in Augustine's willingness to take a critical approach to peace. Indeed, the first half of the *City of God Against the Pagans* is dedicated to deconstructing the *Pax Romana*. Moreover, while just war theorists of today seem to be shocked by the brutality of the post-war situation in Iraq, Augustine was well aware of the fact that 'post war peace' can sometimes be more horrific than the war itself. This is particularly evident in Book III of the *City of God*: 'Although the blood of so many citizens had been shed to secure this victory … hostility, continued even when the war was over, and the ensuing peace was more bloody than ever' (Dyson 1998) He continues:

> These things were done in time of peace, when war was ended! … Peace vied with war in cruelty, and conquered. For the war brought armed men low, but the peace destroyed unarmed ones. During the war, he who was struck might at least strike back if he could; but the object of the peace was to ensure that those who had survived the war might live, but that they should die without being able to resist.

At the heart of Augustine's commentary is a warning to be wary of the many horrors that 'can traffic under the cover of "peace"' (Elshtain 2003). An important lesson to draw from this is, as Jean Bethke Elshtain (2003) has argued: 'peace should not be universally lauded even as war is universally condemned. Each must be evaluated critically.' It is this brand of scepticism, which is absent in current understandings of peace, and in the efforts to establish a *jus post bellum*.

With respect to the charge that there was an undue focus on the *jus ad bellum* level in Augustine's writings, much of this has to do with the context in which Augustine wrote. Above all, Augustine was concerned with providing a justification for Christian participation in war, as well as sanctioning the sovereign's right to use force. Consequently, there was an urgent need to address principles pertaining to proper authority, and the matter of just cause in his writings. Yet, this did not translate into a wholesale abandonment of *in bello* concerns, or a disconnection from the aftermath of war. This would only be the case if Augustine viewed war according to the categories just war theorists employ today; however, this was not the case. There was, rather, a sense of fluidity in Augustine's thought that allowed for linkages between the resort to war, the end of war and the conduct of war. In book XIX of the *City of God*, he makes these crucial connections between war and peace apparent:

> Just as there can be life without pain, therefore, but no pain without life, so there can be peace without any war, but no war without some degree of peace. This is not because of the nature of war itself, but because war can only be waged by or within persons who are in some sense natural beings: beings who could not exist at all if peace of some kind did not exist within them. (Dyson 1998)

> Wars themselves, then, are conducted with the intention of peace, even when they are conducted by those who are concerned to exercise their martial prowess in command and battle. Hence it is clear that peace is the desired end of war. For every man seeks peace, even in making war; but no one seeks war by making peace. (Dyson 1998)

The connection between the different phases of war is also evident in his advice to Boniface. 'Peace is not sought in order to provoke war, but war is waged in order to attain peace. Be a peacemaker, then, even by fighting, so that through your victory you might bring those whom you defeat to the advantages of peace' (Reichberg et al. 2006). Therefore, it was clearly not the case that Augustine was negligent in terms of the aftermath of war and questions of conduct. Those who critique him in this regard are coming from a highly structured just war model, which is completely out of context in Augustine's time. As this section has demonstrated, there are aspects of Augustine's thought which contemporary just war scholars could learn from. In particular, his critical approach to peace, as well as his ability to see the connections between the different phases of war is something, which those developing a *jus post bellum* should bear in mind.

Conclusion

This chapter has examined the limitations associated with current efforts to develop a *jus post bellum*. Much of the impetus for this recent effort stems from the ongoing situation in Iraq – a situation which has revealed a significant gap in just war thinking with respect to the issue of post-war peace. In this respect, the aftermath of the war has provided a vital opportunity for just war scholars to take stock of the current state of the tradition. Unfortunately, most just war scholars have not availed themselves of this opportunity for critical reflection. Instead, the conventional remedy to the apparent neglect of post war issues within the tradition has been to simply append the *jus post bellum* on as a third just war category, to stand alongside the conventional categories of *jus ad bellum* and *jus in bello*. This approach is significantly flawed for it accepts too easily the inherited structure of just war thinking. The result is that in their elaborations of a *jus post bellum*, just war scholars end up perpetuating the same errors that were committed by policy makers in Iraq, in terms of both, the failure to conceptualise peace in a meaningful way and neglecting to appreciate the fluidity between the different phases of war. On both counts, just war scholars would benefit from becoming reacquainted with St Augustine's rendering of peace.

Bibliography

Atack, I. 2005. *The Ethics of Peace and War: from State Security to World Community*. Edinburgh: Edinburgh University Press.

Bass, G.J. 2004. Jus post bellum. *Philosophy and Public Affairs* 32 (4), 384–412.

Bellamy, A. 2006. *Just Wars from Cicero to Iraq*. Cambridge/Malden, MA: Polity Press.

Boon, K. 2005. Legislative reform in post-conflict zones: *jus post bellum* and the contemporary occupant's law-making powers. *McGill Law Journal* 50, 286–326.

Bush, G.W., 2002. The National Security Strategy of the USA. Available at: http://www.globalsecurity.org/military/library/policy/national/nss-020920.pdf (accessed: 15 March 2009).

Chesterman, S. 2004. Occupation as liberation: international humanitarian law and regime change. *Ethics and International Affairs* 18 (3), 51–64.

Christopher, P. 1994. *The Ethics of War and Peace: An Introduction to Legal and Moral Issues*. Englewood Cliffs, NJ: Prentice Hall.

Clark, I. 1988. *Waging War: A Philosophical Introduction*. Oxford: Clarendon Press.

Coker, C. 1997. How wars end. *Millennium Journal of International Studies* 26 (3), 615–29.

Dodge, T. 2003. *Inventing Iraq: The Failure of Nation Building and a History Denied*. New York: Columbia University Press.

Dyson, R.W. 1998. *Augustine, The City of God against the Pagans.* Cambridge: Cambridge University Press.

Elshtain, J.B. 2003. *Just War Against Terror: The Burden of American Power in a Violent World.* New York: Basic Books.

Evans, M. 2005. *Just War Theory: A Reappraisal.* Edinburgh: Edinburgh University Press.

Feldman, F. 2004. *What We Owe Iraq: War and the Ethics of Nation Building.* Princeton, NJ: Princeton University Press.

Freedman, L. 2003. Prevention, not pre-emption. *The Washington Quarterly* 2 (26), 105–14.

Gardiner, N. and Rivkin, D.B. 2003. *Blueprint for Freedom: Limiting the Role of the United Nations in Post War Iraq*. Washington, DC: The Heritage Foundation.

Guthrie, C. and Quinlan, M. 2007. *Just War: The Just War Tradition: Ethics and Modern Warfare*. London: Bloomsbury.

Ikle, F.C. 2005. *Every War Must End*, 2nd edn. New York: Columbia University Press.

Independent International Commission on Kosovo 2000. *The Kosovo Report.* Oxford: Oxford University Press.

International Commission on Intervention and State Sovereignty 2001. *The Responsibility to Protect*. Ottawa: International Development Research Council.

Johnson, J.T. 1975. *Ideology, Reason and the Limitation of War: Religious and Secular Concepts, 1200–1740*. Princeton, NJ: Princeton University Press.

Johnson, J.T. 1996. The broken tradition. *The National Interest*, 22 September.

Kaufman, W. 2005. What's wrong with preventive war? The moral and legal basis for the preventive use of force. *Ethics and International Affairs* 19 (3), 23–38.

Kolb, R. 1997. Origins of the twin terms *jus ad bellum/jus in bello*. *International Review of the Red Cross* 320, 553–62.

Litchenberg, J. 2006. Some central problems in just war theory. In R.J. Hoffman (ed.) *The Just War and Jihad: Violence in Judaism, Christianity, and Islam*. Amherst: Prometheus Books.

Litwak, R.S. 2002. The new calculus of preemption. *Survival* 44 (4), 53–80.

Luban, D. 2004. Preventive war. *Philosophy and Public Affairs* 32 (3), 207–48.

Mckeogh, C. 2002. *Innocent Civilians: The Morality of Killing in War.* New York: Palgrave.

National Intelligence Council. 2005. Mapping the global future. Report of the National Intelligence Council's 2020 Project. Available at http://www.foia.cia.gov/2020/ 2020.pdf (accessed: 15 March 2009).

Orend, B. 2000. *War and International Justice: A Kantian Perspective.* Waterloo: Wilfred Laurier University Press.

Reichberg, G.M, Syse, H. and Begby, E. 2006. *The Ethics of War: Classical and Contemporary Readings.* Malden: Blackwell.

Richmond, O. 2007. *The Transformation of Peace.* London: Palgrave.

Ricks, T.E. 2006. *Fiasco: The American Military Adventure in Iraq*. London: Penguin.

Russell, F.H. 1975. *The Just War in the Middle Ages*. Cambridge: Cambridge University Press.

Schuck, M.J. 1994. Missing elements in just war theory. *Christian Century* 3, 26 October.

Slevin, P., and Priest, D. 2003. Wolfowitz concedes Iraq errors. *Washington Post*, 24 July, A1.

Stahn, C. 2006. *Jus ad Bellum, jus in bello, jus post bellum*? Rethinking the conception of the law of armed force. *European Journal of International Law* 17 (5), 921–43.

Third Infantry Division (Mechanized) After Action Report: Operation Iraqi Freedom. 2003. Available at: www.globalsecurity.org/military/library/report/2003/3id-aar-jul03.pdf (accessed: 15 March 2009).

Walzer, M. 2000. *Just and Unjust Wars*. 3rd edn. New York: Basic Books.

Walzer, M. 2006. *Arguing About War*. New Haven, CT/London: Yale Nota Bene.

Williams, R.E. and Caldwell, D. 2006, *Jus Post Bellum:* just war theory and the principle of just peace. *International Studies Perspective* 7 (4), 309–20.

Zwanenburg, M. 2004. Existentialism in Iraq: security council resolution 1483 and the law of occupation. *International Review of the Red Cross* 856, 745–69.

Index